Building Basic Skills in Mathematics

Building Basic Skills in Mathematics

CB

CONTEMPORARY BOOKS

a division of NTC/CONTEMPORARY PUBLISHING GROUP
Lincolnwood, Illinois USA

Library of Congress Cataloging-in-Publication Data

Main entry under title:

Building basic skills in math.

    1. Mathematics—1961–   I. Contemporary Books, inc.
QA39.2.B82   510   81-704
ISBN 0-8092-5877-3 (pbk.) AACR2

ISBN: 0-8092-5877-3

Published by Contemporary Books,
a division of NTC/Contemporary Publishing Group, Inc.,
4255 West Touhy Avenue,
Lincolnwood (Chicago), Illinois 60646-1975 U.S.A.

9 0 1 2 3 4 5 CU 37 36 35 34 33 32 31

ACKNOWLEDGMENTS

The thoughtful efforts of a great many people went into the preparation of Contemporary Books' *Building Basic Skills* series. We gratefully acknowledge their contributions and continued involvement in Adult Education.

Adult Education Division

Lillian J. Fleming, Editorial Director
Barbara Drazin, Editor
Wendy Harris, Marketing Services Coordinator

Production Department

Deborah Eisel, Production Editor

Reading and Readability Editors

Jane L. Evanson
Helen B. Ward
Norma Libman

Deborah Nathan
Jane Friedland
Donna Wynbrandt

Authors and Contributors

Writing: Rob Sax

Social Studies: Robert Schambier
Carol Hagel
Phil Smolik
Jack Lesar
Nora Ishibashi
Helen T. Bryant
Jo Ann Kawell
Deborah Brewster
Mary E. Bromage
Sheldon B. Silver
Patricia Miripol

Science: Ronald LeMay
Cynthia Talbert
Jeffrey Miripol
John Gloor
William Collien
Charles Nissim-Sabat

Reading: Timothy A. Foote
Raymond Traynor
Pamela D. Drell (Editor)

Mathematics: Jerry Howett

Project Assistance
Sara Plath

Graphic Art: Louise Hodges
Cover Design: Jeff Barnes

CONTENTS

DECIMALS

PERCENT

TO THE LEARNER

Building Basic Skills in Mathematics is a good way to start your study in four areas of mathematics. This book will help you learn how to use WHOLE NUMBERS, FRACTIONS, DECIMALS and PERCENTS. Understanding these four areas will prepare you to build later skills in algebra and geometry.

Depending on what you already know, you may use this book in different ways.

Some people prefer to study only what they need to learn. Taking the PRE-TEST will help you decide which areas you need to study most. One hundred questions and problems make up the PRE-TEST. This will give you a good idea of all the skills you can learn with this book. Do not worry if you cannot work all the problems. The purpose of any pre-test is to show you where to start and what to study. If the test is too long to finish at one time, feel free to divide the problems into two or three parts.

After finishing the problems, turn to ANSWERS AND SOLUTIONS—PRE-TEST and make a list of mistakes you made and problems you could not work. Then turn to the PRE-TEST EVALUATION to find the skills you need to study.

2. Other people prefer to start at the beginning and work through the whole book. This is a good method, since math skills build upon each other. You may decide to skip the PRE-TEST and begin your work right away. You will find that the book will give you step-by-step instruction and plenty of practice.

Whichever way you decide to start building basic skills in mathematics, take plenty of time using this book. Be sure you know the material in each section before you go on to the next part. The skills test at the end of each section will help you decide how well you have learned the material.

When you have finished all four sections, the POST-TEST will help determine how much you have learned and what you need to review.

We hope you enjoy *Building Basic Skills in Mathematics*.

The Editors of Contemporary Books

PRE-TEST: Finding Out What You Know about Whole Numbers, Fractions, Decimals and Percent

Solve each problem. Use either the margin space or a separate piece of paper. There also is additional work space on page 10. Then write your answers on the blank beside the number of the problem. Answers to these problems begin on page 11.

1. _____   1.   In 7,265 the 2 is in what place?

2. _____   2.   What is the value of the 3 in 43,817?

3. _____   3.   Write eighty thousand, four hundred sixty as a whole number.

4. _____   4.   24,735   5. $973 + 28 + 16,382 =$
                          $+ 52,164$
5. _____

6. _____   6.   At Dave's Diner Joseph ordered the fish dinner for $3.35, a cup of coffee for 40¢, and a piece of chocolate cake for 85¢. The tax on his bill was 27¢. What was the total bill for Joseph's lunch including tax?

7. _____   7.   The highway distance from Miami to Atlanta is 604 miles. The distance from Atlanta to Memphis is 366 miles. What is the distance from Miami to Memphis by way of Atlanta?

8. _____   8.   4,963   9. $81,276 - 9,358 =$
                          $- 2,742$
9. _____

1

10. _____   10. $300,200 - 176,158 =$

11. _____   11.   Petra makes \$475 every two weeks. From her wages, her employer deducts \$51.96 for taxes and social security. How much does Petra take home every two weeks?

12. _____   12.   In 1800 the population of the United States was 5,308,000. In 1900 the population was 75,995,000. By how much did the population of the U.S. increase from 1800 to 1900?

13. _____   13.   84   14.   608   15. $763 \times 48 =$

14. _____ $\times\ 21$ $\times\ 37$

15. _____

16. _____   16. $19 \times 2,078 =$ 17. $984 \times 100 =$

17. _____

18. _____   18.   Joyce is paying \$48.70 a month for 16 months for her new furniture. What is the total price she is paying for the furniture?

19. _____   19.   There are 16 ounces in a pound. How many ounces are there in 15 pounds?

20. _____   20. $8\overline{)504}$ 21. $27\overline{)1,247}$

21. _____

22. _____   22. 31,262 ÷ 82 =   23.   13,338 ÷ 234 =

23. _____

24. _____   24. Last year Vito earned $14,244. How much did he earn each month?

25. _____   25. Patty bought three pounds of chicken for $2.67. What was the price of a pound of chicken?

26. _____   26. Reduce $\frac{48}{64}$ 27.   Raise $\frac{5}{7}$ to 42nds.

27. _____

28. _____   28. Change $\frac{66}{9}$ to a mixed number and reduce.

29. _____   29. Change $4\frac{7}{9}$ to an improper fraction.

30. _____   30. A foot contains 12 inches. 10 inches is what fractional part of a foot?

31. _____   31. $9\frac{3}{8}$ 32. $7\frac{11}{12}$ 33. $5\frac{2}{3}$

                        $+\ 4\frac{1}{8}$ $+\ 8\frac{2}{3}$ $7\frac{5}{9}$

32. _____

                                                              $+\ 4\frac{1}{2}$

33. _____

34. _____ 34. Alice bought $2\frac{3}{4}$ pounds of ground chuck, $3\frac{1}{2}$ pounds of chicken, and $1\frac{7}{16}$ pounds of cheese. Find the total weight of her purchases.

35. _____ 35. The distance from Valerie's home to her children's school is $2\frac{9}{10}$ miles. The distance from the school to her office is $5\frac{7}{10}$ miles. What is the distance from Valerie's home to her office by way of the school?

36. _____ 36. $\begin{array}{r} 6\frac{11}{12} \\ -2\frac{5}{12} \\ \hline \end{array}$ 37. $\begin{array}{r} 12\frac{3}{16} \\ -7\frac{9}{16} \\ \hline \end{array}$ 38. $\begin{array}{r} 8\frac{4}{9} \\ -4\frac{5}{6} \\ \hline \end{array}$

37. _____

38. _____

39. _____ 39. From a board $6\frac{1}{2}$ feet long, Jeff cut a piece $3\frac{11}{12}$ feet long. How long was the remaining piece?

40. _____ 40. Colette weighed $140\frac{1}{2}$ pounds last summer. She went on a diet and lost $18\frac{3}{4}$ pounds by Christmas. How much did she weigh at Christmas?

41. _____ 41. $\frac{4}{9} \times \frac{15}{16} =$ 42. $\frac{5}{8} \times 12 =$ 43. $2\frac{6}{7} \times 5\frac{1}{4} =$

42. _____

43. _____

44. _____   44. Carlos takes home $668 a month. He spends $\frac{1}{4}$ of his income on rent. How much does Carlos pay in rent each month?

45. _____   45. One yard of lumber costs $1.35. Find the cost of $8\frac{2}{3}$ yards of lumber.

46. _____   46. $\frac{11}{12} \div \frac{1}{2} =$ 47. $12 \div \frac{8}{9} =$

47. _____

48. _____   48. $2\frac{2}{7} \div 8 =$ 49. $2\frac{2}{9} \div 5\frac{1}{3} =$

49. _____

50. _____   50. $5\frac{1}{2}$ yards of material cost $26.40. What is the cost of one yard of the material?

51. _____   51. Sylvia has 12 pounds of peas from her garden. She wants to put them in cans that each contain $\frac{3}{4}$ pound of peas. How many cans will she fill?

52. _____   52. Write .012 in words.

53. _____   53. Write four hundred eight thousandths as a decimal.

54. _____   54. Write two hundred six and four ten-thousandths as a mixed decimal.

55. _____   55. Change .016 to a fraction and reduce.

56. _____   56. Change $\frac{9}{20}$ to a decimal.

57. _____   57. Which decimal is larger: .046 or .05?

58. _____   58. $.327 + 16 + 2.84 =$

59. _____   59. Adrienne's suitcase weighs 6.4 pounds. The clothes she packed for a trip weigh 7.25 pounds. The other items she packed weigh 3 pounds. What is the weight of Adrienne's suitcase when it is full?

60. _____   60. The population of Central County was 2.3 million people in 1970. In 1980 there were .85 million more people in the county. What was the population of Central County in 1980?

61. _____   61. $26 - 4.978 =$

62. _____   62. The yearly budget for Central City is $10.4 million. By June the city had spent $6.9 million. How much money was left in the budget for the rest of the year?

63. _____   63. On Friday morning the reading on the mileage gauge of John's car was 10,648.2 miles. On Sunday night the reading was 11,023.1 miles. How far did John drive between Friday morning and Sunday night?

64. _____   64. $12 \times 4.38 =$ 65. $.049 \times 4.6 =$

65. _____

66. _____   66. $8.27 \times 10 =$ 67. $.375 \times 100 =$

67. _____

68. _____   68. Ed earns \$5.60 an hour. How much does he earn for 38.5 hours of work?

69. _____   69. $9\overline{)66.6}$ 70. $.7\overline{).336}$ 71. $.015\overline{)9.45}$

70. _____

71. _____

72. _____   72. $.006\overline{)12}$ 73. $4.8 \div 10 =$ 74. $2.67 \div 100 =$

73. _____

74. _____

75. _____   75. Manny drove 243 miles in 4.5 hours. What was his average speed in miles per hour?

76. _____   76. Change .085 to a percent.

77. _____   77. Change 45% to a decimal.

78. _____   78. Change $\frac{7}{12}$ to a percent.

79. _____   79. Change 52% to a fraction and reduce.

80. _____   80. Change $41\frac{2}{3}$% to a fraction and reduce.

81. _____   81. Find 30% of 180.   82. Find 4.8% of 2000.

82. _____

83. _____   83. Find $62\frac{1}{2}$% of 96.   84. Find $7\frac{1}{2}$% of 400.

84. _____

85. _____   85. James earns $14,500 a year. He spends 20% of his income on food. How much does James spend on food in one year?

86. _____   86. Beverly bought a jacket for $24.59. The tax in her state is 8%. Find the price of the jacket including tax. Round off to the nearest cent.

87. _____   87. Albert earns $315 a week. His employer deducts 19% of Albert's salary for taxes and social security. What is Albert's weekly take-home pay?

88. _____   88. Find the interest on $800 at 7% annual interest for nine months.

89. _____   89. 21 is what % of 35?   90.   27 is what % of 81?

90. _____

91. _____   91. 150 is what % of 200?   92.   56 is what % of 64?

92. _____

93. _____   93. Jason borrowed $4000 to pay for his car. So far he has paid back $2500. What percent of the loan has Jason paid back?

94. _____   94. In 1970 the population of Middletown was 15,000 people. In 1980 the population was 21,000. By what percent did the population of Middletown increase from 1970 to 1980?

95. _____   95. 25% of what number is 32?

96. _____   96. 80% of what number is 48?

97. _____   97. 65% of what number is 39?

98. _____   98. $16\frac{2}{3}$% of what number is 24?

99. _____   99. The evening of a major snow storm, there were 12 students in Jerry's night school math class. The 12 are 60% of the number of students who are registered. How many students are registered in Jerry's class?

100. _____   100. Isabella paid $189 for an electric typewriter that was on sale. The $189 price was 90% of the original price. What was the original price of the typewriter?

Do your work here.

ANSWERS AND SOLUTIONS—PRE-TEST

1. hundreds

2. 3000

3. 80,460

4. 76,899

```
   24,735
 + 52,164
   76,899
```

5. 17,383

```
     973
      28
 + 16,382
   17,383
```

6. $4.87

```
 $3.35
   .40
   .85
 + .27
 $4.87
```

7. 970 miles

```
   604
 + 366
   970
```

8. 2,221

```
   4,963
 - 2,742
   2,221
```

9. 71,918

```
   81,276
 -  9,358
   71,918
```

10. 124,042

```
   300,200
 - 176,158
   124,042
```

11. $423.04

```
 $475.00
 -  51.96
 $423.04
```

12. 70,687,000

```
   75,995,000
 -  5,308,000
   70,687,000
```

13. 1,764

```
    84
 ×  21
    84
   168
  1,764
```

14. 22,496

```
    608
 ×   37
   4 256
  18 24
  22,496
```

15. 36,624

```
      763
    ×  48
    6 104
   30 52
   36,624
```

16. 39,482

```
      2,078
    ×    19
    18 702
    20 78
    39,482
```

17. 98,400

18. $779.20

```
     $48.70
    ×    16
    292 20
    487 0
    $779.20
```

19. 240 ounces

```
      16
    × 15
      80
      16
     240
```

20. 63

```
        63
    8)504
      48
      24
      24
```

21. 46 remainder 5

```
          46 remainder 5
    27)1,247
       1 08
        167
        162
          5
```

22. 381 remainder 20

```
           381 remainder 20
    82)31,262
       24 6
        6 66
        6 56
         102
          82
          20
```

23. 57

```
           57
    234)13,338
        11 70
         1 638
         1 638
```

24. $1,187

```
         $ 1,187
    12)$14,244
       12
        2 2
        1 2
        1 04
          96
          84
          84
```

25. $.89

$$\begin{array}{r} \$\ .89 \\ 3\overline{)\$2.67} \\ 2\ 4 \\ \hline 27 \\ 27 \\ \hline \end{array}$$

26. $\frac{3}{4}$

$$\frac{48}{64} = \frac{3}{4}$$

27. $\frac{30}{42}$

$$\frac{5}{7} = \frac{30}{42}$$

28. $7\frac{1}{3}$

$$7\frac{3}{9} = 7\frac{1}{3}$$
$$\begin{array}{r} 9\overline{)66} \\ 63 \\ \hline 3 \\ \hline \end{array}$$

29. $\frac{43}{9}$

$$4\frac{7}{9} = \frac{43}{9}$$

30. $\frac{5}{6}$

$$\frac{10}{12} = \frac{5}{6}$$

31. $13\frac{1}{2}$

$$\begin{array}{r} 9\frac{3}{8} \\ +\ 4\frac{1}{8} \\ \hline 13\frac{4}{8} = 13\frac{1}{2} \end{array}$$

32. $16\frac{7}{12}$

$$\begin{array}{r} 7\frac{11}{12} = 7\frac{11}{12} \\ +\ 8\frac{2}{3} = 8\frac{8}{12} \\ \hline 15\frac{19}{12} = 16\frac{7}{12} \end{array}$$

33. $17\frac{13}{18}$

$$\begin{array}{r} 5\frac{2}{3} = 5\frac{12}{18} \\ 7\frac{5}{9} = 7\frac{10}{18} \\ +\ 4\frac{1}{2} = 4\frac{9}{18} \\ \hline 16\frac{31}{18} = 17\frac{13}{18} \end{array}$$

34. $7\frac{11}{16}$ lb.

$$\begin{array}{r} 2\frac{3}{4} = 2\frac{12}{16} \\ 3\frac{1}{2} = 3\frac{8}{16} \\ +\ 1\frac{7}{16} = 1\frac{7}{16} \\ \hline 6\frac{27}{16} = 7\frac{11}{16} \end{array}$$

35. $8\frac{3}{5}$ mi.

$$2\frac{9}{10}$$
$$+ 5\frac{7}{10}$$
$$7\frac{16}{10} = 8\frac{6}{10} = 8\frac{3}{5}$$

36. $4\frac{1}{2}$

$$6\frac{11}{12}$$
$$- 2\frac{5}{12}$$
$$4\frac{6}{12} = 4\frac{1}{2}$$

37. $4\frac{5}{8}$

$$12\frac{3}{16} = 11\frac{19}{16}$$
$$- 7\frac{9}{16} = 7\frac{9}{16}$$
$$4\frac{10}{16} = 4\frac{5}{8}$$

38. $3\frac{11}{18}$

$$8\frac{4}{9} = 8\frac{8}{18} = 7\frac{26}{18}$$
$$- 4\frac{5}{6} = 4\frac{15}{18} = 4\frac{15}{18}$$
$$3\frac{11}{18}$$

39. $2\frac{7}{12}$ ft.

$$6\frac{1}{2} = 6\frac{6}{12} = 5\frac{18}{12}$$
$$- 3\frac{11}{12} = 3\frac{11}{12} = 3\frac{11}{12}$$
$$2\frac{7}{12}$$

40. $121\frac{3}{4}$ lb.

$$140\frac{1}{2} = 140\frac{2}{4} = 139\frac{6}{4}$$
$$- 18\frac{3}{4} = 18\frac{3}{4} = 18\frac{3}{4}$$
$$121\frac{3}{4}$$

41. $\frac{5}{12}$

$$\overset{1}{\underset{3}{\cancel{4}}}\over 9 \times \overset{5}{\underset{4}{\cancel{15}}}\over 16 = \frac{5}{12}$$

42. $7\frac{1}{2}$

$$\frac{5}{8} \times 12 =$$

$$\frac{5}{\underset{2}{\cancel{8}}} \times \frac{\overset{3}{\cancel{12}}}{1} = \frac{15}{2} = 7\frac{1}{2}$$

43. 15

$$2\frac{6}{7} \times 5\frac{1}{4} =$$

$$\frac{\overset{5}{\cancel{20}}}{\underset{1}{\cancel{7}}} \times \frac{\overset{3}{\cancel{21}}}{\underset{1}{\cancel{4}}} = 15$$

44. $167

$$\frac{1}{\underset{1}{\cancel{4}}} \times \frac{\overset{167}{\cancel{668}}}{1} = 167$$

45. $11.70

$$8\frac{2}{3} \times \frac{1.35}{1}$$

$$\frac{26}{\cancel{3}} \times \frac{\cancel{1.35}^{.45}}{1} = 11.70$$
$$\phantom{\frac{26}{3}}_1$$

46. $1\frac{5}{6}$

$$\frac{11}{\cancel{12}_6} \times \frac{\cancel{2}^1}{1} = \frac{11}{6} = 1\frac{5}{6}$$

47. $13\frac{1}{2}$

$$\frac{\cancel{12}^3}{1} \times \frac{9}{\cancel{8}_2} = \frac{27}{2} = 13\frac{1}{2}$$

48. $\frac{2}{7}$

$$\frac{\cancel{16}^2}{7} \times \frac{1}{\cancel{8}_1} = \frac{2}{7}$$

49. $\frac{5}{12}$

$$\frac{20}{9} \div \frac{16}{3} =$$

$$\frac{\cancel{20}^5}{\cancel{9}_3} \times \frac{\cancel{3}^1}{\cancel{16}_4} = \frac{5}{12}$$

50. $4.80

$$\$26.40 \div 5\frac{1}{2} =$$

$$\frac{26.40}{1} \div \frac{11}{2} =$$

$$\frac{\cancel{26.40}^{2.40}}{1} \times \frac{2}{\cancel{11}_1} = 4.80$$

51. 16 cans

$$12 \div \frac{3}{4} =$$

$$\frac{\cancel{12}^4}{1} \times \frac{4}{\cancel{3}_1} = 16$$

52. twelve thousandths

53. .408

54. 206.0004

55. $\frac{2}{125}$

$$\frac{16}{1000} = \frac{2}{125}$$

56. .45

$$20\overline{)9.00}^{\,.45}$$

57. .05

    .046 or <u>.050</u>

58. 19.167

$$
\begin{array}{r}
.327 \\
16.0 \\
+\ 2.84 \\
\hline
19.167
\end{array}
$$

59. 16.65 lbs.

$$
\begin{array}{r}
6.4 \\
7.25 \\
+\ 3.0 \\
\hline
16.65
\end{array}
$$

60. 3.15 million

$$
\begin{array}{r}
2.3 \text{ million} \\
+\ .85 \\
\hline
3.15 \text{ million}
\end{array}
$$

61. 21.022

$$
\begin{array}{r}
26.000 \\
-\ 4.978 \\
\hline
21.022
\end{array}
$$

62. $3.5 million

$$
\begin{array}{r}
\$10.4 \text{ million} \\
-\ 6.9 \\
\hline
\$\ 3.5 \text{ million}
\end{array}
$$

63. 374.9 mi.

$$
\begin{array}{r}
11,023.1 \\
-\ 10,648.2 \\
\hline
374.9
\end{array}
$$

64. 52.56

$$
\begin{array}{r}
4.38 \\
\times\ 12 \\
\hline
8\ 76 \\
43\ 8 \\
\hline
52.56
\end{array}
$$

65. .2254

$$
\begin{array}{r}
.049 \\
\times\ 4.6 \\
\hline
294 \\
196 \\
\hline
.2254
\end{array}
$$

66. 82.7

67. 37.5

68. $215.60

$$
\begin{array}{r}
\$5.60 \\
\times\ 38.5 \\
\hline
2\ 800 \\
44\ 80 \\
168\ 0 \\
\hline
\$215.60\cancel{0}
\end{array}
$$

69. 7.4

$$
\begin{array}{r}
7.4 \\
9\overline{)66.6} \\
63 \\
\hline
36 \\
36 \\
\hline
\end{array}
$$

70. .48

$$
\begin{array}{r}
.48 \\
.7\overline{).336} \\
28 \\
\hline
56 \\
56 \\
\hline
\end{array}
$$

71. 630

$$
\begin{array}{r}
630 \\
.015\overline{)9.450} \\
9\,0 \\
\hline
45 \\
45 \\
\hline
\end{array}
$$

72. 2000

$$
\begin{array}{r}
2000 \\
.006\overline{)12.000}
\end{array}
$$

73. .48

74. .0267

75. 54 mph

$$
\begin{array}{r}
5\,4 \\
4.5\overline{)243.0} \\
225 \\
\hline
18\,0 \\
18\,0 \\
\hline
\end{array}
$$

76. 8.5%

$$.085 = .08\,5 = 8.5\%$$

77. .45

$$45\% = 45. = .45$$

78. $58\frac{1}{3}\%$

$$\frac{7}{\cancel{12}}_{3} \times \frac{\overset{25}{\cancel{100}}}{1} = \frac{175}{3} = 58\frac{1}{3}\%$$

79. $\frac{13}{25}$

$$\frac{52}{100} = \frac{13}{25}$$

80. $\frac{5}{12}$

$$41\frac{2}{3} \div 100 =$$

$$\frac{\overset{5}{\cancel{125}}}{3} \times \frac{1}{\underset{4}{\cancel{100}}} = \frac{5}{12}$$

81. 54

$$30\% = .30 \qquad \begin{array}{r} 180 \\ \times\, .30 \\ \hline 54.\cancel{0}\cancel{0} \end{array}$$

82. 96

$$4.8\% = .048 \qquad \begin{array}{r} 2000 \\ \times\, .048 \\ \hline 16\,000 \\ 80\,00 \\ \hline 96.\cancel{0}\cancel{0}\cancel{0} \end{array}$$

83. 60

$$62\tfrac{1}{2}\% = \frac{5}{8}$$

$$\frac{5}{\cancel{8}} \times \frac{\overset{12}{\cancel{96}}}{1} = 60$$
$$\phantom{\frac{5}{8}}_{1}$$

84. 30

$$\frac{15}{\cancel{2}} \times \frac{\overset{\overset{2}{\cancel{4}}}{\cancel{400}}}{\cancel{100}} = 30$$
$$_{1}_{1}$$

85. $2,900

$$20\% = .2 \qquad \begin{array}{r} \$\,14,500 \\ \times\, .2 \\ \hline \$2,900.\cancel{0} \end{array}$$

86. $26.56

$$\begin{array}{r} \$24.59 \\ \times\, .08 \\ \hline 1.9672 \end{array} \qquad \begin{array}{r} \$24.59 \\ +\, 1.97 \\ \hline \$26.56 \end{array}$$

$1.9672 rounds off to $1.97

87. $255.15

$$\begin{array}{r} \$315 \\ \times\, .19 \\ \hline 2835 \\ 315 \\ \hline \$59.85 \end{array} \qquad \begin{array}{r} \$315.00 \\ -\, 59.85 \\ \hline \$255.15 \end{array}$$

88. $42

$$9 \text{ mos.} = \frac{9}{12} = \frac{3}{4}$$

$$\frac{\overset{\overset{2}{\cancel{8}}}{\cancel{800}}}{1} \times \frac{7}{\cancel{100}} \times \frac{3}{\cancel{4}} = 42$$
$$_{1}_{1}$$

89. 60%

$$\frac{21}{35} = \frac{3}{5}$$

$$\frac{3}{\cancel{5}} \times \frac{\overset{20}{\cancel{100}}}{1} = 60\%$$
$$\phantom{\frac{3}{5}}_{1}$$

90. $33\tfrac{1}{3}\%$

$$\frac{27}{81} = \frac{1}{3}$$

$$\frac{1}{3} \times \frac{100}{1} = \frac{100}{3} = 33\tfrac{1}{3}\%$$

91. 75%

$$\frac{150}{200} = \frac{3}{4}$$

$$\frac{3}{\cancel{4}} \times \frac{\overset{25}{\cancel{100}}}{1} = 75\%$$
$$\phantom{\frac{3}{4}}_{1}$$

92. $87\tfrac{1}{2}\%$

$$\frac{56}{64} = \frac{7}{8}$$

$$\frac{7}{\cancel{8}} \times \frac{\overset{25}{\cancel{100}}}{1} = \frac{175}{2} = 87\tfrac{1}{2}\%$$
$$\phantom{\frac{7}{8}}_{2}$$

93. $62\frac{1}{2}\%$

$$\frac{2500}{4000} = \frac{5}{8}$$

$$\frac{5}{\cancel{8}} \times \frac{\overset{25}{\cancel{100}}}{1} = \frac{125}{2} = 62\frac{1}{2}\%$$

94. 40%

$$\begin{array}{r} 21,000 \\ -\ 15,000 \\ \hline 6,000 \end{array} \qquad \frac{6,000}{15,000} = \frac{2}{5}$$

$$\frac{2}{\cancel{5}} \times \frac{\overset{20}{\cancel{100}}}{1} = 40\%$$

95. 128

$$25\% = \frac{1}{4}$$

$$32 \div \frac{1}{4} = 32 \times \frac{4}{1} = 128$$

96. 60

$$80\% = \frac{4}{5}$$

$$48 \div \frac{4}{5} = \overset{12}{\cancel{48}} \times \frac{5}{\cancel{4}} = 60$$

97. 60

$$65\% = .65$$

$$\begin{array}{r} 60 \\ .65\overline{)39.00} \\ \underline{39\ 0} \end{array}$$

98. 144

$$16\frac{2}{3}\% = \frac{1}{6}$$

$$24 \div \frac{1}{6} = 24 \times \frac{6}{1} = 144$$

99. 20 students

$$60\% = \frac{3}{5}$$

$$12 \div \frac{3}{5} = \overset{4}{\cancel{12}} \times \frac{5}{\cancel{3}} = 20$$

100. $210

$$90\% = \frac{9}{10}$$

$$189 \div \frac{9}{10} = \overset{21}{\cancel{189}} \times \frac{10}{\cancel{9}} = 210$$

PRE-TEST EVALUATION

Following is a list of the problems on the test and the topics to which each problem belongs. It is important to study the entire book since mathematics builds upon previously developed skills. However, by comparing the problems you got wrong to the topics, you can determine the areas in which you need the most work.

Problems	*Topics*
	WHOLE NUMBERS
1, 2, 3	Understanding Whole Numbers
4, 5	Adding Whole Numbers

WHOLE NUMBERS

UNDERSTANDING WHOLE NUMBERS

The population of New York City is 7895563. This number is not easy to read. It needs commas to help us understand the *place value* of each *digit*.

A *digit* is one of the numerals (0, 1, 2, 3, 4, 5, 6, 7, 8, or 9) that combines to make a whole number. The population of New York City is a seven-digit number.

To make numbers easy to read, we put commas after every three digits beginning from the right. The population of New York City becomes 7,895,563 which we read as seven million, eight hundred ninety-five thousand, five hundred sixty-three. The *place value* of each digit tells us what the digit is worth. Here are the names of the first ten places in our number system.

units or ones
tens
hundreds
thousands
ten thousands
hundred thousands
millions
ten millions
hundred millions
billions

—, — — —, — — —, — — —

If we write the population of New York in the blanks, we get:

—, — — 7, 8 9 5, 5 6 3

Since the 3 is in the units place, the value of 3 is 3 ones or 3.
Since the 6 is in the tens place, the value of 6 is 6 tens or 60.
Since the 9 is in the ten-thousands place, the value of 9 is 9 ten-thousands or 90,000.

EXAMPLE: In the number 2,564 the 5 is in what place?

ANSWER: hundreds

EXAMPLE: What is the value of the 5 in 2,564?

ANSWER: 500

---

1.   In 213 the 2 is in what place?

2.   In 74 the 7 is in what place?

3.   In 4,362 the 4 is in what place?

4.   In 985 the 5 is in what place?

5.   In 62,597 the 6 is in what place?

6.   What is the value of the 4 in 4,658?

7.   What is the value of the 9 in 20,962?

8.   What is the value of the 7 in 3,672?

9.   What is the value of the 2 in 1,269,408?

10.   What is the value of the 1 in 418,295,463?

Answers begin on page 65.

WRITING WHOLE NUMBERS

The Ohio-Allegheny River system is one thousand, three hundred six miles long. Because it's easier, we write large numbers with digits, not words. The length of the Ohio-Allegheny River becomes 1,306 miles. Since the number has no tens, we *hold* the tens place with a zero.

EXAMPLE: Write two hundred three thousand, seventy-six as a whole number.

SOLUTION: Since the number contains no ten-thousands and no hundreds, we hold those places with zeros.
203,076

Write each of the following as whole numbers.

11. six hundred four

12. four thousand, three hundred twenty

13. eighty

14. nine million, five hundred fifty thousand, seventeen

15. ten thousand, ninety

16. five thousand, two

17. eight million, nine hundred two thousand

18. three million, eighty-seven thousand, nine hundred

19. seven hundred thousand, two hundred six

20. eighty-nine million, four hundred fifty thousand

Answers begin on page 65.

ADDING WHOLE NUMBERS

Basic Addition Facts

The basic building blocks of mathematics are the addition, subtraction, multiplication, and division facts. In order to work with numbers in your everyday life, you must know these basic facts. You must know that 9 plus 7 is 16. Counting—in your head or on your fingers—takes too long.

The following exercise gives practice with the addition facts. Write every fact that you know. Check your answers and practice any facts that you did not know. Then cover your answers and repeat this exercise until you know every fact.

1. $\begin{array}{r}4\\+2\\\hline\end{array}$ $\begin{array}{r}9\\+6\\\hline\end{array}$ $\begin{array}{r}2\\+8\\\hline\end{array}$ $\begin{array}{r}7\\+3\\\hline\end{array}$ $\begin{array}{r}0\\+6\\\hline\end{array}$ $\begin{array}{r}1\\+8\\\hline\end{array}$ $\begin{array}{r}3\\+3\\\hline\end{array}$ $\begin{array}{r}5\\+7\\\hline\end{array}$ $\begin{array}{r}8\\+5\\\hline\end{array}$

2. $\begin{array}{r}3\\+4\\\hline\end{array}$ $\begin{array}{r}8\\+8\\\hline\end{array}$ $\begin{array}{r}6\\+4\\\hline\end{array}$ $\begin{array}{r}2\\+0\\\hline\end{array}$ $\begin{array}{r}7\\+6\\\hline\end{array}$ $\begin{array}{r}9\\+3\\\hline\end{array}$ $\begin{array}{r}4\\+1\\\hline\end{array}$ $\begin{array}{r}8\\+2\\\hline\end{array}$ $\begin{array}{r}1\\+5\\\hline\end{array}$

3. $\begin{array}{r}6\\+8\\\hline\end{array}$ $\begin{array}{r}9\\+9\\\hline\end{array}$ $\begin{array}{r}3\\+1\\\hline\end{array}$ $\begin{array}{r}5\\+4\\\hline\end{array}$ $\begin{array}{r}2\\+2\\\hline\end{array}$ $\begin{array}{r}0\\+8\\\hline\end{array}$ $\begin{array}{r}4\\+7\\\hline\end{array}$ $\begin{array}{r}1\\+1\\\hline\end{array}$ $\begin{array}{r}3\\+7\\\hline\end{array}$

4. $\begin{array}{r}4\\+5\\\hline\end{array}$ $\begin{array}{r}1\\+3\\\hline\end{array}$ $\begin{array}{r}0\\+7\\\hline\end{array}$ $\begin{array}{r}9\\+2\\\hline\end{array}$ $\begin{array}{r}5\\+9\\\hline\end{array}$ $\begin{array}{r}2\\+6\\\hline\end{array}$ $\begin{array}{r}8\\+7\\\hline\end{array}$ $\begin{array}{r}5\\+2\\\hline\end{array}$ $\begin{array}{r}6\\+6\\\hline\end{array}$

5. $\begin{array}{r}7\\+8\\\hline\end{array}$ $\begin{array}{r}4\\+4\\\hline\end{array}$ $\begin{array}{r}6\\+1\\\hline\end{array}$ $\begin{array}{r}2\\+5\\\hline\end{array}$ $\begin{array}{r}9\\+8\\\hline\end{array}$ $\begin{array}{r}1\\+0\\\hline\end{array}$ $\begin{array}{r}8\\+4\\\hline\end{array}$ $\begin{array}{r}5\\+3\\\hline\end{array}$ $\begin{array}{r}2\\+4\\\hline\end{array}$

6. $\begin{array}{r}1\\+7\\\hline\end{array}$ $\begin{array}{r}4\\+6\\\hline\end{array}$ $\begin{array}{r}5\\+0\\\hline\end{array}$ $\begin{array}{r}7\\+7\\\hline\end{array}$ $\begin{array}{r}2\\+1\\\hline\end{array}$ $\begin{array}{r}3\\+6\\\hline\end{array}$ $\begin{array}{r}7\\+4\\\hline\end{array}$ $\begin{array}{r}6\\+5\\\hline\end{array}$ $\begin{array}{r}9\\+0\\\hline\end{array}$

7. $\begin{array}{r}8\\+3\\\hline\end{array}$ $\begin{array}{r}1\\+9\\\hline\end{array}$ $\begin{array}{r}9\\+5\\\hline\end{array}$ $\begin{array}{r}8\\+1\\\hline\end{array}$ $\begin{array}{r}5\\+6\\\hline\end{array}$ $\begin{array}{r}2\\+3\\\hline\end{array}$ $\begin{array}{r}4\\+9\\\hline\end{array}$ $\begin{array}{r}9\\+7\\\hline\end{array}$ $\begin{array}{r}3\\+2\\\hline\end{array}$

8. $\begin{array}{r}1\\+4\\\hline\end{array}$ $\begin{array}{r}6\\+7\\\hline\end{array}$ $\begin{array}{r}8\\+6\\\hline\end{array}$ $\begin{array}{r}6\\+3\\\hline\end{array}$ $\begin{array}{r}1\\+2\\\hline\end{array}$ $\begin{array}{r}3\\+5\\\hline\end{array}$ $\begin{array}{r}2\\+7\\\hline\end{array}$ $\begin{array}{r}5\\+5\\\hline\end{array}$ $\begin{array}{r}7\\+1\\\hline\end{array}$

9. $\begin{array}{r}8\\+9\\\hline\end{array}$ $\begin{array}{r}0\\+4\\\hline\end{array}$ $\begin{array}{r}1\\+6\\\hline\end{array}$ $\begin{array}{r}9\\+1\\\hline\end{array}$ $\begin{array}{r}7\\+5\\\hline\end{array}$ $\begin{array}{r}5\\+8\\\hline\end{array}$ $\begin{array}{r}4\\+3\\\hline\end{array}$ $\begin{array}{r}6\\+9\\\hline\end{array}$ $\begin{array}{r}2\\+9\\\hline\end{array}$

10.
5	7	3	6	3	4	7	9	3
+ 1	+ 2	+ 0	+ 2	+ 9	+ 8	+ 9	+ 4	+ 8

Answers begin on page 66.

Adding Larger Numbers

PROBLEM: When Sylvia went shopping she spent $46 for groceries and $32 for household supplies. What was her total bill?

SOLUTION: Add the two amounts. Begin with the units, and add each column as you move to the left.

Step 1. $6 + 2 = 8$ $46

Step 2. $4 + 3 = 7$ + 32

$78

PROBLEM: Sam ironed 10 shirts on Friday. The next day he ironed 15 handkerchiefs and 14 cloth napkins. In two days how many items did Sam iron?

SOLUTION: Add the three amounts. Write the problem so that for each number, units are over units and tens are over tens. Add the first two numbers. Then add the third number to their sum.

Step 1. $0 + 5 = 5$

Step 2. $5 + 4 = 9$ 10 shirts

Step 3. $1 + 1 = 2$ 15 handkerchiefs
                   + 14 cloth napkins

Step 4. $2 + 1 = 3$ 39 items

Add the following numbers.

11.
3	6	5	3	8	2	4	1	9
4	2	5	6	2	3	8	7	6
+ 5	+ 1	+ 8	+ 2	+ 5	+ 8	+ 5	+ 6	+ 2

12.
24	76	45	31	20	14
51	11	32	22	51	30
+ 10	+ 12	+ 10	+ 12	+ 13	+ 23

Checking Addition

To check an addition problem, add the numbers in each column from the bottom.

Step 1. $2 + 6 = 8$

Step 2. $3 + 4 = 7$

$$
\begin{array}{r}
78\checkmark \\
46 \\
+\ 32 \\
\hline
78\checkmark
\end{array}
$$

Add and check.

13.
32	48	54	82	70	36	15
+ 46	+ 31	+ 22	+ 17	+ 20	+ 61	+ 54

14.
734	580	416	582	561	492
+ 234	+ 219	+ 333	+ 216	+ 407	+ 306

15.
8,634	4,575	6,892	2,150	7,063
+ 1,332	+ 2,403	+ 3,106	+ 6,807	+ 3,426

16.
73,208	57,423	16,256	50,874	33,486
+ 24,501	+ 30,466	+ 81,032	+ 49,122	+ 30,503

17.
9,604	419	6,193	120	3,241
+ 293	+ 7,380	+ 602	+ 4,876	+ 427

Answers begin on page 66.

Adding and Carrying

PROBLEM: On weekends the Midtown Theatre has three shows. Friday night 208 people went to the theatre. Saturday afternoon 97 people went. Saturday night 236 people went. What was the total attendance at the theatre that weekend?

SOLUTION:
$$\begin{array}{r} 12 \\ 208 \\ 97 \\ +\ 236 \\ \hline 541 \end{array}$$

Step 1.   Line up the numbers with units under units, tens under tens, and hundreds under hundreds.

Step 2.   Add the units: $8 + 7 = 15$. $15 + 6 = 21$.

Step 3.   Write the 1 in the units column, and *carry* the 2 tens to the tens column.

Step 4.   Add the tens: $2 + 9 = 11$. $11 + 3 = 14$.

Step 5.   Write the 4 in the tens column, and carry the 1 to the hundreds column.

Step 6.   Add the hundreds: $1 + 2 = 3$. $3 + 2 = 5$. Write the 5 in the hundreds column.

The answer, 541 is called the *sum* or the *total*.

People sometimes run into trouble because they do not line up the numbers in their problems well. When you add the ones, put the answer directly below the ones. When you add the tens, put the answer below the tens. Carefully lining up your work can help prevent errors.

Checking

To check a problem that involves carrying, use the following method.

PROBLEM:
$$\begin{array}{r} 208 \\ 97 \\ +\ 236 \end{array}$$

Step 1.   Add the units: $8 + 7 = 15$. $15 + 6 = 21$. Write down
the entire total to the units.

Step 2.   Add the tens: $9 + 3 = 12$. Write down the entire total
to the tens, but leave the units column blank.

Step 3.   Add the hundreds: $2 + 2 = 4$. Write down the total
but leave the units and tens columns blank.

Step 4.   Add the new figures you wrote down.

$$\begin{array}{r} 21 \\ 12 \\ +\ 4 \\ \hline 541 \end{array}$$

Add and check.

18.

48	69	74	39	67	92
+ 56	+ 82	+ 76	+ 83	+ 66	+ 49

19.

508	763	428	256	758	679
+ 693	+ 547	+ 984	+ 976	+ 457	+ 823

20.

81	53	46	85	52	80
85	49	77	24	46	93
+ 36	+ 70	+ 24	+ 17	+ 25	+ 28

21.

394	649	43	86	781	977
758	80	568	904	59	256
+ 26	+ 506	+ 257	+ 25	+ 643	+ 458

22.

3,487	2,286	5,842	3,095	4,306
4,908	536	10,493	635	8,340
2,864	83	388	827	9,755
+ 1,335	+ 2,947	+ 59	+ 3,046	+ 2,647

Answers begin on page 67.

Adding Numbers Written Horizontally

So far in this book the adding problems have been lined up for you, but in everyday situations, numbers are not often set up for you to add. The exercise below contains numbers written side by side. You must rewrite the problem so that the units are under the units, the tens are under the tens, and everything is in its right place.

EXAMPLE: $48 + 7 + 206 =$ Rewrite as:

$$\begin{array}{r} 2 \\ 48 \\ 7 \\ + \ 206 \\ \hline 261 \end{array}$$

Add and check.

23. $49 + 8 + 56 =$ $3 + 95 + 207 =$

24. $47 + 286 + 9 =$ $16 + 427 + 38 =$

25. $68 + 341 + 2,094 =$ $10 + 834 + 5,845 =$

26. $5,732 + 26 + 47 + 208 =$ $83 + 191 + 40 + 6,072 =$

27. $9,823 + 50,474 + 335 =$ $204 + 60,713 + 2,056 =$

Answers begin on page 68.

Applying Your Addition Skills

To solve any word problem, read the problem carefully and watch for the words that give you clues about which operation or operations you will need to use. For addition, some of the key words are *total, sum, altogether,* and *combined.*

Many problems involve adding money. Be sure to line up money problems with cents under cents and dollars under dollars.

EXAMPLE: Find the total bill for a pen that costs $1.79, another pen that costs $4 and tax of 29¢.

SOLUTION:

$$\begin{array}{r} 1\ 1 \\ \$1.79 \\ 4.00 \\ +\ .29 \\ \hline \$6.08 \end{array}$$

Be sure to put the correct label, such as $, pounds, or miles, next to each answer.

Add and check.

28. Manny is 72 inches tall. Jack is 3 inches taller than Manny. How tall is Jack?

29. At the Rigby Bindery there are 127 people in the shop, fourteen people in the office, eight traveling salesmen, and four custodians. What is the combined number of employees working for the bindery?

30. If a ship weighs 1,875,000 pounds when it is not loaded, how much does it weigh with 727,500 pounds of cargo?

31. The Brooklyn Bridge has a span of 1,596 feet. The George Washington Bridge spans 1,904 feet farther. What is the span of the George Washington Bridge?

32. In December Heather's phone bill included $9.19 for monthly service, $20.43 for long-distance calls, and $1.62 for tax. What was the total amount of her phone bill?

33. When Carl and Lois went out to lunch, Carl had a cheeseburger platter for $2.35 and a beer for 75¢. Lois ordered a salad for $1.10, soup for 95¢, and iced tea for 50¢. The tax on their bill was 34¢, and they left a tip of 85¢. How much did they spend altogether?

34. Every week Ms. Stroud's employer deducts $15.68 for federal tax, $11.54 for social security, and $4.73 for state tax. What are the combined deductions from her weekly paycheck?

35. For every person in New York, the city government each year spends $99.38 for police and fire protection, $151.41 for health and hospitals, $295.63 for education, and $314.81 for welfare. Find the total of these amounts.

Answers begin on page 68.

SUBTRACTING WHOLE NUMBERS

Basic Subtraction Facts

The following exercise gives practice with the subtraction facts. Write every fact that you know, but do not count to get the answers.

Check your answers and practice any facts that you did not know.
Then cover your answers and repeat this exercise until you know
every fact.

1.
$$\begin{array}{r} 14 \\ -6 \\ \hline \end{array} \quad \begin{array}{r} 8 \\ -2 \\ \hline \end{array} \quad \begin{array}{r} 6 \\ -5 \\ \hline \end{array} \quad \begin{array}{r} 7 \\ -4 \\ \hline \end{array} \quad \begin{array}{r} 15 \\ -9 \\ \hline \end{array} \quad \begin{array}{r} 12 \\ -3 \\ \hline \end{array} \quad \begin{array}{r} 13 \\ -4 \\ \hline \end{array} \quad \begin{array}{r} 11 \\ -5 \\ \hline \end{array} \quad \begin{array}{r} 6 \\ -6 \\ \hline \end{array}$$

2.
$$\begin{array}{r} 12 \\ -9 \\ \hline \end{array} \quad \begin{array}{r} 9 \\ -6 \\ \hline \end{array} \quad \begin{array}{r} 10 \\ -4 \\ \hline \end{array} \quad \begin{array}{r} 3 \\ -2 \\ \hline \end{array} \quad \begin{array}{r} 6 \\ -2 \\ \hline \end{array} \quad \begin{array}{r} 9 \\ -9 \\ \hline \end{array} \quad \begin{array}{r} 8 \\ -0 \\ \hline \end{array} \quad \begin{array}{r} 9 \\ -3 \\ \hline \end{array} \quad \begin{array}{r} 10 \\ -7 \\ \hline \end{array}$$

3.
$$\begin{array}{r} 3 \\ -0 \\ \hline \end{array} \quad \begin{array}{r} 11 \\ -2 \\ \hline \end{array} \quad \begin{array}{r} 12 \\ -7 \\ \hline \end{array} \quad \begin{array}{r} 6 \\ -3 \\ \hline \end{array} \quad \begin{array}{r} 17 \\ -9 \\ \hline \end{array} \quad \begin{array}{r} 1 \\ -0 \\ \hline \end{array} \quad \begin{array}{r} 10 \\ -1 \\ \hline \end{array} \quad \begin{array}{r} 14 \\ -9 \\ \hline \end{array} \quad \begin{array}{r} 8 \\ -8 \\ \hline \end{array}$$

4.
$$\begin{array}{r} 16 \\ -8 \\ \hline \end{array} \quad \begin{array}{r} 7 \\ -1 \\ \hline \end{array} \quad \begin{array}{r} 13 \\ -6 \\ \hline \end{array} \quad \begin{array}{r} 2 \\ -0 \\ \hline \end{array} \quad \begin{array}{r} 10 \\ -3 \\ \hline \end{array} \quad \begin{array}{r} 15 \\ -7 \\ \hline \end{array} \quad \begin{array}{r} 11 \\ -7 \\ \hline \end{array} \quad \begin{array}{r} 8 \\ -5 \\ \hline \end{array} \quad \begin{array}{r} 6 \\ -0 \\ \hline \end{array}$$

5.
$$\begin{array}{r} 10 \\ -8 \\ \hline \end{array} \quad \begin{array}{r} 5 \\ -3 \\ \hline \end{array} \quad \begin{array}{r} 12 \\ -5 \\ \hline \end{array} \quad \begin{array}{r} 13 \\ -9 \\ \hline \end{array} \quad \begin{array}{r} 9 \\ -8 \\ \hline \end{array} \quad \begin{array}{r} 14 \\ -7 \\ \hline \end{array} \quad \begin{array}{r} 7 \\ -0 \\ \hline \end{array} \quad \begin{array}{r} 10 \\ -5 \\ \hline \end{array} \quad \begin{array}{r} 8 \\ -3 \\ \hline \end{array}$$

6.
$$\begin{array}{r} 4 \\ -4 \\ \hline \end{array} \quad \begin{array}{r} 9 \\ -1 \\ \hline \end{array} \quad \begin{array}{r} 12 \\ -4 \\ \hline \end{array} \quad \begin{array}{r} 9 \\ -4 \\ \hline \end{array} \quad \begin{array}{r} 2 \\ -2 \\ \hline \end{array} \quad \begin{array}{r} 12 \\ -6 \\ \hline \end{array} \quad \begin{array}{r} 11 \\ -8 \\ \hline \end{array} \quad \begin{array}{r} 7 \\ -2 \\ \hline \end{array} \quad \begin{array}{r} 5 \\ -5 \\ \hline \end{array}$$

7.
$$\begin{array}{r} 13 \\ -5 \\ \hline \end{array} \quad \begin{array}{r} 11 \\ -6 \\ \hline \end{array} \quad \begin{array}{r} 12 \\ -8 \\ \hline \end{array} \quad \begin{array}{r} 3 \\ -3 \\ \hline \end{array} \quad \begin{array}{r} 15 \\ -6 \\ \hline \end{array} \quad \begin{array}{r} 8 \\ -1 \\ \hline \end{array} \quad \begin{array}{r} 9 \\ -7 \\ \hline \end{array} \quad \begin{array}{r} 11 \\ -3 \\ \hline \end{array} \quad \begin{array}{r} 16 \\ -9 \\ \hline \end{array}$$

8.
$$\begin{array}{r} 6 \\ -4 \\ \hline \end{array} \quad \begin{array}{r} 10 \\ -6 \\ \hline \end{array} \quad \begin{array}{r} 5 \\ -1 \\ \hline \end{array} \quad \begin{array}{r} 7 \\ -7 \\ \hline \end{array} \quad \begin{array}{r} 4 \\ -3 \\ \hline \end{array} \quad \begin{array}{r} 13 \\ -7 \\ \hline \end{array} \quad \begin{array}{r} 9 \\ -0 \\ \hline \end{array} \quad \begin{array}{r} 3 \\ -1 \\ \hline \end{array} \quad \begin{array}{r} 14 \\ -8 \\ \hline \end{array}$$

9.
18	15	0	8	4	7	11	9	17
−9	−8	−0	−6	−1	−5	−4	−5	−8

10.
5	14	8	2	16	6	13	1	8
−2	−5	−4	−1	−7	−1	−8	−1	−7

11.
4	5	10	7	11	4	7	9	10
−2	−4	−2	−6	−9	−0	−3	−2	−9

Answers begin on page 69.

Subtracting Larger Numbers

PROBLEM: Mr. Powell drives 48 miles to work every morning. After driving 25 miles, he stops to buy gas. How much farther does he have to drive to get to work?

SOLUTION: Subtract the distance he has already driven from the total distance he must drive. First subtract the units, then the tens, and so on until you have subtracted every column.

Step 1. Subtract the units: $8 - 5 = 3$.

Step 2. Subtract the tens: $4 - 2 = 2$.

$$\begin{array}{r} 48 \\ -25 \\ \hline 23 \end{array}$$

The answer to a subtraction problem is called the *difference*.

Checking Subtraction

To check a subtraction problem, add the answer to the bottom number of the original problem. The sum should be the top number of the original problem.

Step 1. $5 + 3 = 8$.

Step 2. $2 + 2 = 4$.

$$\begin{array}{r} 48\checkmark \\ -25 \\ \hline 23 \\ \hline 48\checkmark \end{array}$$

Subtract and check.

12.
| 75 | 62 | 80 | 66 | 73 | 28 | 45 |
| − 23 | − 50 | − 30 | − 41 | − 33 | − 17 | − 22 |

13.
| 47 | 53 | 92 | 87 | 76 | 49 | 58 |
| − 42 | − 21 | − 62 | − 34 | − 35 | − 41 | − 25 |

14.
| 569 | 806 | 964 | 707 | 525 | 748 |
| − 263 | − 403 | − 223 | − 405 | − 114 | − 628 |

15.
| 25,730 | 46,275 | 80,463 | 63,251 | 86,477 |
| − 12,720 | − 33,144 | − 20,361 | − 40,220 | − 71,346 |

16.
| 81,575 | 36,416 | 95,374 | 55,296 | 52,876 |
| − 1,423 | − 2,214 | − 2,322 | − 3,184 | − 1,625 |

Answers begin on page 70.

Subtracting by Borrowing

PROBLEM: Jeff is driving 92 miles from home to his parents' house. He has already driven 58 miles. How far does he have left to go?

SOLUTION: Subtract the distance he has gone from the total distance he wants to go. Since the 8 is too large to subtract from 2, you must *borrow*.

Step 1.   Since you cannot take 8 from 2, borrow one ten from the tens column and add it to the units. (10 + 2 = 12) Cross through the 9 in the tens column and make it an 8 to show that you have borrowed. Put a small 1 beside the 2 to show that it is now 12.

Step 2.   Subtract the units: $12 - 8 = 4$.

Step 3.   Subtract the tens: $8 - 5 = 3$.

$$\begin{array}{r} \overset{8}{\cancel{9}}{}^{1}2 \\ -\,5\ 8 \\ \hline 3\ 4 \end{array}$$

Subtract and check.

17.
76	58	84	35	91	87	53
− 8	− 9	− 7	− 6	− 3	− 9	− 6

18.
38	93	47	52	74	26	61
− 29	− 37	− 39	− 25	− 56	− 19	− 22

Answers begin on page 70.

PROBLEM: The Walek family's monthly income is $734. If they pay $158 a month for rent, how much do they have left each month after paying rent?

SOLUTION: Subtract $158 from $734. In this problem you must borrow twice.

Step 1.   Since you cannot take 8 from 4, borrow one ten from the tens column and add it to the units. $10 + 4 = 14$. Cross through the 3 and make it a 2. Put a small 1 beside the 4.

Step 2.   Subtract the units: $14 - 8 = 6$.

$$\begin{array}{r} \$7\,\overset{2}{\cancel{3}}{}^{1}4 \\ -\,1\ 5\ 8 \\ \hline \$\quad\ \ 6 \end{array}$$

Step 3. Since you cannot take 5 tens from 2 tens, borrow one hundred (or 10 tens) from the hundreds column and add it to the tens. 10 tens + 2 tens = 12 tens. Cross through the 7 and make it a 6. Put a small 1 beside the 2.

Step 4. Subtract the tens: 12 − 5 = 7.

Step 5. Subtract the hundreds: 6 − 1 = 5.

$$\begin{array}{r} 6\ ^1 2\ _1 \\ \$7\ 3\ 4 \\ -\ 1\ 5\ 8 \\ \hline \$5\ 7\ 6 \end{array}$$

Subtract and check.

19.

544	782	647	938	726	583
− 95	− 93	− 88	− 69	− 48	− 94

20.

584	642	533	627	318	976
− 295	− 568	− 347	− 389	− 199	− 288

21.

5,614	2,736	8,370	4,674	5,622
− 3,815	− 1,798	− 2,467	− 3,585	− 4,918

22.

23,475	27,480	52,637	65,124	45,812
− 15,388	− 16,991	− 14,882	− 27,538	− 28,073

23.

837,504	204,376	142,605	381,644	927,345
− 767,652	− 152,488	− 125,894	− 289,579	− 469,329

Answers begin on page 70.

Subtracting Numbers Written Horizontally

Often the numbers you want to subtract will not be lined up as they are in the previous exercises. When the numbers are not lined up, rewrite them with the units under the units, the tens under the tens, and so on.

EXAMPLE: $3,642 - 758 =$ Rewrite as: 3,642
                                                      − 758

SOLUTION: 3,642
                   − 758
                   ─────
                   2,884

Subtract and check.

24. $2,366 - 487 =$ $1,475 - 856 =$ $9,641 - 855 =$

25. $4,876 - 4,297 =$ $9,856 - 9,578 =$ $8,654 - 3,756 =$

26. $2,366 - 1,467 =$ $5,712 - 2,588 =$ $4,638 - 4,549 =$

27. $14,480 - 8,529 =$ $35,826 - 9,757 =$ $26,150 - 7,483 =$

28. $43,117 - 24,898 =$ $65,014 - 26,307 =$ $83,576 - 44,879 =$

Answers begin on page 71.

Subtracting from Zeros

PROBLEM: Max earns $9000 a year. His employer withholds $1785 for taxes and social security. What is Max's yearly take-home pay?

SOLUTION: Subtract the deductions from the yearly earnings.

Step 1. Since thousands is the first column you can borrow from, borrow 1 from the thousands column and take it to the hundreds column. This leaves 8 thousands.

$$\begin{array}{r} \overset{8\;\;1}{\$\cancel{9}\,\cancel{0}\,0\,0} \\ -\,1\,7\,8\,5 \end{array}$$

Step 2. Borrow 1 from the hundreds column and take it to the tens column. This leaves 9 hundreds.

$$\begin{array}{r} \overset{8\;9\;\;1}{\$\cancel{9}\,\cancel{0}\,\cancel{0}\,0} \\ -\,1\,7\,8\,5 \end{array}$$

Step 3. Borrow 1 from the tens column and take it to the units column. This leaves 9 tens.

$$\begin{array}{r} \overset{8\;9\;9\;\;1}{\$\cancel{9}\,\cancel{0}\,\cancel{0}\,\cancel{0}} \\ -\,1\,7\,8\,5 \\ \hline \$7\,2\,1\,5 \end{array}$$

Step 4. Subtract each column:
Units: $10 - 5 = 5$.
Tens: $9 - 8 = 1$.
Hundreds: $9 - 7 = 2$.
Thousands: $8 - 1 = 7$.

Subtract and check.

29.
| 406 | 305 | 208 | 704 | 803 | 902 |
| − 58 | − 66 | − 79 | − 57 | − 64 | − 18 |

30.
| 701 | 602 | 405 | 903 | 807 | 204 |
| − 158 | − 463 | − 277 | − 847 | − 369 | − 197 |

31.
| 600 | 200 | 400 | 500 | 800 | 700 |
| − 527 | − 118 | − 236 | − 423 | − 265 | − 189 |

32.
| 3,060 | 7,040 | 9,050 | 8,010 | 3,020 | 2,080 |
| − 2,186 | − 3,094 | − 3,557 | − 6,956 | − 1,987 | − 1,193 |

33.
| 5,002 | 3,008 | 9,001 | 6,005 | 4,004 | 8,005 |
| − 2,654 | − 1,559 | − 2,108 | − 4,569 | − 2,378 | − 4,336 |

34.
| 20,000 | 40,000 | 50,000 | 60,000 | 30,000 |
| − 13,654 | − 38,562 | − 20,751 | − 33,045 | − 19,720 |

Answers begin on page 71.

Applying Your Subtraction Skills

In the following exercise you will apply both your addition and subtraction skills. Pay close attention to the language that tells you to subtract. Watch for phrases such as: *How much more? How much less? How much bigger? How much smaller? Find the balance. Find the difference.*

Be sure to line up problems carefully and to label each answer.

Subtract and check.

35. A gas range that regularly sells for $529.95 was on sale for $479.95. How much can a customer save buying the range on sale?

36. Connecticut has an area of 5,009 square miles; Rhode Island has an area of 1,214 square miles. How much larger is Connecticut than Rhode Island?

37. Al bought a portable television for $79.95. He paid $6.40 sales tax. How much change should he receive from $90?

38. Chicago became a town in 1833. What was the age of Chicago in 1980?

39. Don Johnson makes $240 a week. His employer deducts $39.72 from each check. Find the balance that Don takes home each week.

40. In 1960 the population of Manhattan was 1,698,281 people; in 1970 it was 1,539,233. By how much did the population of Manhattan decrease in ten years?

41. The Miller family has a monthly budget of $708. If they pay $187.50 for rent, how much do they have left for other expenses?

42. The Bennetts bought a house for $38,500. They made a down payment of $4750. What is the difference between the total price and the Bennett's down payment?

43. In one week a Los Angeles record store sold 5,072 rock records; 2,981 country music records, and 1,079 jazz records. The number of rock records sold that week was how many more than the combined number of country and jazz records?

Answers begin on page 72.

MULTIPLYING WHOLE NUMBERS

Basic Multiplication Facts

Of all the arithmetic facts, the multiplication facts (or the multiplication tables) cause people the most trouble. The following exercise will test your knowledge of the multiplication facts. Do not try to add the problems quickly. Write down the answers that you know. If you get any of these problems wrong, study the multiplication facts that you missed. Then cover your answers, and repeat the exercise until you can get every problem correct.

Be sure you know the multiplication facts before you go on. The time you spend memorizing these facts will be saved later when you do longer multiplication and division problems.

1.
$$\begin{array}{r} 7 \\ \times\,1 \end{array} \quad \begin{array}{r} 5 \\ \times\,5 \end{array} \quad \begin{array}{r} 2 \\ \times\,7 \end{array} \quad \begin{array}{r} 9 \\ \times\,4 \end{array} \quad \begin{array}{r} 3 \\ \times\,5 \end{array} \quad \begin{array}{r} 1 \\ \times\,2 \end{array} \quad \begin{array}{r} 8 \\ \times\,6 \end{array} \quad \begin{array}{r} 6 \\ \times\,7 \end{array} \quad \begin{array}{r} 1 \\ \times\,4 \end{array}$$

2.
$$\begin{array}{r} 2 \\ \times\,5 \end{array} \quad \begin{array}{r} 8 \\ \times\,4 \end{array} \quad \begin{array}{r} 5 \\ \times\,3 \end{array} \quad \begin{array}{r} 3 \\ \times\,9 \end{array} \quad \begin{array}{r} 2 \\ \times\,4 \end{array} \quad \begin{array}{r} 7 \\ \times\,8 \end{array} \quad \begin{array}{r} 4 \\ \times\,4 \end{array} \quad \begin{array}{r} 6 \\ \times\,1 \end{array} \quad \begin{array}{r} 9 \\ \times\,8 \end{array}$$

3.
$$\begin{array}{r} 9 \\ \times\,9 \end{array} \quad \begin{array}{r} 5 \\ \times\,4 \end{array} \quad \begin{array}{r} 6 \\ \times\,8 \end{array} \quad \begin{array}{r} 3 \\ \times\,1 \end{array} \quad \begin{array}{r} 0 \\ \times\,8 \end{array} \quad \begin{array}{r} 2 \\ \times\,2 \end{array} \quad \begin{array}{r} 6 \\ \times\,6 \end{array} \quad \begin{array}{r} 4 \\ \times\,7 \end{array} \quad \begin{array}{r} 6 \\ \times\,2 \end{array}$$

4.
$$\begin{array}{r} 3 \\ \times\,0 \end{array} \quad \begin{array}{r} 3 \\ \times\,7 \end{array} \quad \begin{array}{r} 0 \\ \times\,7 \end{array} \quad \begin{array}{r} 9 \\ \times\,2 \end{array} \quad \begin{array}{r} 5 \\ \times\,9 \end{array} \quad \begin{array}{r} 2 \\ \times\,6 \end{array} \quad \begin{array}{r} 1 \\ \times\,1 \end{array} \quad \begin{array}{r} 8 \\ \times\,7 \end{array} \quad \begin{array}{r} 5 \\ \times\,2 \end{array}$$

5.
$$\begin{array}{r} 5 \\ \times\,1 \end{array} \quad \begin{array}{r} 8 \\ \times\,5 \end{array} \quad \begin{array}{r} 5 \\ \times\,7 \end{array} \quad \begin{array}{r} 3 \\ \times\,3 \end{array} \quad \begin{array}{r} 1 \\ \times\,8 \end{array} \quad \begin{array}{r} 0 \\ \times\,6 \end{array} \quad \begin{array}{r} 7 \\ \times\,3 \end{array} \quad \begin{array}{r} 2 \\ \times\,8 \end{array} \quad \begin{array}{r} 9 \\ \times\,6 \end{array}$$

Answers begin on page 72.

6. | 3 | 2 | 6 | 4 | 5 | 7 | 9 | 1 | 0 |
|---|---|---|---|---|---|---|---|---|
| × 8 | × 9 | × 9 | × 3 | × 8 | × 5 | × 1 | × 6 | × 4 |

7. | 7 | 3 | 9 | 4 | 2 | 5 | 8 | 9 | 1 |
|---|---|---|---|---|---|---|---|---|
| × 9 | × 2 | × 7 | × 9 | × 3 | × 6 | × 1 | × 5 | × 9 |

8. | 4 | 6 | 9 | 7 | 2 | 3 | 5 | 7 | 4 |
|---|---|---|---|---|---|---|---|---|
| × 8 | × 5 | × 0 | × 4 | × 1 | × 6 | × 0 | × 7 | × 6 |

9. | 8 | 2 | 6 | 9 | 7 | 8 | 1 | 7 | 4 |
|---|---|---|---|---|---|---|---|---|
| × 8 | × 0 | × 4 | × 3 | × 6 | × 2 | × 5 | × 2 | × 1 |

10. | 6 | 1 | 4 | 1 | 4 | 8 | 8 | 1 | 3 |
|---|---|---|---|---|---|---|---|---|
| × 3 | × 0 | × 5 | × 3 | × 2 | × 9 | × 3 | × 7 | × 4 |

Answers begin on page 73.

Multiplying by One-Digit Numbers

PROBLEM: John saves $132 a month. How much can he save in three months?

SOLUTION: Multiply $132 by 3.

Step 1. Multiply the units by 3: $3 \times 2 = 6$.

Step 2. Multiply the tens by 3: $3 \times 3 = 9$.

Step 3. Multiply the hundreds by 3: $3 \times 1 = 3$.

$$\begin{array}{r} \$132 \\ \times\ 3 \\ \hline \$396 \end{array}$$

The answer to a multiplication problem is called the *product*.

Checking Multiplication

One common method for checking a multiplication problem is to go over every step you have made to try to find errors. Another method is to divide your answer by the number you multiplied by. If the answer to the division problem is the top number of the multiplying problem, you were correct.

EXAMPLE:
$$\begin{array}{r} 132 \\ \times\ 3 \\ \hline 396 \end{array}$$

CHECK:
$$\begin{array}{r} 132 \\ 3\overline{)396} \end{array}$$

If you are not sure about your division skills at this point, don't try to use this method to check multiplication.

Multiply and check.

11.
$$\begin{array}{r} 32 \\ \times\ 4 \\ \hline \end{array} \qquad \begin{array}{r} 81 \\ \times\ 9 \\ \hline \end{array} \qquad \begin{array}{r} 60 \\ \times\ 7 \\ \hline \end{array} \qquad \begin{array}{r} 43 \\ \times\ 3 \\ \hline \end{array} \qquad \begin{array}{r} 71 \\ \times\ 8 \\ \hline \end{array} \qquad \begin{array}{r} 52 \\ \times\ 4 \\ \hline \end{array} \qquad \begin{array}{r} 91 \\ \times\ 2 \\ \hline \end{array}$$

12.
$$\begin{array}{r} 312 \\ \times\ 3 \\ \hline \end{array} \qquad \begin{array}{r} 423 \\ \times\ 2 \\ \hline \end{array} \qquad \begin{array}{r} 321 \\ \times\ 4 \\ \hline \end{array} \qquad \begin{array}{r} 501 \\ \times\ 7 \\ \hline \end{array} \qquad \begin{array}{r} 731 \\ \times\ 3 \\ \hline \end{array} \qquad \begin{array}{r} 820 \\ \times\ 4 \\ \hline \end{array}$$

13.
$$\begin{array}{r} 9{,}103 \\ \times\ 2 \\ \hline \end{array} \qquad \begin{array}{r} 2{,}312 \\ \times\ 3 \\ \hline \end{array} \qquad \begin{array}{r} 6{,}201 \\ \times\ 4 \\ \hline \end{array} \qquad \begin{array}{r} 3{,}324 \\ \times\ 2 \\ \hline \end{array} \qquad \begin{array}{r} 5{,}230 \\ \times\ 3 \\ \hline \end{array}$$

Answers begin on page 73.

Multiplying by Larger Numbers

PROBLEM: An auditorium contains 34 rows of seats with 21 seats in each row. How many seats are in the auditorium?

SOLUTION: Multiply the number of rows by the number of seats in each row.

Step 1. Start at the right and multiply both top digits by 1. $1 \times 4 = 4$
$1 \times 3 = 3$

Step 2. Multiply both top digits by 2 and begin your answer under the tens column. $2 \times 4 = 8$
$2 \times 3 = 6$

Step 3. Add the partial products.

$$
\begin{array}{r}
34 \\
\times\ 21 \\
\hline
34 \\
68 \\
\hline
714
\end{array}
$$

partial products $\big\}$

Multiply and check.

14.
32	24	52	81	63	92	41
× 34	× 21	× 34	× 65	× 32	× 24	× 97

15.
50	90	40	70	20	60	80
× 63	× 89	× 72	× 28	× 36	× 45	× 51

Answers begin on page 73.

When multiplying by zero, you can save time by putting a zero directly under the zero in the problem and going on to multiply by the next digit.

EXAMPLE:

$$
\begin{array}{r}
42 \\
\times\ 30 \\
\hline
1260
\end{array}
$$

Answers begin on page 74.

16.
84	63	51	42	81	93	72
× 20	× 30	× 90	× 40	× 80	× 20	× 40

Multiplying and Carrying

PROBLEM: Pete is paying $36 a month for 24 months to buy a used car. How much will he have paid in 24 months?

SOLUTION: The multiplication of this problem involves *carrying* because some of the products are two-digit numbers.

Step 1.   4 × 6 = 24. Write the 4 and carry the 2 to the tens column.

Step 2.   4 × 3 = 12. Add the 2 that you carried.

$$12 + 2 = 14$$

Step 3.   2 × 6 = 12. Write the 2 under the tens and carry the 1.

Step 4.   2 × 3 = 6. Add the 1 that you carried.

$$6 + 1 = 7$$

Step 5.   Add the partial products.

$$
\begin{array}{r}
\overset{2}{} \\
\$36 \\
\times\ 24 \\
\hline
144 \\
72 \\
\hline
\$864
\end{array}
$$

partial products }

Multiply and check.

17.
36	75	13	39	86	74	39
× 4	× 9	× 5	× 6	× 7	× 8	× 3

18.
266	593	834	427	542	349
× 8	× 3	× 9	× 4	× 6	× 5

19.
53	69	84	53	74	28	96
× 56	× 74	× 37	× 49	× 68	× 93	× 57

20.
$$\begin{array}{r} 99 \\ \times\ 25 \end{array}$$ $$\begin{array}{r} 48 \\ \times\ 64 \end{array}$$ $$\begin{array}{r} 78 \\ \times\ 72 \end{array}$$ $$\begin{array}{r} 34 \\ \times\ 33 \end{array}$$ $$\begin{array}{r} 85 \\ \times\ 48 \end{array}$$ $$\begin{array}{r} 17 \\ \times\ 93 \end{array}$$ $$\begin{array}{r} 83 \\ \times\ 94 \end{array}$$

21.
$$\begin{array}{r} 754 \\ \times\ 28 \end{array}$$ $$\begin{array}{r} 679 \\ \times\ 89 \end{array}$$ $$\begin{array}{r} 472 \\ \times\ 36 \end{array}$$ $$\begin{array}{r} 617 \\ \times\ 64 \end{array}$$ $$\begin{array}{r} 728 \\ \times\ 57 \end{array}$$ $$\begin{array}{r} 536 \\ \times\ 92 \end{array}$$

Answers begin on page 74.

Multiplying Zeros

Zeros sometimes cause trouble. They shouldn't if you remember that any number multiplied by 0 is 0.

PROBLEM: A plane flew at an average speed of 307 miles per hour. At that rate, how many miles did it fly in six hours?

SOLUTION:

Step 1. $6 \times 7 = 42$. Write the 2. Carry the 4.

Step 2. $6 \times 0 = 0$. Add the 4. $0 + 4 = 4$

Step 3. $6 \times 3 = 18$.

$$\begin{array}{r} 4 \\ 307 \\ \times\ 6 \\ \hline 1842 \text{ miles} \end{array}$$

Multiply and check.

22.
$$\begin{array}{r} 703 \\ \times\ 9 \end{array}$$ $$\begin{array}{r} 604 \\ \times\ 6 \end{array}$$ $$\begin{array}{r} 805 \\ \times\ 4 \end{array}$$ $$\begin{array}{r} 106 \\ \times\ 7 \end{array}$$ $$\begin{array}{r} 504 \\ \times\ 3 \end{array}$$ $$\begin{array}{r} 802 \\ \times\ 9 \end{array}$$

23.
$$\begin{array}{r} 4{,}606 \\ \times\ 8 \end{array}$$ $$\begin{array}{r} 8{,}091 \\ \times\ 3 \end{array}$$ $$\begin{array}{r} 5{,}104 \\ \times\ 7 \end{array}$$ $$\begin{array}{r} 6{,}053 \\ \times\ 6 \end{array}$$ $$\begin{array}{r} 7{,}028 \\ \times\ 9 \end{array}$$

24.
5,705	4,033	8,062	5,607	3,094
$\times$ 95	$\times$ 84	$\times$ 76	$\times$ 36	$\times$ 87

Answers begin on page 74.

Multiplying Numbers Written Horizontally

If a multiplying problem is written horizontally, line the numbers up for easy multiplication.

PROBLEM: 42 $\times$ 327 =

SOLUTION: Put the number with the most digits on top.

$$\begin{array}{r} 327 \\ \times\ \ 42 \\ \hline 654 \\ 13\ 08 \\ \hline 13{,}734 \end{array}$$

Multiply and check.

25. 7 $\times$ 456 =   928 $\times$ 5 =   374 $\times$ 8 =

26. 597 $\times$ 34 =   67 $\times$ 842 =   902 $\times$ 56 =

27. 4,608 $\times$ 53 =   96 $\times$ 8,477 =   5,928 $\times$ 80 =

Answers begin on page 75.

Multiplying by 10, 100, and 1000

PROBLEM: If one carton weighs 36 pounds, how much do ten cartons weigh?

SOLUTION: To multiply a number by 10, put a zero to the right of the number. 36 $\times$ 10 = 360 pounds.

To multiply a number by 100, put two zeros to the right of the number.

EXAMPLE: $29 \times 100 = 2,900$

To multiply a number by 1000, put three zeros to the right of the number.

EXAMPLE: $58 \times 1000 = 58,000$

Put commas in any answers that contain more than three digits.

28. $10 \times 83 =$ $456 \times 10 =$ $10 \times 250 =$ $3,498 \times 10 =$

29. $100 \times 54 =$ $286 \times 100 =$ $100 \times 207 =$ $80 \times 100 =$

30. $1000 \times 9 =$ $47 \times 1000 =$ $1000 \times 803 =$ $970 \times 1000 =$

Answers begin on page 75.

Applying Your Multiplication Skills

In the following exercise you will apply your addition, subtraction, and multiplication skills. Pay close attention to the language that tells you to multiply. There are no simple phrases that you can depend on to indicate multiplication. Usually you will be given information for one thing (such as the amount of money someone makes in one hour) and you will be asked to find an amount for several things (such as the amount a person would make for several hours of work).

31. If one pound of ground beef costs $1.49, what is the cost of four pounds of ground beef?

32. If an airplane flies at an average speed of 389 miles per hour, how far can it fly in 6 hours?

33. Bill makes $62.75 a day as a carpenter. How much can he make in five days?

34. Debbie earns $4.67 an hour for overtime work. Her weekly base salary is $194.50. How much did she make altogether last week if she worked six hours overtime?

35. Pete's gas tank holds 16 gallons. If he averages 19 miles for one gallon of gas, how many miles can he travel on a full tank?

36. Find the total cost of three pounds of chicken at 89¢ a pound, two pounds of beef chuck at $1.59 a pound, and four pounds of frankfurters at $1.35 a pound.

37. There are 5,280 feet in one mile. How many feet are there in 27 miles?

38.   Jose pays $62.50 each month on his car loan and $15 each month on his school loan. In one year, how much does Jose spend in loan repayments?

39.   Which of the following loan payments costs more: $36 a month for 24 months or $48 a month for 18 months?

Answers begin on page 75.

DIVIDING WHOLE NUMBERS

Basic Division Facts

The division facts are the multiplication facts in reverse. Write the answers to the following exercise as quickly as you can. Check your answers. If you miss any of the problems, study them. Then cover your answers, and repeat this exercise until you get every fact correct.

1. $4\overline{)36}$ $1\overline{)7}$ $5\overline{)25}$ $7\overline{)14}$ $5\overline{)15}$ $2\overline{)2}$ $3\overline{)18}$

2. $8\overline{)32}$ $5\overline{)30}$ $9\overline{)0}$ $4\overline{)28}$ $6\overline{)18}$ $1\overline{)2}$ $7\overline{)49}$

3. $6\overline{)36}$ $3\overline{)0}$ $7\overline{)56}$ $6\overline{)12}$ $9\overline{)45}$ $2\overline{)10}$ $2\overline{)18}$

4. $9\overline{)27}$ $4\overline{)8}$ $3\overline{)15}$ $4\overline{)32}$ $5\overline{)45}$ $8\overline{)72}$ $5\overline{)10}$

5. $2\overline{)12}$ $7\overline{)21}$ $1\overline{)1}$ $7\overline{)28}$ $8\overline{)0}$ $2\overline{)4}$ $4\overline{)20}$

6. $8\overline{)24}$ $9\overline{)18}$ $9\overline{)54}$ $3\overline{)12}$ $8\overline{)40}$ $5\overline{)35}$ $1\overline{)9}$

7. $1\overline{)5}$ $5\overline{)40}$ $7\overline{)35}$ $3\overline{)9}$ $8\overline{)8}$ $6\overline{)0}$ $3\overline{)21}$

8. $2\overline{)14}$ $5\overline{)5}$ $2\overline{)16}$ $1\overline{)4}$ $3\overline{)27}$ $6\overline{)42}$ $3\overline{)24}$

9. $9\overline{)63}$ $2\overline{)6}$ $7\overline{)63}$ $9\overline{)36}$ $3\overline{)6}$ $6\overline{)30}$ $1\overline{)8}$

10. $6\overline{)48}$ $7\overline{)42}$ $4\overline{)4}$ $5\overline{)0}$ $6\overline{)24}$ $7\overline{)7}$ $3\overline{)3}$

11. $5\overline{)20}$ $1\overline{)6}$ $4\overline{)16}$ $8\overline{)56}$ $9\overline{)81}$ $8\overline{)48}$ $6\overline{)6}$

12. $9\overline{)72}$ $8\overline{)16}$ $6\overline{)54}$ $2\overline{)8}$ $4\overline{)24}$ $8\overline{)64}$ $4\overline{)12}$

Answers begin on page 76.

Dividing by One-Digit Numbers

PROBLEM: Mr. Fields paid off a $324 loan in six equal installments. How much did he pay each time?

SOLUTION: Divide $324 by 6. Division is the most difficult of the basic arithmetic operations. Study the steps to this solution carefully.

Step 1.   Divide: $32 \div 6 = 5$ plus a remainder. Write the 5 over the tens place.

$$\begin{array}{r} 5 \\ 6\overline{)324} \end{array}$$

Step 2.   Multiply: $5 \times 6 = 30$. Write the 30 under the 32.

$$\begin{array}{r} 5 \\ 6\overline{)324} \\ 30 \end{array}$$

Step 3.   Subtract: $32 - 30 = 2$.

$$\begin{array}{r} 5 \\ 6\overline{)324} \\ \underline{30} \\ 2 \end{array}$$

Step 4.   Bring down the next number in the problem (4).

$$\begin{array}{r} 5 \\ 6\overline{)324} \\ \underline{30} \\ 24 \end{array}$$

Step 5.   Divide: $24 \div 6 = 4$. Write the 4 over the units place.

$$\begin{array}{r} 54 \\ 6\overline{)324} \\ \underline{30} \\ 24 \end{array}$$

Step 6.   Multiply: $4 \times 6 = 24$. Write the 24 under the 24 in the problem.

$$\begin{array}{r} 54 \\ 6\overline{)324} \\ \underline{30} \\ 24 \\ 24 \end{array}$$

Step 7.   Subtract: $24 - 24 = 0$.

$$\begin{array}{r} 54 \\ 6\overline{)324} \\ 30 \\ \hline 24 \\ 24 \\ \hline \end{array}$$

The answer to a division problem is called the *quotient*.

The example above shows the steps in *long division* which means that every step is written down. Often when you divide by a one-digit number, it is possible to use *short division* which means that the multiplying and subtracting steps are done mentally. Write the number that you carry in the number you divide. Study these examples:

$$6\overline{)3\ 2^24} \quad 7\overline{)1,8^47^56} \quad 4\overline{)5,1^5^38^24}$$
$$\quad 54 \qquad\qquad 268 \qquad\qquad 1,396$$

Checking Division

To check a division problem, multiply your answer by the number you divided by. You should get the number you divided into.

For the examples above:

$$\begin{array}{r} 54 \\ \times\ 6 \\ \hline 324 \end{array} \qquad \begin{array}{r} 268 \\ \times\ 7 \\ \hline 1,876 \end{array} \qquad \begin{array}{r} 1,396 \\ \times\ 4 \\ \hline 5,584 \end{array}$$

Divide and check.

13. $6\overline{)318}$ $9\overline{)252}$ $4\overline{)244}$ $7\overline{)525}$ $8\overline{)448}$

14. $5\overline{)145}$ $7\overline{)322}$ $2\overline{)146}$ $3\overline{)108}$ $4\overline{)112}$

15. $8\overline{)3408}$ $6\overline{)3186}$ $5\overline{)1290}$ $9\overline{)1233}$ $4\overline{)1692}$

16. $3\overline{)2562}$ $7\overline{)2604}$ $6\overline{)2502}$ $8\overline{)2632}$ $5\overline{)3075}$

17. $4\overline{)816}$ $6\overline{)3018}$ $9\overline{)2889}$ $3\overline{)1290}$ $7\overline{)4249}$

18. $8\overline{)7600}$ $5\overline{)2115}$ $6\overline{)2280}$ $7\overline{)1463}$ $2\overline{)1412}$

Answers begin on page 77.

Division with Remainders

PROBLEM: How many rows, each containing 10 chairs, can be made from 103 chairs?

SOLUTION: If you divide the total number of chairs by the number of chairs in each row, you will find the number of rows, but in this problem the answer is not even.

$$
\begin{array}{r}
10\text{r}3 \\
10\overline{)103} \\
\underline{10} \\
3 \\
\underline{0} \\
3
\end{array}
$$

The 3 that is left is called the *remainder*. This means that you could make 10 rows of chairs, but there would be 3 chairs left over.

To check a division problem with a remainder, multiply the answer by the number you divided by and add the remainder.

$$
\begin{array}{r}
\text{CHECK:} \quad 10 \\
\times\ 10 \\
\hline
100 \\
+\ \ \ 3 \\
\hline
103
\end{array}
$$

Divide and check.

19. $7\overline{)181}$ $8\overline{)341}$ $5\overline{)344}$ $6\overline{)225}$ $4\overline{)238}$

20. $6\overline{)495}$ $9\overline{)466}$ $3\overline{)145}$ $2\overline{)151}$ $7\overline{)466}$

21. $5\overline{)2,087}$ $4\overline{)1,239}$ $8\overline{)1,733}$ $3\overline{)1,498}$ $9\overline{)2,949}$

22. $6\overline{)25,253}$ $7\overline{)17,971}$ $4\overline{)13,923}$ $8\overline{)16,782}$ $5\overline{)17,303}$

Answers begin on page 77.

Dividing by Larger Numbers

PROBLEM: Verva pays $42 a month for her new furniture. How many months will it take her to pay a total of $1512 for the furniture?

SOLUTION: Divide the total amount by the amount of each monthly payment. Dividing by a two-digit or three-digit number is difficult because it requires guessing or *estimating*. Follow this example carefully.

Step 1.   Estimate how many times 42 goes into 151 by asking yourself how many times 4 goes into 15. $15 \div 4 = 3$ plus a remainder.

Step 2.   Place 3 over the tens place and multiply: $3 \times 42 = 126$.

Step 3.   Subtract: $151 - 126 = 25$.

Step 4.   Bring down the 2.

Step 5.   Estimate how many times 42 goes into 252 by asking yourself how many times 4 goes into 25. $25 \div 4 = 6$ plus a remainder.

Step 6.   Place 6 over the units place and multiply: $6 \times 42 = 252$.

Step 7.   Subtract: $252 - 252 = 0$.

```
      36
42)1512
   126
   252
   252
```

Estimating is difficult and not very exact. Be prepared to make mistakes. Very often your first division estimate will be off by one. Erase and try again.

Divide and check.

23. $41\overline{)287}$ $37\overline{)222}$ $69\overline{)552}$ $48\overline{)192}$

24. $89\overline{)466}$ $26\overline{)124}$ $42\overline{)393}$ $37\overline{)307}$

25. $92\overline{)2,116}$ $54\overline{)1,944}$ $18\overline{)756}$ $66\overline{)1,782}$

26. $58\overline{)2,007}$ $72\overline{)1,891}$ $23\overline{)1,210}$ $36\overline{)1,784}$

PROBLEM: Traveling an average speed of 584 miles per hour, how long would it take an airplane pilot to go 11,096 miles?

SOLUTION: Divide the total distance by the average hourly speed.

Step 1. Estimate how many times 584 goes into 1109 by asking yourself how many times 5 goes into 11. $11 \div 5 = 2$ plus a remainder. Multiply: $2 \times 584 = 1168$ which is too large to subtract from 1109.

Step 2. Instead of 2 put 1 over the tens place. Multiply: $1 \times 584 = 584$.

Step 3. Subtract: $1109 - 584 = 525$.

Step 4. Bring down the 6.

Step 5. Estimate how many times 584 goes into 5256 by asking yourself how many times 5 goes into 52. $52 \div 5 = 10$ plus a remainder. Multiply: $10 \times 584 = 5840$ which is too large to subtract from 5256.

Step 6. Instead of 10 put 9 over the units place. Multiply: $9 \times 584 = 5256$.

Step 7. Subtract: $5256 - 5256 = 0$.

$$
\begin{array}{r}
19 \\
584\overline{)11,096} \\
5\,84 \\
\hline
5\,256 \\
5\,256 \\
\hline
\end{array}
$$

Answers begin on page 77.

Divide and check.

27. $285 \overline{)14,820}$ $412 \overline{)10,712}$ $562 \overline{)24,166}$ $326 \overline{)27,384}$

28. $722 \overline{)25,930}$ $908 \overline{)56,188}$ $453 \overline{)11,022}$ $662 \overline{)35,286}$

Answers begin on page 78.

___

Dividing Numbers Written Horizontally

We have already used both symbols for division, $\div$ and $\overline{)}$. A division problem may be written using one or the other. For instance $18 \overline{)756}$ means the same as $756 \div 18$. The numbers come in reverse order with these symbols. We read the first example "eighteen divided into seven hundred fifty-six." We read the second example "Seven hundred fifty-six divided by eighteen."

PROBLEM: Rewrite and divide $592 \div 16$.

SOLUTION:

$$
\begin{array}{r}
37 \\
16 \overline{)592} \\
48 \\
\overline{112} \\
\underline{112}
\end{array}
$$

The following exercise gives practice in using both division symbols.

Rewrite, divide, and check.

29. $2,136 \div 8 =$ $5,424 \div 6 =$ $3,090 \div 5 =$

30. $386 \div 15 =$ $2,572 \div 62 =$ $1,642 \div 29 =$

31. $3,264 \div 48 =$ $1,961 \div 37 =$ $4,968 \div 54 =$

32. $10,040 \div 124 =$ $15,142 \div 362 =$ $29,346 \div 438 =$

Answers begin on page 78.

Applying Your Division Skills

In the following exercise you will apply your division skills. Pay close attention to the language that tells you to divide. As with multiplication, there are no simple clues that you can rely on to tell you to divide. Sometimes you will be given information for several things (such as the cost of several pounds of an item) and you will be asked to find information about one thing (such as the cost of one item). Sometimes you will be asked to find how many of one thing there are in another (such as how many pounds there are in several ounces). Sometimes you will be asked to find an *average* which is a total divided by the number of things in the total.

---

33. If four cans of soup cost $1.96, how much does one can cost?

34. There are 12 inches in a foot. How many feet long is a table that measures 96 inches in length?

35. Last year the McGlynn family paid $2,100 in rent. How much did they pay each month?

36. Valerie has agreed to pay $36 a month for new living-room furniture. How many months will it take her to pay for $756 worth of furniture?

37. Ellis received the following scores on math tests: 86, 94, 77, 83, and 70. What was his average score?

38. Canned tomatoes are packaged with 24 cans in a box. How many boxes are needed to package 6,168 cans of tomatoes?

39. Maxine made $9,640.80 last year. What was her weekly income? (There are 52 weeks in a year.)

40. Jose can read 342 words per minute. How long will Jose take to read an article which contains 9,234 words?

41. On a certain map one inch represents 240 miles. How many inches apart on the map are two cities which are actually 3,120 miles apart?

42. On Monday the high temperature was 62°; on Tuesday it was 75°; on Wednesday, 72°; on Thursday, 68°; and on Friday, 63°. What was the average high temperature for those days?

Answers begin on page 79.

WHOLE NUMBERS SKILLS TEST

Before going on to fractions, try this review of your whole numbers skills. Check your answers using those beginning on page 80. Then use the Whole Numbers Skills Test Evaluation on page 65 to decide what you need to study more.

1. In 356 the 3 is in what place?

2. In 45,073 the 5 is in what place?

3. What is the value of the 9 in 396,508?

4. Write seventy thousand, two hundred six as a whole number.

5. Write eight million, six hundred thirty-three thousand, five hundred ninety as a whole number.

6.
$$\begin{array}{r} 4,261 \\ + 5,327 \\ \hline \end{array}$$

7.
$$\begin{array}{r} 842 \\ 379 \\ + 467 \\ \hline \end{array}$$

8. $862 + 3,408 + 63 + 235 =$

9.
$$\begin{array}{r} 9,867 \\ - 5,327 \\ \hline \end{array}$$

10.
$$\begin{array}{r} 8,725 \\ - 4,986 \\ \hline \end{array}$$

11. $54,136 - 8,529 =$

12.
$$\begin{array}{r} 40,600 \\ - 25,538 \\ \hline \end{array}$$

13.
$$\begin{array}{r} 62 \\ \times 3 \\ \hline \end{array}$$

14.
$$\begin{array}{r} 81 \\ \times 24 \\ \hline \end{array}$$

15. $5{,}736 \times 48 =$

16.
$$\begin{array}{r} 807 \\ \times\ 39 \\ \hline \end{array}$$

17. $356 \times 100 =$

18. $9\overline{)603}$

19. $9\overline{)5{,}954}$

20. $49\overline{)20{,}482}$

21. $13{,}720 \div 46 =$

22. $19{,}494 \div 342 =$

23. The Johnsons' July phone bill included $8.50 for monthly service, $19.63 for long distance calls, and $2.15 for sales tax. What was their total July phone bill?

24. Every week Mark's employer deducts $49.56 for federal tax, $12 for social security, and $10.17 for state tax. What is the combined amount of the deductions from Mark's check?

25. If the weekly salary of Mark (in problem 24) is $265, what is his weekly take-home pay?

26. In 1960 the population of Middletown was 867,943. In 1970 the population was 908,201. By how much did the population increase over those ten years?

27. There are 36 inches in a yard. How many inches are there in 19 yards?

28. Phil earns $6.50 an hour for the first 35 hours of the week. For overtime work he makes $9.75 an hour. Last week Phil worked 42 hours. How much money did he earn?

29. A community group gave three performances of a talent show. The first night, 387 people attended; the second night, 443 attended; the last night, 619 attended. What was the average nightly attendance?

30. Last year Paul took home $11,109.80. What was his weekly take-home pay? (There are 52 weeks in a year.)

Answers begin on page 80.

WHOLE NUMBERS SKILLS TEST EVALUATION

Problem Number	Practice Pages	Problem Number	Practice Pages
1–3	21–22	15	47
4, 5	22–23	16	46–47
6	23–26	17	47–48
7	27–28	18	50–54
8	29	19	54–55
9	31–34	20	56–57
10	34–36	21, 22	58–59
11	37	23, 24	30–31
12	38–39	25, 26	39–40
13	41–43	27, 28	49–50
14	43–46	29, 30	60–61

Passing score: ___24___ right out of 30 problems.

Your score: _____ right out of 30 problems.

If you had less than a passing score, review the practice pages for the problems you got wrong. Then repeat this test before going on to the fractions unit.

If you had a passing score, correct any problem you got wrong, and go to the fractions unit.

ANSWERS AND SOLUTIONS—WHOLE NUMBERS EXERCISES

UNDERSTANDING WHOLE NUMBERS

1. hundreds

2. tens

3. thousands

4. units or ones

5. ten thousands

6. 4,000

7. 900

8. 70

9. 200,000

10. 10,000,000

WRITING WHOLE NUMBERS

11. 604

12. 4,320

13. 80

14. 9,550,017

15. 10,090

16. 5,002

17. 8,902,000

18. 3,087,900

19. 700,206

20. 89,450,000

ADDING WHOLE NUMBERS

1.
$$\begin{array}{r}4\\+2\\\hline6\end{array}\quad\begin{array}{r}9\\+6\\\hline15\end{array}\quad\begin{array}{r}2\\+8\\\hline10\end{array}\quad\begin{array}{r}7\\+3\\\hline10\end{array}\quad\begin{array}{r}0\\+6\\\hline6\end{array}\quad\begin{array}{r}1\\+8\\\hline9\end{array}\quad\begin{array}{r}3\\+3\\\hline6\end{array}\quad\begin{array}{r}5\\+7\\\hline12\end{array}\quad\begin{array}{r}8\\+5\\\hline13\end{array}$$

2.
$$\begin{array}{r}3\\+4\\\hline7\end{array}\quad\begin{array}{r}8\\+8\\\hline16\end{array}\quad\begin{array}{r}6\\+4\\\hline10\end{array}\quad\begin{array}{r}2\\+0\\\hline2\end{array}\quad\begin{array}{r}7\\+6\\\hline13\end{array}\quad\begin{array}{r}9\\+3\\\hline12\end{array}\quad\begin{array}{r}4\\+1\\\hline5\end{array}\quad\begin{array}{r}8\\+2\\\hline10\end{array}\quad\begin{array}{r}1\\+5\\\hline6\end{array}$$

3.
$$\begin{array}{r}6\\+8\\\hline14\end{array}\quad\begin{array}{r}9\\+9\\\hline18\end{array}\quad\begin{array}{r}3\\+1\\\hline4\end{array}\quad\begin{array}{r}5\\+4\\\hline9\end{array}\quad\begin{array}{r}2\\+2\\\hline4\end{array}\quad\begin{array}{r}0\\+8\\\hline8\end{array}\quad\begin{array}{r}4\\+7\\\hline11\end{array}\quad\begin{array}{r}1\\+1\\\hline2\end{array}\quad\begin{array}{r}3\\+7\\\hline10\end{array}$$

4.
$$\begin{array}{r}4\\+5\\\hline9\end{array}\quad\begin{array}{r}1\\+3\\\hline4\end{array}\quad\begin{array}{r}0\\+7\\\hline7\end{array}\quad\begin{array}{r}9\\+2\\\hline11\end{array}\quad\begin{array}{r}5\\+9\\\hline14\end{array}\quad\begin{array}{r}2\\+6\\\hline8\end{array}\quad\begin{array}{r}8\\+7\\\hline15\end{array}\quad\begin{array}{r}5\\+2\\\hline7\end{array}\quad\begin{array}{r}6\\+6\\\hline12\end{array}$$

5.
$$\begin{array}{r}7\\+8\\\hline15\end{array}\quad\begin{array}{r}4\\+4\\\hline8\end{array}\quad\begin{array}{r}6\\+1\\\hline7\end{array}\quad\begin{array}{r}2\\+5\\\hline7\end{array}\quad\begin{array}{r}9\\+8\\\hline17\end{array}\quad\begin{array}{r}1\\+0\\\hline1\end{array}\quad\begin{array}{r}8\\+4\\\hline12\end{array}\quad\begin{array}{r}5\\+3\\\hline8\end{array}\quad\begin{array}{r}2\\+4\\\hline6\end{array}$$

6.
$$\begin{array}{r}1\\+7\\\hline8\end{array}\quad\begin{array}{r}4\\+6\\\hline10\end{array}\quad\begin{array}{r}5\\+0\\\hline5\end{array}\quad\begin{array}{r}7\\+7\\\hline14\end{array}\quad\begin{array}{r}2\\+1\\\hline3\end{array}\quad\begin{array}{r}3\\+6\\\hline9\end{array}\quad\begin{array}{r}7\\+4\\\hline11\end{array}\quad\begin{array}{r}6\\+5\\\hline11\end{array}\quad\begin{array}{r}9\\+0\\\hline9\end{array}$$

7.
$$\begin{array}{r}8\\+3\\\hline11\end{array}\quad\begin{array}{r}1\\+9\\\hline10\end{array}\quad\begin{array}{r}9\\+5\\\hline14\end{array}\quad\begin{array}{r}8\\+1\\\hline9\end{array}\quad\begin{array}{r}5\\+6\\\hline11\end{array}\quad\begin{array}{r}2\\+3\\\hline5\end{array}\quad\begin{array}{r}4\\+9\\\hline13\end{array}\quad\begin{array}{r}9\\+7\\\hline16\end{array}\quad\begin{array}{r}3\\+2\\\hline5\end{array}$$

8.
$$\begin{array}{r}1\\+4\\\hline5\end{array}\quad\begin{array}{r}6\\+7\\\hline13\end{array}\quad\begin{array}{r}8\\+6\\\hline14\end{array}\quad\begin{array}{r}6\\+3\\\hline9\end{array}\quad\begin{array}{r}1\\+2\\\hline3\end{array}\quad\begin{array}{r}3\\+5\\\hline8\end{array}\quad\begin{array}{r}2\\+7\\\hline9\end{array}\quad\begin{array}{r}5\\+5\\\hline10\end{array}\quad\begin{array}{r}7\\+1\\\hline8\end{array}$$

9.
$$\begin{array}{r}8\\+9\\\hline17\end{array}\quad\begin{array}{r}0\\+4\\\hline4\end{array}\quad\begin{array}{r}1\\+6\\\hline7\end{array}\quad\begin{array}{r}9\\+1\\\hline10\end{array}\quad\begin{array}{r}7\\+5\\\hline12\end{array}\quad\begin{array}{r}5\\+8\\\hline13\end{array}\quad\begin{array}{r}4\\+3\\\hline7\end{array}\quad\begin{array}{r}6\\+9\\\hline15\end{array}\quad\begin{array}{r}2\\+9\\\hline11\end{array}$$

10.
$$\begin{array}{r}5\\+1\\\hline6\end{array}\quad\begin{array}{r}7\\+2\\\hline9\end{array}\quad\begin{array}{r}3\\+0\\\hline3\end{array}\quad\begin{array}{r}6\\+2\\\hline8\end{array}\quad\begin{array}{r}3\\+9\\\hline12\end{array}\quad\begin{array}{r}4\\+8\\\hline12\end{array}\quad\begin{array}{r}7\\+9\\\hline16\end{array}\quad\begin{array}{r}9\\+4\\\hline13\end{array}\quad\begin{array}{r}3\\+8\\\hline11\end{array}$$

11.
$$\begin{array}{r}3\\4\\+5\\\hline12\end{array}\quad\begin{array}{r}6\\2\\+1\\\hline9\end{array}\quad\begin{array}{r}5\\5\\+8\\\hline18\end{array}\quad\begin{array}{r}3\\6\\+2\\\hline11\end{array}\quad\begin{array}{r}8\\2\\+5\\\hline15\end{array}\quad\begin{array}{r}2\\3\\+8\\\hline13\end{array}\quad\begin{array}{r}4\\8\\+5\\\hline17\end{array}\quad\begin{array}{r}1\\7\\+6\\\hline14\end{array}\quad\begin{array}{r}9\\6\\+2\\\hline17\end{array}$$

12.
```
   24        76        45        31        20        14
   51        11        32        22        51        30
 + 10      + 12      + 10      + 12      + 13      + 23
   85        99        87        65        84        67
```

13.
```
   32        48        54        82        70        36        15
 + 46      + 31      + 22      + 17      + 20      + 61      + 54
   78        79        76        99        90        97        69
```

14.
```
  734       580       416       582       561       492
+ 234     + 219     + 333     + 216     + 407     + 306
  968       799       749       798       968       798
```

15.
```
  8,634     4,575     6,892     2,150     7,063
+ 1,332   + 2,403   + 3,106   + 6,807   + 3,426
  9,966     6,978     9,998     8,957    10,489
```

16.
```
 73,208    57,423    16,256    50,874    33,486
+ 24,501  + 30,466  + 81,032  + 49,122  + 30,503
 97,709    87,889    97,288    99,996    63,989
```

17.
```
  9,604       419     6,193       120     3,241
+   293    + 7,380   +   602   + 4,876   +   427
  9,897     7,799     6,795     4,996     3,668
```

18.
```
   48        69        74        39        67        92
 + 56      + 82      + 76      + 83      + 66      + 49
  104       151       150       122       133       141
```

19.
```
  508       763       428       256       758       679
+ 693     + 547     + 984     + 976     + 457     + 823
1,201     1,310     1,412     1,232     1,215     1,502
```

20.
```
   81        53        46        85        52        80
   85        49        77        24        46        93
 + 36      + 70      + 24      + 17      + 25      + 28
  202       172       147       126       123       201
```

21.
```
  394       649        43        86       781       977
  758        80       568       904        59       256
+  26     + 506     + 257     +  25     + 643     + 458
1,178     1,235       868     1,015     1,483     1,691
```

22.
3,487	2,286	5,842	3,095	4,306
4,908	536	10,493	635	8,340
2,864	83	388	827	9,755
+ 1,335	+ 2,947	+ 59	+ 3,046	+ 2,647
12,594	5,852	16,782	7,603	25,048

23.
49	3
8	95
+ 56	+ 207
113	305

24.
47	16
286	427
+ 9	+ 38
342	481

25.
68	10
341	834
+ 2,094	+ 5,845
2,503	6,689

26.
5,732	83
26	191
47	40
+ 208	+ 6,072
6,013	6,386

27.
9,823	204
50,474	60,713
+ 335	+ 2,056
60,632	62,973

28.
72
+ 3
75 inches

29.
127
14
8
+ 4
153 employees

30.
1,875,000
+ 727,500
2,602,500 pounds

31.
1,596
+ 1,904
3,500 feet

32.
$ 9.19
20.43
+ 1.62
$31.24

33.
$2.35
.75
1.10
.95
.50
.34
+ .85
$6.84

34.
$15.68
11.54
+ 4.73
$31.95

35. $ 99.38
        151.41
        295.63
  + 314.81
    $861.23

SUBTRACTING WHOLE NUMBERS

1.	14 −6 = 8	8 −2 = 6	6 −5 = 1	7 −4 = 3	15 −9 = 6	12 −3 = 9	13 −4 = 9	11 −5 = 6	6 −6 = 0
2.	12 −9 = 3	9 −6 = 3	10 −4 = 6	3 −2 = 1	6 −2 = 4	9 −9 = 0	8 −0 = 8	9 −3 = 6	10 −7 = 3
3.	3 −0 = 3	11 −2 = 9	12 −7 = 5	6 −3 = 3	17 −9 = 8	1 −0 = 1	10 −1 = 9	14 −9 = 5	8 −8 = 0
4.	16 −8 = 8	7 −1 = 6	13 −6 = 7	2 −0 = 2	10 −3 = 7	15 −7 = 8	11 −7 = 4	8 −5 = 3	6 −0 = 6
5.	10 −8 = 2	5 −3 = 2	12 −5 = 7	13 −9 = 4	9 −8 = 1	14 −7 = 7	7 −0 = 7	10 −5 = 5	8 −3 = 5
6.	4 −4 = 0	9 −1 = 8	12 −4 = 8	9 −4 = 5	2 −2 = 0	12 −6 = 6	11 −8 = 3	7 −2 = 5	5 −5 = 0
7.	13 −5 = 8	11 −6 = 5	12 −8 = 4	3 −3 = 0	15 −6 = 9	8 −1 = 7	9 −7 = 2	11 −3 = 8	16 −9 = 7
8.	6 −4 = 2	10 −6 = 4	5 −1 = 4	7 −7 = 0	4 −3 = 1	13 −7 = 6	9 −0 = 9	3 −1 = 2	14 −8 = 6
9.	18 −9 = 9	15 −8 = 7	0 −0 = 0	8 −6 = 2	4 −1 = 3	7 −5 = 2	11 −4 = 7	9 −5 = 4	17 −8 = 9

10.
$$\begin{array}{r} 5 \\ -2 \\ \hline 3 \end{array} \qquad \begin{array}{r} 14 \\ -5 \\ \hline 9 \end{array} \qquad \begin{array}{r} 8 \\ -4 \\ \hline 4 \end{array} \qquad \begin{array}{r} 2 \\ -1 \\ \hline 1 \end{array} \qquad \begin{array}{r} 16 \\ -7 \\ \hline 9 \end{array} \qquad \begin{array}{r} 6 \\ -1 \\ \hline 5 \end{array} \qquad \begin{array}{r} 13 \\ -8 \\ \hline 5 \end{array} \qquad \begin{array}{r} 1 \\ -1 \\ \hline 0 \end{array} \qquad \begin{array}{r} 8 \\ -7 \\ \hline 1 \end{array}$$

11.
$$\begin{array}{r} 4 \\ -2 \\ \hline 2 \end{array} \qquad \begin{array}{r} 5 \\ -4 \\ \hline 1 \end{array} \qquad \begin{array}{r} 10 \\ -2 \\ \hline 8 \end{array} \qquad \begin{array}{r} 7 \\ -6 \\ \hline 1 \end{array} \qquad \begin{array}{r} 11 \\ -9 \\ \hline 2 \end{array} \qquad \begin{array}{r} 4 \\ -0 \\ \hline 4 \end{array} \qquad \begin{array}{r} 7 \\ -3 \\ \hline 4 \end{array} \qquad \begin{array}{r} 9 \\ -2 \\ \hline 7 \end{array} \qquad \begin{array}{r} 10 \\ -9 \\ \hline 1 \end{array}$$

12.
$$\begin{array}{r} 75 \\ -23 \\ \hline 52 \end{array} \qquad \begin{array}{r} 62 \\ -50 \\ \hline 12 \end{array} \qquad \begin{array}{r} 80 \\ -30 \\ \hline 50 \end{array} \qquad \begin{array}{r} 66 \\ -41 \\ \hline 25 \end{array} \qquad \begin{array}{r} 73 \\ -33 \\ \hline 40 \end{array} \qquad \begin{array}{r} 28 \\ -17 \\ \hline 11 \end{array} \qquad \begin{array}{r} 45 \\ -22 \\ \hline 23 \end{array}$$

13.
$$\begin{array}{r} 47 \\ -42 \\ \hline 5 \end{array} \qquad \begin{array}{r} 53 \\ -21 \\ \hline 32 \end{array} \qquad \begin{array}{r} 92 \\ -62 \\ \hline 30 \end{array} \qquad \begin{array}{r} 87 \\ -34 \\ \hline 53 \end{array} \qquad \begin{array}{r} 76 \\ -35 \\ \hline 41 \end{array} \qquad \begin{array}{r} 49 \\ -41 \\ \hline 8 \end{array} \qquad \begin{array}{r} 58 \\ -25 \\ \hline 33 \end{array}$$

14.
$$\begin{array}{r} 569 \\ -263 \\ \hline 306 \end{array} \qquad \begin{array}{r} 806 \\ -403 \\ \hline 403 \end{array} \qquad \begin{array}{r} 964 \\ -223 \\ \hline 741 \end{array} \qquad \begin{array}{r} 707 \\ -405 \\ \hline 302 \end{array} \qquad \begin{array}{r} 525 \\ -114 \\ \hline 411 \end{array} \qquad \begin{array}{r} 748 \\ -628 \\ \hline 120 \end{array}$$

15.
$$\begin{array}{r} 25{,}730 \\ -12{,}720 \\ \hline 13{,}010 \end{array} \qquad \begin{array}{r} 46{,}275 \\ -33{,}144 \\ \hline 13{,}131 \end{array} \qquad \begin{array}{r} 80{,}463 \\ -20{,}361 \\ \hline 60{,}102 \end{array} \qquad \begin{array}{r} 63{,}251 \\ -40{,}220 \\ \hline 23{,}031 \end{array} \qquad \begin{array}{r} 86{,}477 \\ -71{,}346 \\ \hline 15{,}131 \end{array}$$

16.
$$\begin{array}{r} 81{,}575 \\ -1{,}423 \\ \hline 80{,}152 \end{array} \qquad \begin{array}{r} 36{,}416 \\ -2{,}214 \\ \hline 34{,}202 \end{array} \qquad \begin{array}{r} 95{,}374 \\ -2{,}322 \\ \hline 93{,}052 \end{array} \qquad \begin{array}{r} 55{,}296 \\ -3{,}184 \\ \hline 52{,}112 \end{array} \qquad \begin{array}{r} 52{,}876 \\ -1{,}625 \\ \hline 51{,}251 \end{array}$$

17.
$$\begin{array}{r} 76 \\ -8 \\ \hline 68 \end{array} \qquad \begin{array}{r} 58 \\ -9 \\ \hline 49 \end{array} \qquad \begin{array}{r} 84 \\ -7 \\ \hline 77 \end{array} \qquad \begin{array}{r} 35 \\ -6 \\ \hline 29 \end{array} \qquad \begin{array}{r} 91 \\ -3 \\ \hline 88 \end{array} \qquad \begin{array}{r} 87 \\ -9 \\ \hline 78 \end{array} \qquad \begin{array}{r} 53 \\ -6 \\ \hline 47 \end{array}$$

18.
$$\begin{array}{r} 38 \\ -29 \\ \hline 9 \end{array} \qquad \begin{array}{r} 93 \\ -37 \\ \hline 56 \end{array} \qquad \begin{array}{r} 47 \\ -39 \\ \hline 8 \end{array} \qquad \begin{array}{r} 52 \\ -25 \\ \hline 27 \end{array} \qquad \begin{array}{r} 74 \\ -56 \\ \hline 18 \end{array} \qquad \begin{array}{r} 26 \\ -19 \\ \hline 7 \end{array} \qquad \begin{array}{r} 61 \\ -22 \\ \hline 39 \end{array}$$

19.
$$\begin{array}{r} 544 \\ -95 \\ \hline 449 \end{array} \qquad \begin{array}{r} 782 \\ -93 \\ \hline 689 \end{array} \qquad \begin{array}{r} 647 \\ -88 \\ \hline 559 \end{array} \qquad \begin{array}{r} 938 \\ -69 \\ \hline 869 \end{array} \qquad \begin{array}{r} 726 \\ -48 \\ \hline 678 \end{array} \qquad \begin{array}{r} 583 \\ -94 \\ \hline 489 \end{array}$$

20.
$$\begin{array}{r} 584 \\ -295 \\ \hline 289 \end{array} \qquad \begin{array}{r} 642 \\ -568 \\ \hline 74 \end{array} \qquad \begin{array}{r} 533 \\ -347 \\ \hline 186 \end{array} \qquad \begin{array}{r} 627 \\ -389 \\ \hline 238 \end{array} \qquad \begin{array}{r} 318 \\ -199 \\ \hline 119 \end{array} \qquad \begin{array}{r} 976 \\ -288 \\ \hline 688 \end{array}$$

21.
5,614	2,736	8,370	4,674	5,622
− 3,815	− 1,798	− 2,467	− 3,585	− 4,918
1,799	938	5,903	1,089	704

22.
23,475	27,480	52,637	65,124	45,812
− 15,388	− 16.991	− 14,882	− 27,538	− 28,073
8,087	10,489	37,755	37,586	17,739

23.
837,504	204,376	142,605	381,644	927,345
− 767,652	− 152,488	− 125,894	− 289,579	− 469,329
69,852	51,888	16,711	92,065	458,016

24.
2,366		1,475		9,641
− 487		− 856		− 855
1,879		619		8,786

25.
4,876		9,856		8,654
− 4,297		− 9,578		− 3,756
579		278		4,898

26.
2,366		5,712		4,638
− 1,467		− 2,588		− 4,549
899		3,124		89

27.
14,480		35,826		26,150
− 8,529		− 9,757		− 7,483
5,951		26,069		18,667

28.
43,117		65,014		83,576
− 24,898		− 26,307		− 44,879
18,219		38,707		38,697

29.
406	305	208	704	803	902
− 58	− 66	− 79	− 57	− 64	− 18
348	239	129	647	739	884

30.
701	602	405	903	807	204
− 158	− 463	− 277	− 847	− 369	− 197
543	139	128	56	438	7

31.
600	200	400	500	800	700
− 527	− 118	− 236	− 423	− 265	− 189
73	82	164	77	535	511

32.
3,060	7,040	9,050	8,010	3,020	2,080
− 2,186	− 3,094	− 3,557	− 6,956	− 1,987	− 1,193
874	3,946	5,493	1,054	1,033	887

33.
5,002	3,008	9,001	6,005	4,004	8,005
− 2,654	− 1,559	− 2,108	− 4,569	− 2,378	− 4,336
2,348	1,449	6,893	1,436	1,626	3,669

34.
20,000	40,000	50,000	60,000	30,000
− 13,654	− 38,562	− 20,751	− 33,045	− 19,720
6,346	1,438	29,249	26,955	10,280

35.
$529.95
− 479.95
$ 50.00

36.
5,009
− 1,214
3,795 sq. mi.

37.
$79.95	$90.00
+ 6.40	− 86.35
$86.35	$ 3.65

38.
1980
− 1833
147 years old

39.
$240.00
− 39.72
$200.28

40.
1,698,281
− 1,539,233
159,048 people

41.
$708.00
− 187.50
$520.50

42.
$38,500
− 4,750
$33,750

43.
2,981	5,072
+ 1,079	− 4,060
4,060	1,012 records

MULTIPLYING WHOLE NUMBERS

1.
7	5	2	9	3	1	8	6	1
× 1	× 5	× 7	× 4	× 5	× 2	× 6	× 7	× 4
7	25	14	36	15	2	48	42	4

2.
2	8	5	3	2	7	4	6	9
× 5	× 4	× 3	× 9	× 4	× 8	× 4	× 1	× 8
10	32	15	27	8	56	16	6	72

3.
9	5	6	3	0	2	6	4	6
× 9	× 4	× 8	× 1	× 8	× 2	× 6	× 7	× 2
81	20	48	3	0	4	36	28	12

4.
$$
\begin{array}{r} 3 \\ \times\,0 \\ \hline 0 \end{array}
\quad
\begin{array}{r} 3 \\ \times\,7 \\ \hline 21 \end{array}
\quad
\begin{array}{r} 0 \\ \times\,7 \\ \hline 0 \end{array}
\quad
\begin{array}{r} 9 \\ \times\,2 \\ \hline 18 \end{array}
\quad
\begin{array}{r} 5 \\ \times\,9 \\ \hline 45 \end{array}
\quad
\begin{array}{r} 2 \\ \times\,6 \\ \hline 12 \end{array}
\quad
\begin{array}{r} 1 \\ \times\,1 \\ \hline 1 \end{array}
\quad
\begin{array}{r} 8 \\ \times\,7 \\ \hline 56 \end{array}
\quad
\begin{array}{r} 5 \\ \times\,2 \\ \hline 10 \end{array}
$$

5.
$$
\begin{array}{r} 5 \\ \times\,1 \\ \hline 5 \end{array}
\quad
\begin{array}{r} 8 \\ \times\,5 \\ \hline 40 \end{array}
\quad
\begin{array}{r} 5 \\ \times\,7 \\ \hline 35 \end{array}
\quad
\begin{array}{r} 3 \\ \times\,3 \\ \hline 9 \end{array}
\quad
\begin{array}{r} 1 \\ \times\,8 \\ \hline 8 \end{array}
\quad
\begin{array}{r} 0 \\ \times\,6 \\ \hline 0 \end{array}
\quad
\begin{array}{r} 7 \\ \times\,3 \\ \hline 21 \end{array}
\quad
\begin{array}{r} 2 \\ \times\,8 \\ \hline 16 \end{array}
\quad
\begin{array}{r} 9 \\ \times\,6 \\ \hline 54 \end{array}
$$

6.
$$
\begin{array}{r} 3 \\ \times\,8 \\ \hline 24 \end{array}
\quad
\begin{array}{r} 2 \\ \times\,9 \\ \hline 18 \end{array}
\quad
\begin{array}{r} 6 \\ \times\,9 \\ \hline 54 \end{array}
\quad
\begin{array}{r} 4 \\ \times\,3 \\ \hline 12 \end{array}
\quad
\begin{array}{r} 5 \\ \times\,8 \\ \hline 40 \end{array}
\quad
\begin{array}{r} 7 \\ \times\,5 \\ \hline 35 \end{array}
\quad
\begin{array}{r} 9 \\ \times\,1 \\ \hline 9 \end{array}
\quad
\begin{array}{r} 1 \\ \times\,6 \\ \hline 6 \end{array}
\quad
\begin{array}{r} 0 \\ \times\,4 \\ \hline 0 \end{array}
$$

7.
$$
\begin{array}{r} 7 \\ \times\,9 \\ \hline 63 \end{array}
\quad
\begin{array}{r} 3 \\ \times\,2 \\ \hline 6 \end{array}
\quad
\begin{array}{r} 9 \\ \times\,7 \\ \hline 63 \end{array}
\quad
\begin{array}{r} 4 \\ \times\,9 \\ \hline 36 \end{array}
\quad
\begin{array}{r} 2 \\ \times\,3 \\ \hline 6 \end{array}
\quad
\begin{array}{r} 5 \\ \times\,6 \\ \hline 30 \end{array}
\quad
\begin{array}{r} 8 \\ \times\,1 \\ \hline 8 \end{array}
\quad
\begin{array}{r} 9 \\ \times\,5 \\ \hline 45 \end{array}
\quad
\begin{array}{r} 1 \\ \times\,9 \\ \hline 9 \end{array}
$$

8.
$$
\begin{array}{r} 4 \\ \times\,8 \\ \hline 32 \end{array}
\quad
\begin{array}{r} 6 \\ \times\,5 \\ \hline 30 \end{array}
\quad
\begin{array}{r} 9 \\ \times\,0 \\ \hline 0 \end{array}
\quad
\begin{array}{r} 7 \\ \times\,4 \\ \hline 28 \end{array}
\quad
\begin{array}{r} 2 \\ \times\,1 \\ \hline 2 \end{array}
\quad
\begin{array}{r} 3 \\ \times\,6 \\ \hline 18 \end{array}
\quad
\begin{array}{r} 5 \\ \times\,0 \\ \hline 0 \end{array}
\quad
\begin{array}{r} 7 \\ \times\,7 \\ \hline 49 \end{array}
\quad
\begin{array}{r} 4 \\ \times\,6 \\ \hline 24 \end{array}
$$

9.
$$
\begin{array}{r} 8 \\ \times\,8 \\ \hline 64 \end{array}
\quad
\begin{array}{r} 2 \\ \times\,0 \\ \hline 0 \end{array}
\quad
\begin{array}{r} 6 \\ \times\,4 \\ \hline 24 \end{array}
\quad
\begin{array}{r} 9 \\ \times\,3 \\ \hline 27 \end{array}
\quad
\begin{array}{r} 7 \\ \times\,6 \\ \hline 42 \end{array}
\quad
\begin{array}{r} 8 \\ \times\,2 \\ \hline 16 \end{array}
\quad
\begin{array}{r} 1 \\ \times\,5 \\ \hline 5 \end{array}
\quad
\begin{array}{r} 7 \\ \times\,2 \\ \hline 14 \end{array}
\quad
\begin{array}{r} 4 \\ \times\,1 \\ \hline 4 \end{array}
$$

10.
$$
\begin{array}{r} 6 \\ \times\,3 \\ \hline 18 \end{array}
\quad
\begin{array}{r} 1 \\ \times\,0 \\ \hline 0 \end{array}
\quad
\begin{array}{r} 4 \\ \times\,5 \\ \hline 20 \end{array}
\quad
\begin{array}{r} 1 \\ \times\,3 \\ \hline 3 \end{array}
\quad
\begin{array}{r} 4 \\ \times\,2 \\ \hline 8 \end{array}
\quad
\begin{array}{r} 8 \\ \times\,9 \\ \hline 72 \end{array}
\quad
\begin{array}{r} 8 \\ \times\,3 \\ \hline 24 \end{array}
\quad
\begin{array}{r} 1 \\ \times\,7 \\ \hline 7 \end{array}
\quad
\begin{array}{r} 3 \\ \times\,4 \\ \hline 12 \end{array}
$$

11.
$$
\begin{array}{r} 32 \\ \times\,4 \\ \hline 128 \end{array}
\quad
\begin{array}{r} 81 \\ \times\,9 \\ \hline 729 \end{array}
\quad
\begin{array}{r} 60 \\ \times\,7 \\ \hline 420 \end{array}
\quad
\begin{array}{r} 43 \\ \times\,3 \\ \hline 129 \end{array}
\quad
\begin{array}{r} 71 \\ \times\,8 \\ \hline 568 \end{array}
\quad
\begin{array}{r} 52 \\ \times\,4 \\ \hline 208 \end{array}
\quad
\begin{array}{r} 91 \\ \times\,2 \\ \hline 182 \end{array}
$$

12.
$$
\begin{array}{r} 312 \\ \times\,3 \\ \hline 936 \end{array}
\quad
\begin{array}{r} 423 \\ \times\,2 \\ \hline 846 \end{array}
\quad
\begin{array}{r} 321 \\ \times\,4 \\ \hline 1{,}284 \end{array}
\quad
\begin{array}{r} 501 \\ \times\,7 \\ \hline 3{,}507 \end{array}
\quad
\begin{array}{r} 731 \\ \times\,3 \\ \hline 2{,}193 \end{array}
\quad
\begin{array}{r} 820 \\ \times\,4 \\ \hline 3{,}280 \end{array}
$$

13.
$$
\begin{array}{r} 9{,}103 \\ \times\,2 \\ \hline 18{,}206 \end{array}
\quad
\begin{array}{r} 2{,}312 \\ \times\,3 \\ \hline 6{,}936 \end{array}
\quad
\begin{array}{r} 6{,}201 \\ \times\,4 \\ \hline 24{,}804 \end{array}
\quad
\begin{array}{r} 3{,}324 \\ \times\,2 \\ \hline 6{,}648 \end{array}
\quad
\begin{array}{r} 5{,}230 \\ \times\,3 \\ \hline 15{,}690 \end{array}
$$

14.
$$
\begin{array}{r} 32 \\ \times\,34 \\ \hline 128 \\ 96 \\ \hline 1{,}088 \end{array}
\quad
\begin{array}{r} 24 \\ \times\,21 \\ \hline 24 \\ 48 \\ \hline 504 \end{array}
\quad
\begin{array}{r} 52 \\ \times\,34 \\ \hline 208 \\ 156 \\ \hline 1{,}768 \end{array}
\quad
\begin{array}{r} 81 \\ \times\,65 \\ \hline 405 \\ 486 \\ \hline 5{,}265 \end{array}
\quad
\begin{array}{r} 63 \\ \times\,32 \\ \hline 126 \\ 189 \\ \hline 2{,}016 \end{array}
\quad
\begin{array}{r} 92 \\ \times\,24 \\ \hline 368 \\ 184 \\ \hline 2{,}208 \end{array}
\quad
\begin{array}{r} 41 \\ \times\,97 \\ \hline 287 \\ 369 \\ \hline 3{,}977 \end{array}
$$

15.
50	90	40	70	20	60	80
× 63	× 89	× 72	× 28	× 36	× 45	× 51
150	810	80	560	120	300	80
300	720	280	140	60	240	400
3,150	8,010	2,880	1,960	720	2,700	4,080

16.
84	63	51	42	81	93	72
× 20	× 30	× 90	× 40	× 80	× 20	× 40
1,680	1,890	4,590	1,680	6,480	1,860	2,880

17.
36	75	13	39	86	74	39
× 4	× 9	× 5	× 6	× 7	× 8	× 3
144	675	65	234	602	592	117

18.
266	593	834	427	542	349
× 8	× 3	× 9	× 4	× 6	× 5
2,128	1,779	7,506	1,708	3,252	1,745

19.
53	69	84	53	74	28	96
× 56	× 74	× 37	× 49	× 68	× 93	× 57
318	276	588	477	592	84	672
265	483	252	212	444	252	480
2,968	5,106	3,108	2,597	5,032	2,604	5,472

20.
99	48	78	34	85	17	83
× 25	× 64	× 72	× 33	× 48	× 93	× 94
495	192	156	102	680	51	332
198	288	546	102	340	153	747
2,475	3,072	5,616	1,122	4,080	1,581	7,802

21.
754	679	472	617	728	536
× 28	× 89	× 36	× 64	× 57	× 92
6032	6111	2832	2468	5096	1072
1508	5432	1416	3702	3640	4824
21,112	60,431	16,992	39,488	41,496	49,312

22.
703	604	805	106	504	809
× 9	× 6	× 4	× 7	× 3	× 2
6,327	3,624	3,220	742	1,512	1,618

23.
4,606	8,091	5,104	6,053	7,028
× 8	× 3	× 7	× 6	× 9
36,848	24,273	35,728	36,318	63,252

24.
```
    5,705        4,033        8,062        5,607        3,094
 ×     95     ×     84     ×     76     ×     36     ×     87
   28 525       16 132       48 372       33 642       21 658
  513 45       322 64       564 34       168 21       247 52
  541,975      338,772      612,712      201,852      269,178
```

25.
```
    456          928          374
 ×    7       ×    5       ×    8
  3,192        4,640        2,992
```

26.
```
    597          842          902
 ×   34       ×   67       ×   56
  2 388        5 894        5 412
 17 91        50 52        45 10
 20,298       56,414       50,512
```

27.
```
  4,608        8,477        5,928
 ×   53       ×   96       ×   80
 13 824       50 862      474,240
230 40       762 93
244,224      813,792
```

28. 830   4,560   2,500   34,980

29. 5,400   28,600   20,700   8,000

30. 9,000   47,000   803,000   970,000

31.
```
  $1.49
 ×    4
  $5.96
```
32.
```
    389
 ×    6
  2,334 miles
```

33.
```
  $ 62.75
 ×      5
  $313.75
```
34.
```
  $  4.67        $  28.02
 ×     6       + 194.50
  $28.02        $222.52
```

35.
```
     16
 ×   19
    144
     16
    304 miles
```
36.
```
  $ .89        $1.59        $ 1.35
 ×   3       ×    2       ×    4
  $2.67        $3.18        $5.40
                            3.18
                            2.67
                           $11.25
```

37.   5,280
      ×   27
      36 960
      105 60
      142,560 feet

38. $62.50
      + 15.00
      $77.50
      ×   12
      155 00
      775 0
      $930.00

39. $ 36 $ 48
      ×   24   ×   18   They are the same.
         144   384
          72   48
       $864 $864

DIVIDING WHOLE NUMBERS

1. $\frac{9}{4\overline{)36}}$ $\frac{7}{1\overline{)7}}$ $\frac{5}{5\overline{)25}}$ $\frac{2}{7\overline{)14}}$ $\frac{3}{5\overline{)15}}$ $\frac{1}{2\overline{)2}}$ $\frac{6}{3\overline{)18}}$

2. $\frac{4}{8\overline{)32}}$ $\frac{6}{5\overline{)30}}$ $\frac{0}{9\overline{)0}}$ $\frac{7}{4\overline{)28}}$ $\frac{3}{6\overline{)18}}$ $\frac{2}{1\overline{)2}}$ $\frac{7}{7\overline{)49}}$

3. $\frac{6}{6\overline{)36}}$ $\frac{0}{3\overline{)0}}$ $\frac{8}{7\overline{)56}}$ $\frac{2}{6\overline{)12}}$ $\frac{5}{9\overline{)45}}$ $\frac{5}{2\overline{)10}}$ $\frac{9}{2\overline{)18}}$

4. $\frac{3}{9\overline{)27}}$ $\frac{2}{4\overline{)8}}$ $\frac{5}{3\overline{)15}}$ $\frac{8}{4\overline{)32}}$ $\frac{9}{5\overline{)45}}$ $\frac{9}{8\overline{)72}}$ $\frac{2}{5\overline{)10}}$

5. $\frac{6}{2\overline{)12}}$ $\frac{3}{7\overline{)21}}$ $\frac{1}{1\overline{)1}}$ $\frac{4}{7\overline{)28}}$ $\frac{0}{8\overline{)0}}$ $\frac{2}{2\overline{)4}}$ $\frac{5}{4\overline{)20}}$

6. $\frac{3}{8\overline{)24}}$ $\frac{2}{9\overline{)18}}$ $\frac{6}{9\overline{)54}}$ $\frac{4}{3\overline{)12}}$ $\frac{5}{8\overline{)40}}$ $\frac{7}{5\overline{)35}}$ $\frac{9}{1\overline{)9}}$

7. $\frac{5}{1\overline{)5}}$ $\frac{8}{5\overline{)40}}$ $\frac{5}{7\overline{)35}}$ $\frac{3}{3\overline{)9}}$ $\frac{1}{8\overline{)8}}$ $\frac{0}{6\overline{)0}}$ $\frac{7}{3\overline{)21}}$

8. $\frac{7}{2\overline{)14}}$ $\frac{1}{5\overline{)5}}$ $\frac{8}{2\overline{)16}}$ $\frac{4}{1\overline{)4}}$ $\frac{9}{3\overline{)27}}$ $\frac{7}{6\overline{)42}}$ $\frac{8}{3\overline{)24}}$

9. $\frac{7}{9\overline{)63}}$ $\frac{3}{2\overline{)6}}$ $\frac{9}{7\overline{)63}}$ $\frac{4}{9\overline{)36}}$ $\frac{2}{3\overline{)6}}$ $\frac{5}{6\overline{)30}}$ $\frac{8}{1\overline{)8}}$

10. $\frac{8}{6\overline{)48}}$ $\frac{6}{7\overline{)42}}$ $\frac{1}{4\overline{)4}}$ $\frac{0}{5\overline{)0}}$ $\frac{4}{6\overline{)24}}$ $\frac{1}{7\overline{)7}}$ $\frac{1}{3\overline{)3}}$

11. $\quad$ 4 $\quad$ 6 $\quad$ 4 $\quad$ 7 $\quad$ 9 $\quad$ 6 $\quad$ 1

$5\overline{)20}\qquad 1\overline{)6}\qquad 4\overline{)16}\qquad 8\overline{)56}\qquad 9\overline{)81}\qquad 8\overline{)48}\qquad 6\overline{)6}$

12. $\quad$ 8 $\quad$ 2 $\quad$ 9 $\quad$ 4 $\quad$ 6 $\quad$ 8 $\quad$ 3

$9\overline{)72}\qquad 8\overline{)16}\qquad 6\overline{)54}\qquad 2\overline{)8}\qquad 4\overline{)24}\qquad 8\overline{)64}\qquad 4\overline{)12}$

13. $\quad$ 5 3 $\qquad$ 2 8 $\qquad$ 6 1 $\qquad$ 7 5 $\qquad$ 5 6

$6\overline{)3\ 1^18}\qquad 9\overline{)2\ 5^72}\qquad 4\overline{)2\ 4\ 4}\qquad 7\overline{)5\ 2^35}\qquad 8\overline{)4\ 4^48}$

14. $\quad$ 2 9 $\qquad$ 4 6 $\qquad$ 7 3 $\qquad$ 3 6 $\qquad$ 2 8

$5\overline{)1\ 4^45}\qquad 7\overline{)3\ 2^42}\qquad 2\overline{)1\ 4\ 6}\qquad 3\overline{)1\ 0^18}\qquad 4\overline{)1\ 1^32}$

15. $\quad$ 4 2 6 $\qquad$ 5 3 1 $\qquad$ 2 5 8 $\qquad$ 1 3 7 $\qquad$ 4 2 3

$8\overline{)3\ 4^20^48}\qquad 6\overline{)3\ 1^18\ 6}\qquad 5\overline{)1\ 2^29^40}\qquad 9\overline{)1\ 2^33^63}\qquad 4\overline{)1\ 6\ 9^12}$

16. $\quad$ 8 5 4 $\qquad$ 3 7 2 $\qquad$ 4 1 7 $\qquad$ 3 2 9 $\qquad$ 6 1 5

$3\overline{)2\ 5^16^12}\qquad 7\overline{)2\ 6^50^14}\qquad 6\overline{)2\ 5^10^42}\qquad 8\overline{)2\ 6^23^72}\qquad 5\overline{)3\ 0\ 7^25}$

17. $\quad$ 2 0 4 $\qquad$ 5 0 3 $\qquad$ 3 2 1 $\qquad$ 4 3 0 $\qquad$ 6 0 7

$4\overline{)8\ 1\ 6}\qquad 6\overline{)3\ 0\ 1\ 8}\qquad 9\overline{)2\ 8^18\ 9}\qquad 3\overline{)1\ 2\ 9\ 0}\qquad 7\overline{)4\ 2\ 4\ 9}$

18. $\quad$ 9 5 0 $\qquad$ 4 2 3 $\qquad$ 3 8 0 $\qquad$ 2 0 9 $\qquad$ 7 0 6

$8\overline{)7\ 6^40\ 0}\qquad 5\overline{)2\ 1^11^15}\qquad 6\overline{)2\ 2^48\ 0}\qquad 7\overline{)1\ 4\ 6\ 3}\qquad 2\overline{)1\ 4\ 1\ 2}$

19. $\quad$ 2 5r6 $\qquad$ 4 2r5 $\qquad$ 6 8r4 $\qquad$ 3 7r3 $\qquad$ 5 9r2

$7\overline{)1\ 8^41}\qquad 8\overline{)3\ 4^21}\qquad 5\overline{)3\ 4^44}\qquad 6\overline{)2\ 2^45}\qquad 4\overline{)2\ 3^38}$

20. $\quad$ 8 2r3 $\qquad$ 5 1r7 $\qquad$ 4 8r1 $\qquad$ 7 5r1 $\qquad$ 6 6r4

$6\overline{)4\ 9^15}\qquad 9\overline{)4\ 6^16}\qquad 3\overline{)1\ 4^25}\qquad 2\overline{)1\ 5^11}\qquad 7\overline{)4\ 6^46}$

21. $\quad$ 4 1 7r2 $\qquad$ 3 0 9r3 $\qquad$ 2 1 6r5 $\qquad$ 4 9 9r1 $\qquad$ 3 2 7r6

$5\overline{)2,0\ 8^37}\qquad 4\overline{)1,2\ 3\ 9}\qquad 8\overline{)1,7^13^53}\qquad 3\overline{)1,4^29^28}\qquad 9\overline{)2,9^24^69}$

22. $\quad$ 4, 2 0 8r5 $\qquad$ 2, 5 6 7r2 $\qquad$ 3, 4 8 0r3 $\qquad$ 2, 0 9 7r6 $\qquad$ 3, 4 6 0r3

$6\overline{)25,^12\ 5\ 3}\qquad 7\overline{)17,3^94^75^1}\qquad 4\overline{)13,^19^32\ 3}\qquad 8\overline{)16,\ 7\ 8^62}\qquad 5\overline{)17,2^33^03}$

23. $\quad$ 7 $\qquad\qquad$ 6 $\qquad\qquad$ 8 $\qquad\qquad$ 4

$41\overline{)287}\qquad 37\overline{)222}\qquad 69\overline{)552}\qquad 48\overline{)192}$

$\quad\ \underline{287}\qquad\quad\ \ \underline{222}\qquad\quad\ \ \underline{552}\qquad\quad\ \ \underline{192}$

24. $\quad$ 5r21 $\qquad\qquad$ 4r20 $\qquad\qquad$ 9r15 $\qquad\qquad$ 8r11

$89\overline{)466}\qquad 26\overline{)124}\qquad 42\overline{)393}\qquad 37\overline{)307}$

$\quad\ \underline{445}\qquad\quad\ \ \underline{104}\qquad\quad\ \ \underline{378}\qquad\quad\ \ \underline{296}$

$\quad\quad\ \overline{21}\qquad\quad\quad\ \overline{20}\qquad\quad\quad\ \overline{15}\qquad\quad\quad\ \overline{11}$

25.
```
        23                  36                  42                  27
    92)2,116            54)1,944            18)756              66)1,782
       1 84                1 62                72                  1 32
        276                 324                 36                  462
        276                 324                 36                  462
```

26.
```
        34r35               26r19               52r14               49r20
    58)2,007            72)1,891            23)1,210            36)1,784
       1 74                1 44                1 15                1 44
        267                 451                 60                  344
        232                 432                 46                  324
         35                  19                  14                   20
```

27.
```
         52                  26                  43                  84
    285)14,820          412)10,712          562)24,166          326)27,384
        14 25               8 24                22 48               26 08
         570               2 472              1 686              1 304
         570               2 472              1 686              1 304
```

28.
```
         35r660                          61r800
    722)25,930                       908)56,188
        21 66                            54 48
         4 270                           1 708
         3 610                             908
           660                             800
```

```
         24r150                          53r200
    453)11,022                       662)35,286
        9 06                             33 10
        1 962                            2 186
        1 812                            1 986
          150                             200
```

29.
```
        267                 904                 618
     8)2,136             6)5,424             5)3,090
```

30.
```
        25r11               41r30               56r18
    15)386              62)2,572            29)1,642
       30                  2 48                1 45
        86                  92                  192
        75                  62                  174
        11                  30                   18
```

31.
```
          68                53                 92
   48)3,264          37)1,961          54)4,968
      2 88              1 85              4 86
       384               111               108
       384               111               108
```

32.
```
        80r120              41r300                 67
  124)10,040          362)15,142          438)29,346
      9 92                14 48              26 28
       120                 662               3 066
                           362               3 066
                           300
```

33.
```
     $ .49
   4)$1.96
```

34.
```
      8 feet
   12)96
```

35.
```
     $  175
  12)$2,100
     1 2
       90
       84
       60
       60
```

36.
```
      21 months
   36)756
      72
      36
      36·
```

37.
```
      86        82
      94      5)410
      77
      83
   +  70
      410
```

38.
```
      257 boxes
  24)6,168
     4 8
     1 36
     1 20
       168
       168
```

39.
```
     $  185.40
  52)$9,640.80
     5 2
     4 44
     4 16
       280
       260
        20 8
        20 8
```

40.
```
      27 minutes
  342)9,234
      6 84
      2 394
      2 394
```

41.   13 inches
      240)3,120
            2 40
            ─────
             720
             720
             ───

42.   62   68°
             75   5)340
             72
             68
           + 63
           ─────
            340

ANSWERS AND SOLUTIONS—WHOLE NUMBERS SKILLS TEST

1. hundreds

2. thousands

3. 90,000

4. 70,206

5. 8,633,590

6.   4,261
      + 5,327
      ───────
        9,588

7.   842
          379
        + 467
        ─────
        1,688

8.   862
        3,408
           63
        + 235
        ─────
        4,568

9.   9,867
      − 5,327
      ───────
        4,540

10.   8,725
      − 4,986
      ───────
        3,739

11.   54,136
      − 8,529
      ───────
       45,607

12.   40,600
      − 25,538
      ────────
       15,062

13.   62
         × 3
         ────
          186

14.   81
         × 24
         ────
          324
          162
         ─────
        1,944

15.   5,736
        × 48
       ──────
       45 888
      229 44
      ───────
      275,328

16.   807
         × 39
        ─────
        7 263
       24 21
       ──────
       31,473

17.   356
        × 100
       ──────
       35,600

18.   67
        9)603
          54
          ──
          63
          63
          ──

19.   661r5
        9)5,954
          5 4
          ───
           55
           54
           ──
           14
            9
           ──
            5

20.   418
       49)20,482
          19 6
          ────
            88
            49
           ───
           392
           392
           ───

21.
```
          298r12
    46)13,720
       9 2
       ────
       4 52
       4 14
       ────
         380
         368
         ────
          12
```

22.
```
             57
    342)19,494
        17 10
        ─────
         2 394
         2 394
         ─────
```

23.
```
    $  8.50
      19.63
    +  2.15
    ───────
    $30.28
```

24.
```
    $49.56
     12.00
    + 10.17
    ───────
    $71.73
```

25.
```
    $265.00
    −  71.73
    ───────
    $193.27
```

26.
```
     908,201
    − 867,943
    ────────
      40,258 people
```

27.
```
        36
    ×   19
    ──────
       324
        36
    ──────
       684 inches
```

28.
```
        42        $6.50          $9.75
    −   35      ×    35        ×     7
    ──────      ───────        ───────
         7        32 50        $ 68.25
                 195 0         +227.50
                 ──────        ───────
                $227.50        $295.75
```

29.
```
    387        483 people
    443      3)1449
    619
    ─────
    1,449
```

30.
```
         $   213.65
    52)$11,109.80
        10 4
        ────
          70
          52
          ───
          189
          156
          ───
           33 8
           31 2
           ────
            2 60
            2 60
            ────
```

FRACTIONS

UNDERSTANDING FRACTIONS

A fraction is a part of something. A foot is a fraction of a yard; it is one of the three equal parts of a yard or $\frac{1}{3}$ of a yard. 70¢ is a fraction of a dollar; it is seven of the ten equal parts in a dollar or $\frac{7}{10}$ of a dollar.

The two numbers in a fraction are called the:

<u>**numerator**</u> —tells how many parts you have.
denominator—tells how many parts in the whole.

PROBLEM: Write a fraction that represents what part of the square at the right is shaded.

SOLUTION: Write the number of parts that are shaded (3) over the total number of parts in the square (8). The fraction that represents what part of the square is shaded is $\frac{3}{8}$.

Write fractions that represent what part of each figure is shaded.

1. ____   ____    ____

2. 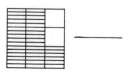 ____   ____   ____

3.  ____   ____   ____

Answers begin on page 116.

FORMS OF FRACTIONS

There are three forms of fractions:

Proper fraction—a fraction in which the top number is *less than* the bottom number.

EXAMPLES: $\frac{2}{3}$ $\frac{9}{10}$ $\frac{7}{15}$ $\frac{3}{20}$

The value of a proper fraction is always *less than one whole*.

Improper fraction—a fraction in which the top number is *equal to or more than* the bottom number.

EXAMPLES: $\frac{5}{2}$ $\frac{20}{4}$ $\frac{6}{6}$ $\frac{100}{99}$

The value of an improper fraction is either *equal to one or more than one*.

Mixed number—a whole number and a fraction written side by side.

EXAMPLES: $2\frac{1}{2}$ $4\frac{3}{5}$ $9\frac{7}{10}$ $3\frac{8}{15}$

Tell whether each of the following is a proper fraction (P), an improper fraction (I), or a mixed number (M).

4. $\frac{3}{5}$ ____ $\frac{5}{3}$ ____ $\frac{7}{7}$ ____ $2\frac{3}{4}$ ____

5. $\frac{30}{6}$ ____ $\frac{9}{90}$ ____ $10\frac{3}{4}$ ____ $\frac{11}{12}$ ____

6. $5\frac{13}{14}$ ____ $\frac{10}{10}$ ____ $\frac{1}{60}$ ____ $\frac{16}{15}$ ____

Answers begin on page 116.

Reducing Fractions

Reducing a fraction means dividing both the top and bottom numbers of a fraction by a number that goes into them evenly.

EXAMPLE: Reduce $\frac{8}{10}$.

Step 1.   Divide both 8 and 10 by a number that goes into them evenly. The number is 2.

$$\frac{8 \div 2}{10 \div 2} = \frac{4}{5}$$

Step 2.   Check to see whether another number divides evenly into the top and bottom numbers of the new fraction. No number, other than one, divides evenly into both the top and bottom. $\frac{4}{5}$ is reduced as far as it will go.

Often a fraction can be reduced more than once.

EXAMPLE: Reduce $\frac{32}{48}$.

Step 1.   Divide both 32 and 48 by a number that goes into them evenly. The number is 8.

$$\frac{32 \div 8}{48 \div 8} = \frac{4}{6}$$

Step 2.   Check to see whether another number divides evenly into both the top and bottom of the new fraction. 2 divides evenly into both.

$$\frac{4 \div 2}{6 \div 2} = \frac{2}{3}$$

Step 3.   Check to see whether another number divides evenly into both the top and bottom of the new fraction. $\frac{2}{3}$ is reduced as far as it will go.

Remember:

Every answer to an addition, subtraction, multiplication, or division fraction problem should be reduced.

A fraction that is reduced as far as it will go is in *lowest terms*.

A reduced fraction is *equal to* the original fraction.

Reduce each fraction to the lowest terms.

7. $\frac{14}{18} =$ $\frac{25}{30} =$ $\frac{15}{45} =$ $\frac{24}{36} =$ $\frac{35}{56} =$

8. $\dfrac{45}{63} =$ $\dfrac{40}{100} =$ $\dfrac{26}{34} =$ $\dfrac{60}{130} =$ $\dfrac{2}{84} =$

9. $\dfrac{35}{60} =$ $\dfrac{12}{28} =$ $\dfrac{18}{27} =$ $\dfrac{25}{75} =$ $\dfrac{40}{200} =$

10. $\dfrac{9}{36} =$ $\dfrac{32}{72} =$ $\dfrac{24}{42} =$ $\dfrac{33}{44} =$ $\dfrac{6}{300} =$

Answers begin on page 116.

Raising Fractions to Higher Terms

In addition and subtraction of fractions, it is often necessary to raise fractions to *higher terms*. This operation is the opposite of reducing fractions. To raise a fraction to higher terms, multiply both the top and bottom number of the fraction.

EXAMPLE: Raise $\dfrac{3}{4}$ to 20ths.

Step 1. Divide the old bottom number into the new bottom number.

$$4\overline{)20} \quad (5)$$

Step 2. Multiply both the top and bottom by 5.

$$\dfrac{3 \times 5}{4 \times 5} = \dfrac{15}{20}$$

Step 3. Check by reducing the new fraction. The reduced answer should be the original fraction.

$$\dfrac{15 \div 5}{20 \div 5} = \dfrac{3}{4}$$

EXAMPLE: $\dfrac{3}{7} = \dfrac{}{28}$ Find the new top number.

Step 1. Divide 7 into 28.

$$7\overline{)28} \quad (4)$$

Step 2.   Multiply both the top and bottom by 4. $\dfrac{3 \times 4}{7 \times 4} = \dfrac{12}{28}$

Step 3.   Check by reducing $\dfrac{12}{28}$ by 4. $\dfrac{12 \div 4}{28 \div 4} = \dfrac{3}{7}$

Find each missing top number.

11. $\dfrac{5}{6} = \dfrac{}{18}$ $\dfrac{9}{10} = \dfrac{}{50}$ $\dfrac{1}{3} = \dfrac{}{6}$ $\dfrac{4}{9} = \dfrac{}{81}$

12. $\dfrac{3}{8} = \dfrac{}{80}$ $\dfrac{7}{20} = \dfrac{}{60}$ $\dfrac{4}{5} = \dfrac{}{75}$ $\dfrac{7}{11} = \dfrac{}{66}$

13. $\dfrac{5}{12} = \dfrac{}{36}$ $\dfrac{3}{4} = \dfrac{}{32}$ $\dfrac{8}{9} = \dfrac{}{27}$ $\dfrac{1}{6} = \dfrac{}{30}$

Answers begin on page 116.

Changing Improper Fractions to Whole or Mixed Numbers

In an improper fraction the top number is as big or bigger than the bottom number. The value of an improper fraction is equal to one or larger than one.

To change an improper fraction to a whole or mixed number, divide the bottom into the top. Put the remainder over the bottom number and reduce.

Every improper fraction answer to an addition, subtraction, multiplication, or division problem should be changed to a whole or mixed number.

EXAMPLE: Change $\dfrac{14}{4}$ to a mixed number.

$$\begin{array}{r} 3 \\ 4\overline{)14} \\ \underline{12} \\ 2 \end{array}$$

Step 1.   Divide the bottom into the top.

Step 2.   Write the remainder over the original bottom number.

Step 3.   Reduce the fraction.

The answer is $3\frac{1}{2}$.

$$\frac{2 \div 2}{4 \div 2} = \frac{1}{2}$$

EXAMPLE: Change $\frac{15}{5}$ to a whole or mixed number.

Step 1.   Divide the bottom into the top. There is no remainder. $\frac{15}{5}$ is equal to the whole number 3.

$$5\overline{)15}^{\,3}$$

Change each improper fraction to a whole or mixed number and reduce.

14. $\frac{16}{6} =$ $\frac{28}{8} =$ $\frac{12}{9} =$ $\frac{14}{3} =$

15. $\frac{35}{7} =$ $\frac{19}{6} =$ $\frac{20}{12} =$ $\frac{40}{15} =$

16. $\frac{9}{9} =$ $\frac{38}{8} =$ $\frac{44}{7} =$ $\frac{51}{20} =$

Answers begin on page 116.

Changing Mixed Numbers to Improper Fractions

In multiplication and division of fractions, it is often necessary to change mixed numbers to improper fractions.

To change a mixed number to an improper fraction:

1.   Multiply the bottom number by the whole number.
2.   Add the top number.
3.   Place the total over the bottom number.

EXAMPLE: Change $3\frac{2}{5}$ to an improper fraction.

Step 1.   Multiply the bottom number by the whole number. $5 \times 3 = 15.$

Step 2.   Add the top number to the result. $15 + 2 = 17.$

Step 3.   Place the total over the bottom number. $\frac{17}{5}$

Change each mixed number to an improper fraction.

17. $2\frac{3}{4} =$ $5\frac{1}{2} =$ $3\frac{5}{7} =$ $4\frac{2}{9} =$ $6\frac{1}{3} =$

18. $1\frac{5}{9} =$ $10\frac{2}{3} =$ $4\frac{3}{7} =$ $5\frac{2}{11} =$ $8\frac{5}{6} =$

19. $9\frac{7}{8} =$ $12\frac{1}{4} =$ $3\frac{4}{5} =$ $2\frac{3}{8} =$ $7\frac{5}{12} =$

Answers begin on page 116.

Finding What Fraction One Number Is of Another

PROBLEM: A yard contains 36 inches. 20 inches is what fraction of a yard?

SOLUTION: Put the *part* over the *whole* and reduce. $\frac{20 \div 4}{36 \div 4} = \frac{5}{9}$

Write fractions for each of the following and reduce.

20.   A foot contains 12 inches. 8 inches is what part of a foot?

21.   Mr. Torres earns $720 a month. He spends $180 a month for rent. What fraction of his income does he spend on rent.

22.   A pound contains 16 ounces. 12 ounces is what fraction of a pound?

23.   75¢ is what fractional part of $1.00?

24.   A ton contains 2000 pounds. 1600 pounds is what part of a ton?

25.   A year contains 52 weeks. 28 weeks is what fractional part of a year?

26.   A meter contains 100 centimeters. 65 centimeters is what part of a meter?

Answers begin on page 117.

ADDING FRACTIONS

Adding Fractions with the Same Denominators

PROBLEM: Sophie walked $\frac{3}{10}$ mile to the grocery. Then she walked $\frac{4}{10}$ mile farther to the post office. Find the total distance that she walked.

SOLUTION: Add the top numbers of each fraction and place the total over the bottom number.

$$\frac{3}{10}$$
$$+\frac{4}{10}$$
$$\overline{\frac{7}{10}}\text{ mile}$$

Step 1.   Add the top numbers: $3 + 4 = 7$.

Step 2.   Place the total, 7, over the bottom number: $\frac{7}{10}$.

Add the following.

1.
$$\frac{3}{6}$$
$$+\frac{2}{6}$$

$$\frac{4}{9}$$
$$+\frac{3}{9}$$

$$3\frac{2}{8}$$
$$+4\frac{5}{8}$$

$$5\frac{2}{5}$$
$$+6\frac{2}{5}$$

$$7\frac{6}{12}$$
$$+3\frac{1}{12}$$

2.
$$\frac{3}{10}$$
$$\frac{2}{10}$$
$$+\frac{4}{10}$$

$$\frac{5}{12}$$
$$\frac{3}{12}$$
$$+\frac{3}{12}$$

$$2\frac{3}{9}$$
$$4\frac{3}{9}$$
$$+6\frac{2}{9}$$

$$5\frac{6}{20}$$
$$3\frac{7}{20}$$
$$+2\frac{4}{20}$$

$$9\frac{3}{16}$$
$$6\frac{4}{16}$$
$$+4\frac{8}{16}$$

Answers begin on page 117.

The answers to addition of fractions problems should be reduced.

EXAMPLE:
$$\frac{2}{9}$$
$$+\frac{4}{9}$$
$$\overline{\frac{6}{9}} = \frac{2}{3}$$

Step 1.   Add the top numbers: $2 + 4 = 6$.

Step 2.   Write the total, 6, over the bottom number: $\frac{6}{9}$.

Step 3.   Reduce: $\dfrac{6 \div 3}{9 \div 3} = \dfrac{2}{3}$

Add and reduce.

3.
$$\begin{array}{r} \frac{4}{8} \\ + \frac{2}{8} \\ \hline \end{array}$$
$$\begin{array}{r} \frac{3}{10} \\ + \frac{2}{10} \\ \hline \end{array}$$
$$\begin{array}{r} 4\frac{3}{9} \\ + 2\frac{3}{9} \\ \hline \end{array}$$
$$\begin{array}{r} 3\frac{5}{12} \\ + 7\frac{3}{12} \\ \hline \end{array}$$
$$\begin{array}{r} 2\frac{4}{15} \\ + 5\frac{8}{15} \\ \hline \end{array}$$

4.
$$\begin{array}{r} \frac{2}{10} \\ \frac{3}{10} \\ + \frac{3}{10} \\ \hline \end{array}$$
$$\begin{array}{r} \frac{5}{18} \\ \frac{4}{18} \\ + \frac{3}{18} \\ \hline \end{array}$$
$$\begin{array}{r} 4\frac{3}{16} \\ 3\frac{4}{16} \\ + 2\frac{5}{16} \\ \hline \end{array}$$
$$\begin{array}{r} 3\frac{2}{12} \\ 5\frac{3}{12} \\ + 4\frac{4}{12} \\ \hline \end{array}$$
$$\begin{array}{r} 6\frac{5}{14} \\ 2\frac{1}{14} \\ + 3\frac{4}{14} \\ \hline \end{array}$$

Answers begin on page 117.

When the sum of an addition problem is an improper fraction, change the sum to a whole number or a mixed number.

EXAMPLE:

$$\begin{array}{r} 4\frac{8}{9} \\ + 3\frac{4}{9} \\ \hline 7\frac{12}{9} = 7 + 1\frac{3}{9} = 8\frac{3}{9} = 8\frac{1}{3} \end{array}$$

Step 1. Add the top numbers of the fractions: $8 + 4 = 12$.

Step 2. Write the total over the bottom number: $\frac{12}{9}$.

Step 3. Add the whole numbers: $4 + 3 = 7$.

Step 4. Change the improper fraction to a mixed number: $\frac{12}{9} = 1\frac{3}{9}$, and add the mixed number to the total of the whole numbers: $7 + 1\frac{3}{9} = 8\frac{3}{9}$.

Step 5. Reduce: $8\frac{3}{9} = 8\frac{1}{3}$.

Add and reduce.

5. $\dfrac{7}{8}$
$+\dfrac{5}{8}$

$\dfrac{8}{9}$
$+\dfrac{7}{9}$

$5\dfrac{5}{6}$
$+\;6\dfrac{1}{6}$

$4\dfrac{9}{10}$
$+\;3\dfrac{6}{10}$

$8\dfrac{7}{12}$
$+\;2\dfrac{11}{12}$

6. $\dfrac{3}{4}$
$\dfrac{2}{4}$
$+\dfrac{1}{4}$

$\dfrac{2}{7}$
$\dfrac{3}{7}$
$+\dfrac{5}{7}$

$3\dfrac{4}{5}$
$4\dfrac{3}{5}$
$+\;5\dfrac{2}{5}$

$8\dfrac{7}{12}$
$7\dfrac{8}{12}$
$+\;4\dfrac{9}{12}$

$3\dfrac{10}{16}$
$6\dfrac{11}{16}$
$+\;2\dfrac{13}{16}$

Answers begin on page 117.

Adding Fractions with Different Denominators

PROBLEM: Jill bought $\dfrac{1}{2}$ pound of ground beef and $\dfrac{3}{4}$ pound of chicken. What was the total weight of her purchases?

SOLUTION: Add the weights of each item. First find a *common denominator*. A common denominator is a number that can be divided evenly by all the denominators in the problem. The smallest number that can be divided evenly by the other denominators is called the *lowest common denominator* or *LCD*. Sometimes the largest denominator in the problem will work as the LCD. In this problem, the lowest number that can be divided evenly by both 2 and 4 is 4.

Step 1.   Find the LCD. 2 and 4 both divide evenly into 4.

Step 2.   Raise $\dfrac{1}{2}$ to 4ths.

Step 3.   Add the fractions with the LCD and change the total to a mixed number.

$$\dfrac{1}{2}=\dfrac{2}{4}$$
$$+\;\dfrac{3}{4}=\dfrac{3}{4}$$
$$\dfrac{5}{4}=1\dfrac{1}{4}\text{ lb.}$$

Add and reduce.

7. $\dfrac{5}{8}$ $\dfrac{1}{3}$ $\dfrac{4}{5}$ $\dfrac{4}{7}$ $\dfrac{5}{9}$

$+\dfrac{3}{4}$ $+\dfrac{5}{6}$ $+\dfrac{4}{15}$ $+\dfrac{9}{28}$ $+\dfrac{11}{36}$

8. $\dfrac{2}{3}$ $\dfrac{3}{5}$ $\dfrac{3}{5}$ $\dfrac{13}{20}$ $\dfrac{5}{8}$

$\dfrac{7}{12}$ $\dfrac{1}{2}$ $\dfrac{8}{15}$ $\dfrac{4}{5}$ $\dfrac{7}{32}$

$+\dfrac{3}{4}$ $+\dfrac{7}{10}$ $+\dfrac{2}{3}$ $+\dfrac{1}{4}$ $+\dfrac{9}{16}$

9. $6\dfrac{5}{8}$ $5\dfrac{6}{35}$ $8\dfrac{1}{6}$ $6\dfrac{5}{48}$

$+7\dfrac{11}{24}$ $+9\dfrac{2}{7}$ $+3\dfrac{7}{24}$ $+2\dfrac{5}{8}$

Answers begin on page 118.

Finding a Common Denominator

There are three basic methods for finding a common denominator.

1. Check the largest denominator to find out whether it can be divided evenly by the other denominators in the problem.
    (This is the method we used in the previous exercise.)

2. Multiply the denominators together.

EXAMPLE:

$$\begin{array}{r} \dfrac{3}{4} = \dfrac{9}{12} \\[2mm] +\dfrac{2}{3} = \dfrac{8}{12} \\[2mm] \hline \dfrac{17}{12} = 1\dfrac{5}{12} \end{array}$$

Step 1.   Multiply the denominators: $4 \times 3 = 12$. 12 is the common denominator.

Step 2.   Raise each fraction to 12ths.

Step 3.   Add the new fractions.

Step 4.   Change the answer to a mixed number.

3.   Go through the multiplication table of the largest denominator.

EXAMPLE:

$$\begin{array}{r} \dfrac{5}{9} = \dfrac{10}{18} \\[2mm] \dfrac{2}{3} = \dfrac{12}{18} \\[2mm] +\dfrac{1}{6} = \dfrac{3}{18} \\[2mm] \hline \dfrac{25}{18} = 1\dfrac{7}{18} \end{array}$$

Step 1.   Go through the multiplication table of the largest denominator, 9.
$9 \times 1 = 9$ which cannot be divided evenly by 6.
$9 \times 2 = 18$ which can be divided evenly by 3, 6, and 9.

Step 2.   Raise each fraction to 18ths.

Step 3.   Add the new fractions.

Step 4.   Change the answer to a mixed number.

Add and reduce.

10. $\dfrac{4}{5}$ $+\dfrac{2}{3}$ $\dfrac{3}{4}$ $+\dfrac{3}{7}$ $\dfrac{5}{6}$ $+\dfrac{4}{5}$ $\dfrac{4}{9}$ $+\dfrac{3}{4}$ $\dfrac{3}{8}$ $+\dfrac{3}{5}$

11. $\dfrac{3}{8}$ $+\dfrac{5}{6}$ $\dfrac{4}{9}$ $+\dfrac{5}{12}$ $\dfrac{7}{8}$ $+\dfrac{9}{10}$ $\dfrac{7}{12}$ $+\dfrac{5}{8}$ $\dfrac{7}{10}$ $+\dfrac{8}{15}$

12. $3\dfrac{1}{6}$ $2\dfrac{4}{7}$ $+\,5\dfrac{1}{2}$ $6\dfrac{3}{4}$ $4\dfrac{2}{3}$ $+\,1\dfrac{1}{2}$ $5\dfrac{1}{3}$ $2\dfrac{1}{4}$ $+\,9\dfrac{3}{5}$ $4\dfrac{5}{12}$ $7\dfrac{2}{9}$ $+\,4\dfrac{2}{3}$

13. $2\dfrac{5}{6}$ $6\dfrac{3}{8}$ $+\,8\dfrac{3}{4}$ $3\dfrac{5}{16}$ $4\dfrac{3}{4}$ $+\,9\dfrac{1}{2}$ $5\dfrac{3}{10}$ $8\dfrac{5}{6}$ $+\,3\dfrac{2}{5}$ $9\dfrac{5}{6}$ $2\dfrac{3}{8}$ $+\,4\dfrac{7}{24}$

Answers begin on page 118.

Applying Addition of Fractions Skills

Watch for the key words *total* and *combine* in the following problems. Put the correct label, such as inches or pounds, next to each answer. Reduce all answers.

14. The Johnson family's house is $24\frac{1}{2}$ feet wide. They built a porch that extends the house by $10\frac{3}{4}$ feet. Find the new width of their house.

15. Jill works part time in the local supermarket. Friday she worked $4\frac{1}{4}$ hours. Saturday she worked $3\frac{2}{3}$ hours. Sunday she worked $5\frac{1}{2}$ hours. What was her total number of hours for those three days?

16. On a normal day, Charles drives $12\frac{3}{10}$ miles to work, $8\frac{1}{2}$ miles to night school, and $7\frac{9}{10}$ miles back home. What is the total distance that he drives each day?

17. Celeste bought $3\frac{1}{2}$ pounds of ground beef, $2\frac{1}{4}$ pounds of chicken, $1\frac{15}{16}$ pounds of tomatoes, and $5\frac{3}{8}$ pounds of apples. Find the combined weight of her purchases.

18. George Allen is $71\frac{1}{2}$ inches tall. His son Jack is $2\frac{3}{4}$ inches taller. How tall is Jack?

19. Harriet usually drives to work in $\frac{3}{4}$ of an hour. On Monday a snowstorm caused her a delay of an extra $\frac{2}{3}$ of an hour. How long did Harriet spend driving to work on Monday?

Answers begin on page 119.

SUBTRACTING FRACTIONS

Subtracting Fractions with the Same Denominators

PROBLEM: From a bag that contained $\frac{7}{8}$ pound of sugar, Kate used $\frac{3}{8}$ pound to bake cakes. How much sugar was left?

SOLUTION: Subtract the amount of sugar Kate used from the amount that she started with.

$$\begin{array}{r} \frac{7}{8} \\ -\frac{3}{8} \\ \hline \frac{4}{8} = \frac{1}{2} \text{ lb.} \end{array}$$

Step 1. Subtract the top numbers: $7 - 3 = 4$.

Step 2. Write the answer over the bottom number: $\frac{4}{8}$.

Step 3. Reduce the final answer: $\frac{4 \div 4}{8 \div 4} = \frac{1}{2}$

Subtract and reduce.

1.
$$\begin{array}{r} \frac{11}{12} \\ -\frac{7}{12} \\ \hline \end{array} \qquad \begin{array}{r} \frac{13}{15} \\ -\frac{4}{15} \\ \hline \end{array} \qquad \begin{array}{r} \frac{5}{9} \\ -\frac{2}{9} \\ \hline \end{array} \qquad \begin{array}{r} \frac{17}{20} \\ -\frac{3}{20} \\ \hline \end{array} \qquad \begin{array}{r} \frac{15}{16} \\ -\frac{9}{16} \\ \hline \end{array}$$

2.
$$\begin{array}{r} 9\frac{7}{8} \\ -6\frac{5}{8} \\ \hline \end{array} \qquad \begin{array}{r} 15\frac{9}{10} \\ -7\frac{7}{10} \\ \hline \end{array} \qquad \begin{array}{r} 14\frac{19}{24} \\ -8\frac{5}{24} \\ \hline \end{array} \qquad \begin{array}{r} 11\frac{5}{6} \\ -5\frac{1}{6} \\ \hline \end{array}$$

Answers begin on page 120.

Subtracting Fractions with Different Denominators

PROBLEM: The distance from Dave's house to his work is $\frac{1}{2}$ mile. He stops to buy a newspaper every morning when he has walked $\frac{3}{8}$ mile. How much farther does Dave have to walk to get to work?

SOLUTION: Subtract the distance Dave has already walked from the total distance he needs to walk. First find a common denominator.

Step 1. Find the LCD. 2 and 8 both divide evenly into 8.

Step 2. Raise $\frac{1}{2}$ to 8ths.

Step 3. Subtract the fractions with the LCD.

$$\frac{1}{2} = \frac{4}{8}$$
$$-\frac{3}{8} = \frac{3}{8}$$
$$\frac{1}{8} \text{ mile}$$

Subtract and reduce.

3.
$$\frac{2}{3} \quad -\frac{2}{9}$$

$$\frac{9}{16} \quad -\frac{1}{4}$$

$$\frac{2}{3} \quad -\frac{1}{4}$$

$$\frac{5}{6} \quad -\frac{3}{7}$$

$$\frac{7}{8} \quad -\frac{5}{6}$$

4.
$$9\frac{11}{12} \quad -2\frac{5}{8}$$

$$8\frac{5}{9} \quad -3\frac{1}{6}$$

$$10\frac{4}{5} \quad -6\frac{3}{4}$$

$$23\frac{11}{16} \quad -19\frac{1}{2}$$

Answers begin on page 120.

Borrowing and Subtracting Fractions

PROBLEM: Phil weighed 167 pounds. He dieted for a month and lost $12\frac{1}{4}$ pounds. Find his new weight.

SOLUTION: Subtract the amount Phil lost from his original weight. Since there is nothing to subtract $\frac{1}{4}$ from, *borrow* 1 from 167.

$$167 = 166\frac{4}{4}$$
$$- 12\frac{1}{4} = 12\frac{1}{4}$$
$$154\frac{3}{4} \text{ lb.}$$

Step 1. Borrow 1 from 167 and rewrite the 1 as $\frac{4}{4}$ because 4 is the LCD.

Step 2. Subtract the fractions and whole numbers.

Subtract and reduce.

5.
$9 - \frac{3}{5}$
$12 - \frac{2}{7}$
$8 - \frac{5}{9}$
$4 - \frac{2}{3}$
$7 - \frac{11}{12}$

6.
$5 - 1\frac{4}{7}$
$6 - 5\frac{7}{10}$
$9 - 2\frac{3}{8}$
$7 - 3\frac{4}{11}$
$8 - 6\frac{5}{13}$

Answers begin on page 120.

PROBLEM: Jack is $72\frac{1}{4}$ inches tall. John is $3\frac{3}{4}$ inches shorter. Find John's height.

SOLUTION: Subtract $3\frac{3}{4}$ inches from Jack's height. Since $\frac{1}{4}$ is not enough to subtract $\frac{3}{4}$ from, borrow 1 from 72.

$$72\tfrac{1}{4} = 71\tfrac{1}{4} + \tfrac{4}{4} = 71\tfrac{5}{4}$$
$$- \quad 3\tfrac{3}{4} = \qquad\qquad 3\tfrac{3}{4}$$
$$\overline{\qquad\qquad\qquad 68\tfrac{2}{4} = 68\tfrac{1}{2} \text{ in.}}$$

Step 1. Borrow 1 from 72. Rewrite the 1 as $\tfrac{4}{4}$ because 4 is the LCD.

Step 2. Add $\tfrac{4}{4}$ to $\tfrac{1}{4}$ $\tfrac{4}{4} + \tfrac{1}{4} = \tfrac{5}{4}$

Step 3. Subtract the fractions and the whole numbers.

Subtract and reduce.

7. $9\tfrac{2}{5}$ $7\tfrac{5}{8}$ $8\tfrac{2}{9}$ $6\tfrac{3}{7}$
    $- 2\tfrac{4}{5}$ $- 3\tfrac{7}{8}$ $- 5\tfrac{8}{9}$ $- 5\tfrac{6}{7}$

8. $5\tfrac{1}{3}$ $6\tfrac{5}{12}$ $7\tfrac{1}{6}$ $9\tfrac{5}{16}$
    $- 1\tfrac{2}{3}$ $- 3\tfrac{11}{12}$ $- 4\tfrac{5}{6}$ $- 8\tfrac{11}{16}$

Answers begin on page 120.

PROBLEM: A crate full of merchandise weighs $97\tfrac{3}{8}$ pounds. The crate itself weighs $15\tfrac{3}{4}$ pounds. Find the weight of the merchandise inside the crate.

SOLUTION: Subtract the weight of the crate from the weight of the crate when it is full. To subtract, first find a common denominator.

$$97\tfrac{3}{8} = 97\tfrac{3}{8} = 96\tfrac{3}{8} + \tfrac{8}{8} = 96\tfrac{11}{8}$$
$$- 15\tfrac{3}{4} = 15\tfrac{6}{8} = \qquad\qquad 15\,\tfrac{6}{8}$$
$$\overline{\qquad\qquad\qquad\qquad\qquad\qquad 81\,\tfrac{5}{8}\ \text{lb.}}$$

Step 1. Find the LCD. 8 and 4 both divide evenly into 8.

Step 2. Raise $\tfrac{3}{4}$ to 8ths. $\tfrac{3}{4} = \tfrac{6}{8}$

Step 3. Since you cannot subtract 6 from 3, borrow 1 from 97 and rewrite 1 as $\tfrac{8}{8}$.

Step 4. Add $\tfrac{8}{8}$ to $\tfrac{3}{8}$ $\qquad\qquad \tfrac{3}{8} + \tfrac{8}{8} = \tfrac{11}{8}$

Step 5. Subtract the fractions and the whole numbers.

Subtract and reduce.

9. $\quad 6\tfrac{1}{4} \qquad\qquad\qquad 10\tfrac{3}{5} \qquad\qquad\qquad 4\tfrac{2}{9} \qquad\qquad\qquad 12\tfrac{1}{4}$

$\quad\ -\ 3\tfrac{1}{3} \qquad\qquad\ -\ 8\tfrac{3}{4} \qquad\qquad\ -\ 1\tfrac{1}{2} \qquad\qquad\ -\ 3\tfrac{5}{6}$

10. $\quad 20\tfrac{5}{12} \qquad\qquad\quad 14\,\tfrac{2}{5} \qquad\qquad\quad 18\tfrac{1}{3} \qquad\qquad\quad 13\tfrac{3}{8}$

$\quad\ -\ 9\,\tfrac{2}{3} \qquad\qquad\ -\ 6\tfrac{8}{15} \qquad\qquad\ -\ 9\,\tfrac{1}{2} \qquad\qquad\ -\ 5\tfrac{7}{10}$

Answers begin on page 121.

Applying Subtraction of Fractions Skills

In the following problems watch for phrases that tell you to subtract such as: *How much more? How much less? Find the difference.* Put the correct label such as dollars or feet next to each answer, and reduce all answers.

11. The distance from Susan's house to work is $2\frac{3}{10}$ miles. She stops for a newspaper after she has gone $1\frac{1}{2}$ miles. How much farther does she have to go to work?

12. Mrs. McManus weighs $118\frac{3}{4}$ pounds. Mr. McManus weighs 162 pounds. Find the difference between their weights.

13. Petra had a 5-pound bag of sugar. She used $2\frac{5}{16}$ pounds of sugar for baking. How much sugar was left?

14. A carpenter had a piece of lumber $62\frac{3}{8}$ inches long. From it he cut a piece $23\frac{7}{8}$ inches long. How long was the piece that was left?

15. Before Mr. and Mrs. Smith left on vacation, the mileage gauge of their car registered $16{,}204\frac{8}{10}$ miles. When they got home, it registered $17{,}310\frac{9}{10}$ miles. How many miles did they drive on their vacation?

16. Jane normally works 8 hours a day in her office. On Tuesday she left work $2\frac{2}{3}$ hours early for a doctor's appointment. How many hours did she work on Tuesday?

17. Fred weighed $185\frac{1}{4}$ pounds on January 1. By February 15 he had lost $20\frac{9}{16}$ pounds. How much did he weigh on February 15?

Answers begin on page 121.

MULTIPLYING FRACTIONS

PROBLEM: Cecelia had $\frac{3}{4}$ of a pound of flour. She used one-half of it to bake bread. How much flour did she use?

SOLUTION: Multiply $\frac{3}{4}$ by $\frac{1}{2}$. To multiply fractions, multiply the top numbers together and the bottom numbers together.

Step 1. Multiply the top numbers: $1 \times 3 = 3$.

Step 2. Multiply the bottom numbers: $2 \times 4 = 8$.

$$\frac{1}{2} \times \frac{3}{4} = \frac{3}{8} \text{ lb.}$$

Step 3. Reduce the answer if possible. $\frac{3}{8}$ is reduced.

Multiply and reduce.

1. $\frac{3}{4} \times \frac{5}{7} =$ 　　　　$\frac{2}{9} \times \frac{1}{5} =$ 　　　　$\frac{4}{11} \times \frac{2}{3} =$ 　　　　$\frac{5}{12} \times \frac{5}{6} =$

2. $\frac{9}{10} \times \frac{3}{8} =$ 　　　　$\frac{2}{3} \times \frac{5}{13} =$ 　　　　$\frac{3}{16} \times \frac{1}{2} =$ 　　　　$\frac{1}{4} \times \frac{7}{8} =$

Answers begin on page 122.

Multiplying Three Fractions

To multiply three fractions together:

1.   Multiply the top numbers of the first two fractions. Then multiply that answer by the top number of the third fraction.

2.   Multiply the bottom numbers of the first two fractions. Then multiply that answer by the bottom number of the third fraction.

3.   Reduce the answer if possible.

Multiply and reduce.

3. $\frac{2}{3} \times \frac{1}{5} \times \frac{1}{3} =$ $\frac{1}{9} \times \frac{5}{6} \times \frac{1}{2} =$ $\frac{1}{3} \times \frac{4}{7} \times \frac{2}{3} =$

4. $\frac{3}{4} \times \frac{1}{2} \times \frac{7}{8} =$ $\frac{1}{2} \times \frac{3}{4} \times \frac{5}{7} =$ $\frac{5}{6} \times \frac{1}{2} \times \frac{5}{8} =$

Answers begin on page 122.

Canceling and Multiplying Fractions

Sometimes the fractions in a multiplication problem can be canceled. Canceling is a shortcut. It is like reducing. To cancel, find a number that divides evenly into both a top and bottom number of your problem.

EXAMPLE:

In this problem 8 and 14 can be canceled by 2. Also, 9 and 15 can be canceled by 3.

Step 1.   Cancel 8 and 14 by 2.
          $8 \div 2 = 4$. Cross out 8 and write 4.
          $14 \div 2 = 7$. Cross out 14 and write 7.

$$\frac{8}{15} \times \frac{9}{14} =$$

$$\frac{\overset{4}{\cancel{8}}}{\underset{5}{\cancel{15}}} \times \frac{\overset{3}{\cancel{9}}}{\underset{7}{\cancel{14}}} = \frac{12}{35}$$

Step 2.   Cancel 9 and 15 by 3.
          $9 \div 3 = 3$. Cross out 9 and write 3.
          $15 \div 3 = 5$. Cross out 15 and write 5.

Step 3.   Multiply across by the new numbers.
          $4 \times 3 = 12$ $5 \times 7 = 35$

Cancel, multiply, and reduce.

5. $\dfrac{3}{4} \times \dfrac{5}{6} =$ $\dfrac{4}{9} \times \dfrac{6}{7} =$ $\dfrac{5}{8} \times \dfrac{9}{10} =$ $\dfrac{7}{12} \times \dfrac{9}{11} =$

6. $\dfrac{3}{8} \times \dfrac{14}{15} =$ $\dfrac{9}{10} \times \dfrac{20}{21} =$ $\dfrac{8}{9} \times \dfrac{15}{16} =$ $\dfrac{25}{32} \times \dfrac{24}{35} =$

7. $\dfrac{5}{9} \times \dfrac{3}{7} \times \dfrac{14}{15} =$ $\dfrac{6}{7} \times \dfrac{7}{8} \times \dfrac{4}{5} =$ $\dfrac{11}{15} \times \dfrac{10}{11} \times \dfrac{3}{4} =$

8. $\dfrac{9}{10} \times \dfrac{1}{4} \times \dfrac{8}{9} =$ $\dfrac{5}{6} \times \dfrac{14}{15} \times \dfrac{2}{21} =$ $\dfrac{20}{21} \times \dfrac{9}{16} \times \dfrac{4}{5} =$

Answers begin on page 122.

Multiplying Fractions by Whole Numbers

PROBLEM: Mr. Lawrence earns \$820 a month. He spends $\frac{1}{4}$ of his income for rent. What does he pay each month for rent?

SOLUTION: Multiply \$820 by $\frac{1}{4}$. Write the whole number 820 as a fraction by putting it over 1.

$$\dfrac{1}{\cancel{4}} \times \dfrac{\overset{205}{\cancel{820}}}{1} = \dfrac{205}{1} = \$205$$

Step 1.   Write 820 as a fraction: $\frac{820}{1}$

Step 2.   Cancel and multiply across.

Step 3.   Change the improper fraction to a whole or mixed number.

Multiply and reduce.

9. $\dfrac{5}{8} \times 24 =$ $\dfrac{9}{10} \times 45 =$ $\dfrac{3}{7} \times 28 =$ $\dfrac{4}{11} \times 55 =$

10. $12 \times \dfrac{7}{9} =$ $35 \times \dfrac{8}{15} =$ $42 \times \dfrac{12}{35} =$ $24 \times \dfrac{5}{16} =$

Answers begin on page 122.

Multiplying Mixed Numbers

PROBLEM: One cubic foot of water weighs $62\dfrac{1}{2}$ pounds. How much does $\dfrac{2}{5}$ cubic foot of water weigh?

SOLUTION: Multiply $62\dfrac{1}{2}$ by $\dfrac{2}{5}$. To multiply mixed numbers, first change each mixed number to an improper fraction.

$$\dfrac{2}{5} \times 62\dfrac{1}{2} =$$

$$\dfrac{\overset{1}{\cancel{2}}}{\underset{1}{\cancel{5}}} \times \dfrac{\overset{25}{\cancel{125}}}{\underset{1}{\cancel{2}}} = \dfrac{25}{1} = 25 \text{ lb.}$$

Step 1.   Change $62\dfrac{1}{2}$ to an improper fraction: $62\dfrac{1}{2} = \dfrac{125}{2}$

Step 2.   Cancel and multiply across.

Step 3.   Change the improper fraction to a whole or mixed number.

Multiply and reduce.

11. $3\dfrac{3}{4} \times \dfrac{2}{3} =$ $3\dfrac{3}{7} \times \dfrac{3}{10} =$ $\dfrac{5}{8} \times 2\dfrac{2}{9} =$ $\dfrac{8}{15} \times 1\dfrac{9}{16} =$

12. $2\dfrac{4}{7} \times 3\dfrac{1}{9} =$ $1\dfrac{9}{11} \times 1\dfrac{1}{6} =$ $1\dfrac{5}{9} \times 1\dfrac{5}{7} =$ $2\dfrac{5}{8} \times 2\dfrac{2}{15} =$

13. $1\frac{5}{16} \times 2\frac{6}{7} \times 2\frac{2}{5} =$ $1\frac{7}{8} \times \frac{3}{4} \times 2\frac{2}{9} =$ $1\frac{7}{20} \times 5\frac{1}{3} \times 1\frac{1}{4} =$

Answers begin on page 123.

Applying Multiplication of Fractions Skills

In the following problems watch for phrases that tell you to multiply such as: *Find a part of something* or *Find the cost or weight of several things* when you have information about one thing. Label and reduce each answer.

---

14.   Matthew earns $12,500 a year. $\frac{2}{5}$ of his earnings go to mortgage payments. How much does he pay yearly on his mortgage?

15.   Pete needs $4\frac{1}{3}$ yards of lumber to build a bookcase. How much lumber does he need to build five bookcases?

16.   Manny works for $7.00 an hour. How much money does he make in $7\frac{1}{2}$ hours?

17.   A pound of apples cost 68¢. How much do $3\frac{3}{4}$ pounds of apples cost?

18.   At the beginning of the week a record dealer had 540 new record albums. By the end of the week he had sold $\frac{2}{3}$ of them. How many of the albums did he sell?

19. One yard of material costs $3.60. Find the cost of $8\frac{2}{3}$ yards of the material.

20. Faye takes home $184 a week. She spends $\frac{3}{8}$ of her pay on food for her family. How much does she spend each week on food?

Answers begin on page 123.

DIVIDING FRACTIONS

Dividing Fractions by Fractions

PROBLEM: How many $\frac{1}{8}$-inch strips of wood can be cut from a piece of wood that is $\frac{3}{4}$ inch long?

SOLUTION: Find how many $\frac{1}{8}$s there are in $\frac{3}{4}$. Divide $\frac{3}{4}$ by $\frac{1}{8}$. To divide fractions, first *invert* the fraction you are dividing by. To invert means to turn the fraction upside down. Put the top number in the bottom position and the bottom number in the top. $\frac{1}{8}$ inverted becomes $\frac{8}{1}$. Then change the division sign to a multiplication sign and follow the rules for multiplication.

$$\frac{3}{4} \div \frac{1}{8} =$$

$$\frac{3}{\underset{1}{4}} \times \frac{\overset{2}{8}}{1} = \frac{6}{1} = 6 \text{ strips}$$

Step 1.   Invert $\frac{1}{8}$ to $\frac{8}{1}$.

Step 2.   Change $\div$ to $\times$.

Step 3.   Cancel and multiply across.

The fraction to invert is always the fraction *at the right* of the division sign.

Divide and reduce.

1. $\dfrac{5}{6} \div \dfrac{2}{3} =$ $\dfrac{3}{8} \div \dfrac{3}{4} =$ $\dfrac{9}{10} \div \dfrac{3}{5} =$ $\dfrac{7}{9} \div \dfrac{5}{6} =$

2. $\dfrac{1}{3} \div \dfrac{1}{6} =$ $\dfrac{5}{9} \div \dfrac{3}{4} =$ $\dfrac{11}{12} \div \dfrac{2}{3} =$ $\dfrac{15}{16} \div \dfrac{9}{14} =$

Answers begin on page 124.

Dividing Whole Numbers by Fractions

PROBLEM: A hardware store owner has 15 pounds of nails. He wants to package them in $\frac{1}{4}$-pound boxes. How many boxes can he fill?

SOLUTION: Find out how many $\frac{1}{4}$s there are in 15. Divide 15 by $\frac{1}{4}$.

$$15 \div \frac{1}{4} =$$
$$\frac{15}{1} \times \frac{4}{1} = \frac{60}{1} = 60 \text{ boxes}$$

Step 1. Write 15 as a fraction, $\frac{15}{1}$.

Step 2. Invert $\frac{1}{4}$ to $\frac{4}{1}$.

Step 3. Change $\div$ to $\times$.

Step 4. Multiply across.

Divide and reduce.

3. $8 \div \dfrac{4}{5} =$ $12 \div \dfrac{2}{3} =$ $9 \div \dfrac{6}{7} =$ $7 \div \dfrac{3}{4} =$

4. $10 \div \dfrac{5}{6} =$ $6 \div \dfrac{4}{9} =$ $4 \div \dfrac{3}{8} =$ $15 \div \dfrac{10}{11} =$

Answers begin on page 124.

Dividing Fractions by Whole Numbers

PROBLEM: Mrs. Miller has $\frac{3}{4}$ pound of chocolate. She wants to divide the chocolate evenly among 6 children. How much chocolate will each child get?

SOLUTION: Divide $\frac{3}{4}$ by 6.

Step 1.   Write 6 as a fraction, $\frac{6}{1}$.

Step 2.   Invert $\frac{6}{1}$ to $\frac{1}{6}$.

Step 3.   Change $\div$ to $\times$.

Step 4.   Cancel and multiply across.

$$\frac{3}{4} \div 6 =$$

$$\frac{\overset{1}{\cancel{3}}}{4} \times \frac{1}{\underset{2}{\cancel{6}}} = \frac{1}{8} \text{ lb.}$$

Divide and reduce.

5. $\frac{1}{5} \div 5 =$ $\frac{2}{3} \div 12 =$ $\frac{3}{4} \div 24 =$ $\frac{5}{8} \div 2 =$

6. $\frac{4}{5} \div 9 =$ $\frac{7}{8} \div 7 =$ $\frac{6}{11} \div 3 =$ $\frac{12}{13} \div 8 =$

Answers begin on page 124.

Dividing with Mixed Numbers

PROBLEM: Bill needs $2\frac{3}{4}$ feet of lumber to make a shelf. How many shelves can he make from a piece of lumber that is $13\frac{3}{4}$ feet long?

SOLUTION: Find out how many times $2\frac{3}{4}$ goes into $13\frac{3}{4}$. Divide $13\frac{3}{4}$ by $2\frac{3}{4}$. To divide with mixed numbers, first change each mixed number to an improper fraction. Then invert the improper fraction at the right of the $\div$ sign.

Step 1. Change the improper fractions to mixed numbers.

$13\frac{3}{4} = \frac{55}{4}$ and $2\frac{3}{4} = \frac{11}{4}$.

Step 2. Invert $\frac{11}{4}$ to $\frac{4}{11}$.

Step 3. Change $\div$ to $\times$.

Step 4. Cancel and multiply across.

$$13\frac{3}{4} \div 2\frac{3}{4} =$$
$$\frac{55}{4} \div \frac{11}{4} =$$
$$\overset{5}{\cancel{\underset{1}{55}}} \times \overset{1}{\cancel{\underset{1}{\frac{4}{11}}}} = 5 \text{ shelves}$$

Divide and reduce.

7. $\dfrac{9}{10} \div 1\frac{1}{2} =$ $\dfrac{5}{6} \div 4\frac{2}{3} =$ $14 \div 2\frac{1}{3} =$ $20 \div 3\frac{1}{5} =$

8. $5\frac{1}{2} \div \dfrac{11}{12} =$ $4\frac{1}{5} \div 21 =$ $3\frac{1}{3} \div \dfrac{25}{27} =$ $2\frac{4}{5} \div \dfrac{1}{7} =$

9. $2\frac{2}{9} \div 2\frac{2}{3} =$ $3\frac{3}{8} \div 5\frac{1}{4} =$ $2\frac{1}{3} \div 1\frac{5}{9} =$ $5\frac{5}{6} \div 3\frac{1}{8} =$

Answers begin on page 125.

Applying Division of Fractions Skills

In the following problems watch for words that tell you to divide such as: *share, cut,* or *split.* Put the thing being divided *first* (to the left of the $\div$ sign). Invert only the number at the right of the $\div$ sign. Label and reduce each answer.

---

10. Ben wants to split a board which is $4\frac{1}{2}$ feet long into three equal pieces. How long will each piece be?

11.   One can contains $\frac{1}{4}$ pound of beets. How many cans can be filled from 20 pounds of beets?

12.   How many strips of cloth each $3\frac{1}{2}$ yards long can be cut from a bolt that is $24\frac{1}{2}$ yards long?

13.   After a weekend spent fishing, Jason brought back $18\frac{3}{4}$ pounds of fish. He wants to share the fish equally among five people. How much will each person get?

14.   How many slices of cheese each $\frac{3}{8}$ of an inch thick can be cut from a piece of cheese that is $13\frac{1}{2}$ inches thick?

15.   A tailor needs $2\frac{1}{3}$ yards of material to make a pair of trousers. How many pairs of trousers can he make from 16 yards of material?

Answers begin on page 125.

FRACTIONS SKILLS TEST

Before going on to decimals, try this review of your fractions skills. Check your answers with those beginning on page 126. Then use the Fractions Skills Test Evaluation to decide what you need to study more.

1. Reduce $\frac{16}{24}$

2. Reduce $\frac{35}{45}$

3. Raise $\frac{3}{8}$ to 40ths

4. Change $\frac{28}{6}$ to a mixed number and reduce.

5. Change $3\frac{5}{8}$ to an improper fraction.

6. A yard contains 36 inches. 18 inches is what fractional part of a yard?

7. $\begin{array}{r} 3\frac{2}{7} \\ + 6\frac{4}{7} \\ \hline \end{array}$

8. $\begin{array}{r} 9\frac{3}{5} \\ + 2\frac{4}{5} \\ \hline \end{array}$

9. $\begin{array}{r} 1\frac{5}{12} \\ + 4\frac{3}{4} \\ \hline \end{array}$

10. $\begin{array}{r} 8\frac{2}{3} \\ 3\frac{7}{9} \\ + 2\frac{1}{2} \\ \hline \end{array}$

11. Before lunch Debbie worked $3\frac{1}{2}$ hours. After lunch she worked $5\frac{3}{4}$ hours. How many hours did she work that day?

12. Maxine is $64\frac{1}{2}$ inches tall. Her daughter Natalie is $5\frac{7}{8}$ inches taller. How tall is Natalie?

13. $\begin{array}{r} 10\frac{5}{12} \\ - \ 6\frac{1}{12} \\ \hline \end{array}$

14. $\begin{array}{r} 7\frac{5}{8} \\ - 2\frac{5}{16} \\ \hline \end{array}$

15. $\begin{array}{r} 12 \\ - 9\frac{3}{7} \\ \hline \end{array}$

16. $\begin{array}{r} 4\frac{2}{9} \\ - 2\frac{5}{9} \\ \hline \end{array}$

17. $\begin{array}{r} 8\frac{2}{3} \\ - 2\frac{4}{5} \\ \hline \end{array}$

18.   A carpenter had a piece of lumber $5\frac{1}{3}$ yards long. From it he cut a piece $2\frac{1}{2}$ yards long. How long was the remaining piece?

19.   Marilyn weighed 132 pounds. She went on a diet and lost $8\frac{3}{4}$ pounds. How much did she weigh after the diet?

20. $\frac{3}{5} \times \frac{4}{7} =$ 21. $\frac{1}{2} \times \frac{5}{6} \times \frac{3}{4} =$ 22. $\frac{9}{10} \times \frac{20}{21} =$

23. $16 \times \frac{5}{6} =$ 24. $\frac{3}{4} \times 3\frac{1}{5} =$ 25. $1\frac{5}{9} \times 3\frac{3}{7} =$

26.   One cubic foot of water weighs $62\frac{1}{2}$ pounds. How much do three cubic feet of water weigh?

27.   Find the cost of $4\frac{2}{3}$ yards of lumber at $2.40 for one yard.

28. $\frac{3}{8} \div \frac{6}{7} =$ 29. $9 \div \frac{6}{11} =$ 30. $\frac{3}{4} \div 2 =$

31. $\frac{3}{10} \div 3\frac{1}{5} =$ 32. $1\frac{7}{15} \div 2\frac{8}{9} =$

33. Mrs. Riedel wants to cut a piece of material that is $5\frac{1}{4}$ yards long into three equal pieces. How long will each piece be?

34. One can contains $\frac{3}{4}$ of a pound of beans. How many cans can be filled from 24 pounds of beans?

FRACTIONS SKILLS TEST EVALUATION

Problem Number	Practice Pages	Problem Number	Practice Pages
1–2	84–85	17	101
3	85–86	18–19	101–103
4	86–87	20	103
5	87–88	21	104
6	88–89	22	104–105
7	89–91	23	105–106
8	91–92	24–25	106–107
9–10	92–95	26–27	107–108
11–12	96	28	108–109
13	97	29	109
14	98	30	110
15	99	31–32	110–111
16	100	33–34	111–112

Passing score: 27 out of 34 problems.

Your score: __ out of 34 problems.

If you had less than a passing score, review the practice pages for the problems you got wrong. Then repeat this test before going on to the decimals unit.

If you had a passing score, correct any problem you got wrong, and go to the decimals unit.

ANSWERS AND SOLUTIONS— FRACTION SKILLS EXERCISES

UNDERSTANDING FRACTIONS

1. $\frac{1}{3}$ $\frac{1}{4}$ $\frac{3}{4}$

2. $\frac{7}{9}$ $\frac{3}{8}$ $\frac{5}{9}$

3. $\frac{1}{2}$ $\frac{2}{5}$ $\frac{5}{6}$

FORMS OF FRACTIONS

4. $\frac{3}{5}$ __P__ $\frac{5}{3}$ __I__ $\frac{7}{7}$ __I__ $2\frac{3}{4}$ __M__

5. $\frac{30}{6}$ __I__ $\frac{9}{90}$ __P__ $10\frac{3}{4}$ __M__ $\frac{11}{12}$ __P__

6. $5\frac{13}{14}$ __M__ $\frac{10}{10}$ __I__ $\frac{1}{60}$ __P__ $\frac{16}{15}$ __I__

7. $\frac{14}{18}=\frac{7}{9}$ $\frac{25}{30}=\frac{5}{6}$ $\frac{15}{45}=\frac{1}{3}$ $\frac{24}{36}=\frac{2}{3}$ $\frac{35}{56}=\frac{5}{8}$

8. $\frac{45}{63}=\frac{5}{7}$ $\frac{40}{100}=\frac{2}{5}$ $\frac{26}{34}=\frac{13}{17}$ $\frac{60}{130}=\frac{6}{13}$ $\frac{2}{84}=\frac{1}{42}$

9. $\frac{35}{60}=\frac{7}{12}$ $\frac{12}{28}=\frac{3}{7}$ $\frac{18}{27}=\frac{2}{3}$ $\frac{25}{75}=\frac{1}{3}$ $\frac{40}{200}=\frac{1}{5}$

10. $\frac{9}{36}=\frac{1}{4}$ $\frac{32}{72}=\frac{4}{9}$ $\frac{24}{42}=\frac{4}{7}$ $\frac{33}{44}=\frac{3}{4}$ $\frac{6}{300}=\frac{1}{50}$

11. $\frac{5}{6}=\frac{15}{18}$ $\frac{9}{10}=\frac{45}{50}$ $\frac{1}{3}=\frac{2}{6}$ $\frac{4}{9}=\frac{36}{81}$

12. $\frac{3}{8}=\frac{30}{80}$ $\frac{7}{20}=\frac{21}{60}$ $\frac{4}{5}=\frac{60}{75}$ $\frac{7}{11}=\frac{42}{66}$

13. $\frac{5}{12}=\frac{15}{36}$ $\frac{3}{4}=\frac{24}{32}$ $\frac{8}{9}=\frac{24}{27}$ $\frac{1}{6}=\frac{5}{30}$

14. $\frac{16}{6}=2\frac{4}{6}=2\frac{2}{3}$ $\frac{28}{8}=3\frac{4}{8}=3\frac{1}{2}$ $\frac{12}{9}=1\frac{3}{9}=1\frac{1}{3}$ $\frac{14}{3}=4\frac{2}{3}$

15. $\frac{35}{7}=5$ $\frac{19}{6}=3\frac{1}{6}$ $\frac{20}{12}=1\frac{8}{12}=1\frac{2}{3}$ $\frac{40}{15}=2\frac{10}{15}=2\frac{2}{3}$

16. $\frac{9}{9}=1$ $\frac{38}{8}=4\frac{6}{8}=4\frac{3}{4}$ $\frac{44}{7}=6\frac{2}{7}$ $\frac{51}{20}=2\frac{11}{20}$

17. $2\frac{3}{4}=\frac{11}{4}$ $5\frac{1}{2}=\frac{11}{2}$ $3\frac{5}{7}=\frac{26}{7}$ $4\frac{2}{9}=\frac{38}{9}$ $6\frac{1}{3}=\frac{19}{3}$

18. $1\frac{5}{9} = \frac{14}{9}$ $10\frac{2}{3} = \frac{32}{3}$ $4\frac{3}{7} = \frac{31}{7}$ $5\frac{2}{11} = \frac{57}{11}$ $8\frac{5}{6} = \frac{53}{6}$

19. $9\frac{7}{8} = \frac{79}{8}$ $12\frac{1}{4} = \frac{49}{4}$ $3\frac{4}{5} = \frac{19}{5}$ $2\frac{3}{8} = \frac{19}{8}$ $7\frac{5}{12} = \frac{89}{12}$

20. $\frac{8}{12} = \frac{2}{3}$ 21. $\frac{180}{720} = \frac{1}{4}$ 22. $\frac{12}{16} = \frac{3}{4}$ 23. $\frac{75}{100} = \frac{3}{4}$

24. $\frac{1600}{2000} = \frac{4}{5}$ 25. $\frac{28}{52} = \frac{7}{13}$ 26. $\frac{65}{100} = \frac{13}{20}$

ADDING FRACTIONS

1.
$$\begin{array}{r} \frac{3}{6} \\ + \frac{2}{6} \\ \hline \frac{5}{6} \end{array}$$
$$\begin{array}{r} \frac{4}{9} \\ + \frac{3}{9} \\ \hline \frac{7}{9} \end{array}$$
$$\begin{array}{r} 3\frac{2}{8} \\ + 4\frac{5}{8} \\ \hline 7\frac{7}{8} \end{array}$$
$$\begin{array}{r} 5\frac{2}{5} \\ + 6\frac{2}{5} \\ \hline 11\frac{4}{5} \end{array}$$
$$\begin{array}{r} 7\frac{6}{12} \\ + 3\frac{1}{12} \\ \hline 10\frac{7}{12} \end{array}$$

2.
$$\begin{array}{r} \frac{3}{10} \\ \frac{2}{10} \\ + \frac{4}{10} \\ \hline \frac{9}{10} \end{array}$$
$$\begin{array}{r} \frac{5}{12} \\ \frac{3}{12} \\ + \frac{3}{12} \\ \hline \frac{11}{12} \end{array}$$
$$\begin{array}{r} 2\frac{3}{9} \\ 4\frac{3}{9} \\ + 6\frac{2}{9} \\ \hline 12\frac{8}{9} \end{array}$$
$$\begin{array}{r} 5\frac{6}{20} \\ 3\frac{7}{20} \\ + 2\frac{4}{20} \\ \hline 10\frac{17}{20} \end{array}$$
$$\begin{array}{r} 9\frac{3}{16} \\ 6\frac{4}{16} \\ + 4\frac{8}{16} \\ \hline 19\frac{15}{16} \end{array}$$

3.
$$\begin{array}{r} \frac{4}{8} \\ + \frac{2}{8} \\ \hline \frac{6}{8} = \frac{3}{4} \end{array}$$
$$\begin{array}{r} \frac{3}{10} \\ + \frac{2}{10} \\ \hline \frac{5}{10} = \frac{1}{2} \end{array}$$
$$\begin{array}{r} 4\frac{3}{9} \\ + 2\frac{3}{9} \\ \hline 6\frac{6}{9} = 6\frac{2}{3} \end{array}$$
$$\begin{array}{r} 3\frac{5}{12} \\ + 7\frac{3}{12} \\ \hline 10\frac{8}{12} = 10\frac{2}{3} \end{array}$$
$$\begin{array}{r} 2\frac{4}{15} \\ + 5\frac{8}{15} \\ \hline 7\frac{12}{15} = 7\frac{4}{5} \end{array}$$

4.
$$\begin{array}{r} \frac{2}{10} \\ \frac{3}{10} \\ + \frac{3}{10} \\ \hline \frac{8}{10} = \frac{4}{5} \end{array}$$
$$\begin{array}{r} \frac{5}{18} \\ \frac{4}{18} \\ + \frac{3}{18} \\ \hline \frac{12}{18} = \frac{2}{3} \end{array}$$
$$\begin{array}{r} 4\frac{3}{16} \\ 3\frac{4}{16} \\ + 2\frac{5}{16} \\ \hline 9\frac{12}{16} = 9\frac{3}{4} \end{array}$$
$$\begin{array}{r} 3\frac{2}{12} \\ 5\frac{3}{12} \\ + 4\frac{4}{12} \\ \hline 12\frac{9}{12} = 12\frac{3}{4} \end{array}$$
$$\begin{array}{r} 6\frac{5}{14} \\ 2\frac{1}{14} \\ + 3\frac{4}{14} \\ \hline 11\frac{10}{14} = 11\frac{5}{7} \end{array}$$

5.
$$\begin{array}{r} \frac{7}{8} \\ + \frac{5}{8} \\ \hline \frac{12}{8} = 1\frac{4}{8} \\ = 1\frac{1}{2} \end{array}$$
$$\begin{array}{r} \frac{8}{9} \\ + \frac{7}{9} \\ \hline \frac{15}{9} = 1\frac{6}{9} \\ = 1\frac{2}{3} \end{array}$$
$$\begin{array}{r} 5\frac{5}{6} \\ + 6\frac{1}{6} \\ \hline 11\frac{6}{6} = 12 \end{array}$$
$$\begin{array}{r} 4\frac{9}{10} \\ + 3\frac{6}{10} \\ \hline 7\frac{15}{10} = 8\frac{5}{10} \\ = 8\frac{1}{2} \end{array}$$
$$\begin{array}{r} 8\frac{7}{12} \\ + 2\frac{11}{12} \\ \hline 10\frac{18}{12} = 11\frac{6}{12} \\ = 11\frac{1}{2} \end{array}$$

6.

$$\begin{array}{r} \frac{3}{4} \\ \frac{2}{4} \\ +\frac{1}{4} \\ \hline \frac{6}{4} = 1\frac{2}{4} \\ = 1\frac{1}{2} \end{array} \qquad \begin{array}{r} \frac{2}{7} \\ \frac{3}{7} \\ +\frac{5}{7} \\ \hline \frac{10}{7} = 1\frac{3}{7} \end{array} \qquad \begin{array}{r} 3\frac{4}{5} \\ 4\frac{3}{5} \\ +5\frac{2}{5} \\ \hline 12\frac{9}{5} = 13\frac{4}{5} \end{array} \qquad \begin{array}{r} 8\frac{7}{12} \\ 7\frac{8}{12} \\ +4\frac{9}{12} \\ \hline 19\frac{24}{12} = 21 \end{array} \qquad \begin{array}{r} 3\frac{10}{16} \\ 6\frac{11}{16} \\ +2\frac{13}{16} \\ \hline 11\frac{34}{16} = 13\frac{2}{16} \\ = 13\frac{1}{8} \end{array}$$

7.

$$\begin{array}{r} \frac{5}{8} = \frac{5}{8} \\ +\frac{3}{4} = \frac{6}{8} \\ \hline \frac{11}{8} = 1\frac{3}{8} \end{array} \qquad \begin{array}{r} \frac{1}{3} = \frac{2}{6} \\ +\frac{5}{6} = \frac{5}{6} \\ \hline \frac{7}{6} = 1\frac{1}{6} \end{array} \qquad \begin{array}{r} \frac{4}{5} = \frac{12}{15} \\ +\frac{4}{15} = \frac{4}{15} \\ \hline \frac{16}{15} = 1\frac{1}{15} \end{array} \qquad \begin{array}{r} \frac{4}{7} = \frac{16}{28} \\ +\frac{9}{28} = \frac{9}{28} \\ \hline \frac{25}{28} \end{array} \qquad \begin{array}{r} \frac{5}{9} = \frac{20}{36} \\ +\frac{11}{36} = \frac{11}{36} \\ \hline \frac{31}{36} \end{array}$$

8.

$$\begin{array}{r} \frac{2}{3} = \frac{8}{12} \\ \frac{7}{12} = \frac{7}{12} \\ +\frac{3}{4} = \frac{9}{12} \\ \hline \frac{24}{12} = 2 \end{array} \qquad \begin{array}{r} \frac{3}{5} = \frac{6}{10} \\ \frac{1}{2} = \frac{5}{10} \\ +\frac{7}{10} = \frac{7}{10} \\ \hline \frac{18}{10} = 1\frac{8}{10} = 1\frac{4}{5} \end{array} \qquad \begin{array}{r} \frac{3}{5} = \frac{9}{15} \\ \frac{8}{15} = \frac{8}{15} \\ +\frac{2}{3} = \frac{10}{15} \\ \hline \frac{27}{15} = 1\frac{12}{15} = 1\frac{4}{5} \end{array}$$

$$\begin{array}{r} \frac{13}{20} = \frac{13}{20} \\ \frac{4}{5} = \frac{16}{20} \\ +\frac{1}{4} = \frac{5}{20} \\ \hline \frac{34}{20} = 1\frac{14}{20} = 1\frac{7}{10} \end{array} \qquad \begin{array}{r} \frac{5}{8} = \frac{20}{32} \\ \frac{7}{32} = \frac{7}{32} \\ +\frac{9}{16} = \frac{18}{32} \\ \hline \frac{45}{32} = 1\frac{13}{32} \end{array}$$

9.

$$\begin{array}{r} 6\frac{5}{8} = 6\frac{15}{24} \\ +7\frac{11}{24} = 7\frac{11}{24} \\ \hline 13\frac{26}{24} = 14\frac{2}{24} \\ = 14\frac{1}{12} \end{array} \qquad \begin{array}{r} 5\frac{6}{35} = 5\frac{6}{35} \\ +9\frac{2}{7} = 9\frac{10}{35} \\ \hline 14\frac{16}{35} \end{array} \qquad \begin{array}{r} 8\frac{1}{6} = 8\frac{4}{24} \\ +3\frac{7}{24} = 3\frac{7}{24} \\ \hline 11\frac{11}{24} \end{array} \qquad \begin{array}{r} 6\frac{5}{48} = 6\frac{5}{48} \\ +2\frac{5}{8} = 2\frac{30}{48} \\ \hline 8\frac{35}{48} \end{array}$$

10.

$$\begin{array}{r} \frac{4}{5} = \frac{12}{15} \\ +\frac{2}{3} = \frac{10}{15} \\ \hline \frac{22}{15} = 1\frac{7}{15} \end{array} \qquad \begin{array}{r} \frac{3}{4} = \frac{21}{28} \\ +\frac{3}{7} = \frac{12}{28} \\ \hline \frac{33}{28} = 1\frac{5}{28} \end{array} \qquad \begin{array}{r} \frac{5}{6} = \frac{25}{30} \\ +\frac{4}{5} = \frac{24}{30} \\ \hline \frac{49}{30} = 1\frac{19}{30} \end{array} \qquad \begin{array}{r} \frac{4}{9} = \frac{16}{36} \\ +\frac{3}{4} = \frac{27}{36} \\ \hline \frac{43}{36} = 1\frac{7}{36} \end{array} \qquad \begin{array}{r} \frac{3}{8} = \frac{15}{40} \\ +\frac{3}{5} = \frac{24}{40} \\ \hline \frac{39}{40} \end{array}$$

11.

$$\begin{array}{r} \frac{3}{8} = \frac{9}{24} \\ +\frac{5}{6} = \frac{20}{24} \\ \hline \frac{29}{24} = 1\frac{5}{24} \end{array} \qquad \begin{array}{r} \frac{4}{9} = \frac{16}{36} \\ +\frac{5}{12} = \frac{15}{36} \\ \hline \frac{31}{36} \end{array} \qquad \begin{array}{r} \frac{7}{8} = \frac{35}{40} \\ +\frac{9}{10} = \frac{36}{40} \\ \hline \frac{71}{40} = 1\frac{31}{40} \end{array} \qquad \begin{array}{r} \frac{7}{12} = \frac{14}{24} \\ +\frac{5}{8} = \frac{15}{24} \\ \hline \frac{29}{24} = 1\frac{5}{24} \end{array} \qquad \begin{array}{r} \frac{7}{10} = \frac{21}{30} \\ +\frac{8}{15} = \frac{16}{30} \\ \hline \frac{37}{30} = 1\frac{7}{30} \end{array}$$

12.

$$3\tfrac{1}{6} = 3\tfrac{7}{42}$$
$$2\tfrac{4}{7} = 2\tfrac{24}{42}$$
$$+\,5\tfrac{1}{2} = 5\tfrac{21}{42}$$
$$10\tfrac{52}{42} = 11\tfrac{10}{42} = 11\tfrac{5}{21}$$

$$6\tfrac{3}{4} = 6\tfrac{9}{12}$$
$$4\tfrac{2}{3} = 4\tfrac{8}{12}$$
$$+\,1\tfrac{1}{2} = 1\tfrac{6}{12}$$
$$11\tfrac{23}{12} = 12\tfrac{11}{12}$$

$$5\tfrac{1}{3} = 5\tfrac{20}{60}$$
$$2\tfrac{1}{4} = 2\tfrac{15}{60}$$
$$+\,9\tfrac{3}{5} = 9\tfrac{36}{60}$$
$$16\tfrac{71}{60} = 17\tfrac{11}{60}$$

$$4\tfrac{5}{12} = 4\tfrac{15}{36}$$
$$7\tfrac{2}{9} = 7\tfrac{8}{36}$$
$$+\,4\tfrac{2}{3} = 4\tfrac{24}{36}$$
$$15\tfrac{47}{36} = 16\tfrac{11}{36}$$

13.

$$2\tfrac{5}{6} = 2\tfrac{20}{24}$$
$$6\tfrac{3}{8} = 6\tfrac{9}{24}$$
$$+\,8\tfrac{3}{4} = 8\tfrac{18}{24}$$
$$16\tfrac{47}{24} = 17\tfrac{23}{24}$$

$$3\tfrac{5}{16} = 3\tfrac{5}{16}$$
$$4\tfrac{3}{4} = 4\tfrac{12}{16}$$
$$+\,9\tfrac{1}{2} = 9\tfrac{8}{16}$$
$$16\tfrac{25}{16} = 17\tfrac{9}{16}$$

$$5\tfrac{3}{10} = 5\tfrac{9}{30}$$
$$8\tfrac{5}{6} = 8\tfrac{25}{30}$$
$$+\,3\tfrac{2}{5} = 9\tfrac{12}{30}$$
$$16\tfrac{46}{30} = 17\tfrac{16}{30} = 17\tfrac{8}{15}$$

$$9\tfrac{5}{6} = 9\tfrac{20}{24}$$
$$2\tfrac{3}{8} = 2\tfrac{9}{24}$$
$$+\,4\tfrac{7}{24} = 4\tfrac{7}{24}$$
$$15\tfrac{36}{24} = 16\tfrac{12}{24} = 16\tfrac{1}{2}$$

14.

$$24\tfrac{1}{2} = 24\tfrac{2}{4}$$
$$\times\,10\tfrac{3}{4} = 10\tfrac{3}{4}$$
$$34\tfrac{5}{4} = 35\tfrac{1}{4} \text{ ft.}$$

15.

$$4\tfrac{1}{4} = 4\tfrac{3}{12}$$
$$3\tfrac{2}{3} = 3\tfrac{8}{12}$$
$$+\,5\tfrac{1}{2} = 5\tfrac{6}{12}$$
$$12\tfrac{17}{12} = 13\tfrac{5}{12} \text{ hrs.}$$

16.

$$12\tfrac{3}{10} = 12\tfrac{3}{10}$$
$$8\tfrac{1}{2} = 8\tfrac{5}{10}$$
$$+\,7\tfrac{9}{10} = 7\tfrac{9}{10}$$
$$27\tfrac{17}{10} = 28\tfrac{7}{10} \text{ mi.}$$

17.

$$3\tfrac{1}{2} = 3\tfrac{8}{16}$$
$$2\tfrac{1}{4} = 2\tfrac{4}{16}$$
$$1\tfrac{15}{16} = 1\tfrac{15}{16}$$
$$+\,5\tfrac{3}{8} = 5\tfrac{6}{16}$$
$$11\tfrac{33}{16} = 13\tfrac{1}{16} \text{ lb.}$$

18.
$$71\tfrac{1}{2} = 71\tfrac{2}{4}$$
$$+\ \ 2\tfrac{3}{4} = \ 2\tfrac{3}{4}$$
$$73\tfrac{5}{4} = 74\tfrac{1}{4}\ \text{in.}$$

19.
$$\tfrac{3}{4} = \tfrac{9}{12}$$
$$+\ \tfrac{2}{3} = \tfrac{8}{12}$$
$$\tfrac{17}{12} = 1\tfrac{5}{12}\ \text{hrs.}$$

SUBTRACTING FRACTIONS

1.
$$\begin{array}{r}\tfrac{11}{12}\\[-2pt]-\ \tfrac{7}{12}\\[-2pt]\hline \tfrac{4}{12} = \tfrac{1}{3}\end{array}$$
$$\begin{array}{r}\tfrac{13}{15}\\[-2pt]-\ \tfrac{4}{15}\\[-2pt]\hline \tfrac{9}{15} = \tfrac{3}{5}\end{array}$$
$$\begin{array}{r}\tfrac{5}{9}\\[-2pt]-\ \tfrac{2}{9}\\[-2pt]\hline \tfrac{3}{9} = \tfrac{1}{3}\end{array}$$
$$\begin{array}{r}\tfrac{17}{20}\\[-2pt]-\ \tfrac{3}{20}\\[-2pt]\hline \tfrac{14}{20} = \tfrac{7}{10}\end{array}$$
$$\begin{array}{r}\tfrac{15}{16}\\[-2pt]-\ \tfrac{9}{16}\\[-2pt]\hline \tfrac{6}{16} = \tfrac{3}{8}\end{array}$$

2.
$$\begin{array}{r}9\tfrac{7}{8}\\[-2pt]-\ 6\tfrac{5}{8}\\[-2pt]\hline 3\tfrac{2}{8} = 3\tfrac{1}{4}\end{array}$$
$$\begin{array}{r}15\tfrac{9}{10}\\[-2pt]-\ 7\tfrac{7}{10}\\[-2pt]\hline 8\tfrac{2}{10} = 8\tfrac{1}{5}\end{array}$$
$$\begin{array}{r}14\tfrac{19}{24}\\[-2pt]-\ 8\tfrac{5}{24}\\[-2pt]\hline 6\tfrac{14}{24} = 6\tfrac{7}{12}\end{array}$$
$$\begin{array}{r}11\tfrac{5}{6}\\[-2pt]-\ 5\tfrac{1}{6}\\[-2pt]\hline 6\tfrac{4}{6} = 6\tfrac{2}{3}\end{array}$$

3.
$$\begin{array}{r}\tfrac{2}{3} = \tfrac{6}{9}\\[-2pt]-\ \tfrac{2}{9} = \tfrac{2}{9}\\[-2pt]\hline \tfrac{4}{9}\end{array}$$
$$\begin{array}{r}\tfrac{9}{16} = \tfrac{9}{16}\\[-2pt]-\ \tfrac{1}{4} = \tfrac{4}{16}\\[-2pt]\hline \tfrac{5}{16}\end{array}$$
$$\begin{array}{r}\tfrac{2}{3} = \tfrac{8}{12}\\[-2pt]-\ \tfrac{1}{4} = \tfrac{3}{12}\\[-2pt]\hline \tfrac{5}{12}\end{array}$$
$$\begin{array}{r}\tfrac{5}{6} = \tfrac{35}{42}\\[-2pt]-\ \tfrac{3}{7} = \tfrac{18}{42}\\[-2pt]\hline \tfrac{17}{42}\end{array}$$
$$\begin{array}{r}\tfrac{7}{8} = \tfrac{21}{24}\\[-2pt]-\ \tfrac{5}{6} = \tfrac{20}{24}\\[-2pt]\hline \tfrac{1}{24}\end{array}$$

4.
$$\begin{array}{r}9\tfrac{11}{12} = 9\tfrac{22}{24}\\[-2pt]-\ 2\tfrac{5}{8} = 2\tfrac{15}{24}\\[-2pt]\hline 7\tfrac{7}{24}\end{array}$$
$$\begin{array}{r}8\tfrac{5}{9} = 8\tfrac{10}{18}\\[-2pt]-\ 3\tfrac{1}{6} = 3\tfrac{3}{18}\\[-2pt]\hline 5\tfrac{7}{18}\end{array}$$
$$\begin{array}{r}10\tfrac{4}{5} = 10\tfrac{16}{20}\\[-2pt]-\ 6\tfrac{3}{4} = 6\tfrac{15}{20}\\[-2pt]\hline 4\tfrac{1}{20}\end{array}$$
$$\begin{array}{r}23\tfrac{11}{16} = 23\tfrac{11}{16}\\[-2pt]-19\tfrac{1}{2} = 19\tfrac{8}{16}\\[-2pt]\hline 4\tfrac{3}{16}\end{array}$$

5.
$$\begin{array}{r}\overset{8}{\cancel{9}}\tfrac{5}{5}\\[-2pt]-\ \tfrac{3}{5}\\[-2pt]\hline 8\tfrac{2}{5}\end{array}$$
$$\begin{array}{r}\overset{11}{\cancel{12}}\tfrac{7}{7}\\[-2pt]-\ \tfrac{2}{7}\\[-2pt]\hline 11\tfrac{5}{7}\end{array}$$
$$\begin{array}{r}\overset{7}{\cancel{8}}\tfrac{9}{9}\\[-2pt]-\ \tfrac{5}{9}\\[-2pt]\hline 7\tfrac{4}{9}\end{array}$$
$$\begin{array}{r}\overset{3}{\cancel{4}}\tfrac{3}{3}\\[-2pt]-\ \tfrac{2}{3}\\[-2pt]\hline 3\tfrac{1}{3}\end{array}$$
$$\begin{array}{r}\overset{6}{\cancel{7}}\tfrac{12}{12}\\[-2pt]-\ \tfrac{11}{12}\\[-2pt]\hline -\ 6\tfrac{1}{12}\end{array}$$

6.
$$\begin{array}{r}\overset{4}{\cancel{5}}\tfrac{7}{7}\\[-2pt]-\ 1\tfrac{4}{7}\\[-2pt]\hline 3\tfrac{3}{7}\end{array}$$
$$\begin{array}{r}\overset{5}{\cancel{6}}\tfrac{10}{10}\\[-2pt]-\ 5\tfrac{7}{10}\\[-2pt]\hline \tfrac{3}{10}\end{array}$$
$$\begin{array}{r}\overset{8}{\cancel{9}}\tfrac{8}{8}\\[-2pt]-\ 2\tfrac{3}{8}\\[-2pt]\hline 6\tfrac{5}{8}\end{array}$$
$$\begin{array}{r}\overset{6}{\cancel{7}}\tfrac{11}{11}\\[-2pt]-\ 3\tfrac{4}{11}\\[-2pt]\hline 3\tfrac{7}{11}\end{array}$$
$$\begin{array}{r}\overset{7}{\cancel{8}}\tfrac{13}{13}\\[-2pt]-\ 6\tfrac{5}{13}\\[-2pt]\hline 1\tfrac{8}{13}\end{array}$$

7.
$$\begin{array}{r}9\tfrac{2}{5} = 8\tfrac{7}{5}\\[-2pt]-\ 2\tfrac{4}{5} = 2\tfrac{4}{5}\\[-2pt]\hline 6\tfrac{3}{5}\end{array}$$
$$\begin{array}{r}7\tfrac{5}{8} = 6\tfrac{13}{8}\\[-2pt]-\ 3\tfrac{7}{8} = 3\tfrac{7}{8}\\[-2pt]\hline 3\tfrac{6}{8} = 3\tfrac{3}{4}\end{array}$$
$$\begin{array}{r}8\tfrac{2}{9} = 7\tfrac{11}{9}\\[-2pt]-5\tfrac{8}{9} = 5\tfrac{8}{9}\\[-2pt]\hline 2\tfrac{3}{9} = 2\tfrac{1}{3}\end{array}$$
$$\begin{array}{r}6\tfrac{3}{7} = 5\tfrac{10}{7}\\[-2pt]-\ 5\tfrac{6}{7} = 5\tfrac{6}{7}\\[-2pt]\hline \tfrac{4}{7}\end{array}$$

8.

$$5\tfrac{1}{3} = 4\tfrac{4}{3}$$
$$-\ 1\tfrac{2}{3} = 1\tfrac{2}{3}$$
$$\overline{\qquad\quad 3\tfrac{2}{3}}$$

$$6\tfrac{5}{12} = 5\tfrac{17}{12}$$
$$-\ 3\tfrac{11}{12} = 3\tfrac{11}{12}$$
$$\overline{\qquad\quad 2\tfrac{6}{12} = 2\tfrac{1}{2}}$$

$$7\tfrac{1}{6} = 6\tfrac{7}{6}$$
$$-\ 4\tfrac{5}{6} = 4\tfrac{5}{6}$$
$$\overline{\qquad\quad 2\tfrac{2}{6} = 2\tfrac{1}{3}}$$

$$9\tfrac{5}{16} = 8\tfrac{21}{16}$$
$$-\ 8\tfrac{11}{16} = 8\tfrac{11}{16}$$
$$\overline{\qquad\quad \tfrac{10}{16} = \tfrac{5}{8}}$$

9.

$$6\tfrac{1}{4} = 6\tfrac{3}{12} = 5\tfrac{15}{12}$$
$$-\ 3\tfrac{1}{3} = 3\tfrac{4}{12} = 3\tfrac{4}{12}$$
$$\overline{\qquad\qquad\qquad 2\tfrac{11}{12}}$$

$$10\tfrac{3}{5} = 10\tfrac{12}{20} = 9\tfrac{32}{20}$$
$$-\ 8\tfrac{3}{4} = 8\tfrac{15}{20} = 8\tfrac{15}{20}$$
$$\overline{\qquad\qquad\qquad 1\tfrac{17}{20}}$$

$$4\tfrac{2}{9} = 4\tfrac{4}{18} = 3\tfrac{22}{18}$$
$$-\ 1\tfrac{1}{2} = 1\tfrac{9}{18} = 1\tfrac{9}{18}$$
$$\overline{\qquad\qquad\qquad 2\tfrac{13}{18}}$$

$$12\tfrac{1}{4} = 12\tfrac{3}{12} = 11\tfrac{15}{12}$$
$$-\ 3\tfrac{5}{6} = 3\tfrac{10}{12} = 3\tfrac{10}{12}$$
$$\overline{\qquad\qquad\qquad 8\tfrac{5}{12}}$$

10.

$$20\tfrac{5}{12} = 20\tfrac{5}{12} = 19\tfrac{17}{12}$$
$$-\ 9\tfrac{2}{3} = 9\tfrac{8}{12} = 9\tfrac{8}{12}$$
$$\overline{\qquad\qquad\qquad 10\tfrac{9}{12} = 10\tfrac{3}{4}}$$

$$14\tfrac{2}{5} = 14\tfrac{6}{15} = 13\tfrac{21}{15}$$
$$-\ 6\tfrac{8}{15} = 6\tfrac{8}{15} = 6\tfrac{8}{15}$$
$$\overline{\qquad\qquad\qquad 7\tfrac{13}{15}}$$

$$18\tfrac{1}{3} = 18\tfrac{2}{6} = 17\tfrac{8}{6}$$
$$-\ 9\tfrac{1}{2} = 9\tfrac{3}{6} = 9\tfrac{3}{6}$$
$$\overline{\qquad\qquad\qquad 8\tfrac{5}{6}}$$

$$13\tfrac{3}{8} = 13\tfrac{15}{40} = 12\tfrac{55}{40}$$
$$-\ 5\tfrac{7}{10} = 5\tfrac{28}{40} = 5\tfrac{28}{40}$$
$$\overline{\qquad\qquad\qquad 7\tfrac{27}{40}}$$

11.

$$2\tfrac{3}{10} = 2\tfrac{3}{10} = 1\tfrac{13}{10}$$
$$-\ 1\tfrac{1}{2} = 1\tfrac{5}{10} = 1\tfrac{5}{10}$$
$$\overline{\qquad\qquad\qquad \tfrac{8}{10} = \tfrac{4}{5}\ \text{mi.}}$$

12.

$$162\ \ = 161\tfrac{4}{4}$$
$$-\ 118\tfrac{3}{4} = 118\tfrac{3}{4}$$
$$\overline{\qquad\qquad 43\tfrac{1}{4}\ \text{lb.}}$$

13.

$$5\ \ = 4\tfrac{16}{16}$$
$$-\ 2\tfrac{5}{16} = 2\tfrac{5}{16}$$
$$\overline{\qquad\quad 2\tfrac{11}{16}\ \text{lb.}}$$

14.

$$62\tfrac{3}{8} = 61\tfrac{11}{8}$$
$$-\ 23\tfrac{7}{8} = 23\tfrac{7}{8}$$
$$\overline{\qquad\quad 38\tfrac{4}{8} = 38\tfrac{1}{2}\ \text{in.}}$$

15.

$$17,310\tfrac{9}{10}$$
$$-\ 16,204\tfrac{8}{10}$$
$$\overline{\quad 1,106\tfrac{1}{10}\ \text{mi.}}$$

16.

$$8\ \ = 7\tfrac{3}{3}$$
$$-\ 2\tfrac{2}{3} = 2\tfrac{2}{3}$$
$$\overline{\qquad\quad 5\tfrac{1}{3}\ \text{hrs.}}$$

17. $185\frac{1}{4} = 185\frac{4}{16} = 184\frac{20}{16}$

   $-\ 20\frac{9}{16} = 20\frac{9}{16} = 20\frac{9}{16}$

   $164\frac{11}{16}$ lb.

MULTIPLYING FRACTIONS

1. $\frac{3}{4} \times \frac{5}{7} = \frac{15}{28}$ $\frac{2}{9} \times \frac{1}{5} = \frac{2}{45}$ $\frac{4}{11} \times \frac{2}{3} = \frac{8}{33}$ $\frac{5}{12} \times \frac{5}{6} = \frac{25}{72}$

2. $\frac{9}{10} \times \frac{3}{8} = \frac{27}{80}$ $\frac{2}{3} \times \frac{5}{13} = \frac{10}{39}$ $\frac{3}{16} \times \frac{1}{2} = \frac{3}{32}$ $\frac{1}{4} \times \frac{7}{8} = \frac{7}{32}$

3. $\frac{2}{3} \times \frac{1}{5} \times \frac{1}{3} = \frac{2}{45}$ $\frac{1}{9} \times \frac{5}{6} \times \frac{1}{2} = \frac{5}{108}$ $\frac{1}{3} \times \frac{4}{7} \times \frac{2}{3} = \frac{8}{63}$

4. $\frac{3}{4} \times \frac{1}{2} \times \frac{7}{8} = \frac{21}{64}$ $\frac{1}{2} \times \frac{3}{4} \times \frac{5}{7} = \frac{15}{56}$ $\frac{5}{6} \times \frac{1}{2} \times \frac{5}{8} = \frac{25}{96}$

5. $\frac{\overset{1}{\cancel{2}}}{4} \times \frac{5}{\underset{2}{\cancel{6}}} = \frac{5}{8}$ $\frac{4}{\underset{3}{\cancel{9}}} \times \frac{\overset{2}{\cancel{6}}}{7} = \frac{8}{21}$ $\frac{\overset{1}{\cancel{2}}}{8} \times \frac{9}{\underset{2}{\cancel{10}}} = \frac{9}{16}$ $\frac{7}{\underset{4}{\cancel{12}}} \times \frac{\overset{3}{\cancel{9}}}{11} = \frac{21}{44}$

6. $\frac{\overset{1}{\cancel{2}}}{\underset{4}{\cancel{8}}} \times \frac{\overset{7}{\cancel{14}}}{\underset{5}{\cancel{15}}} = \frac{7}{20}$ $\frac{\overset{3}{\cancel{9}}}{\underset{1}{\cancel{10}}} \times \frac{\overset{2}{\cancel{20}}}{\underset{7}{\cancel{21}}} = \frac{6}{7}$ $\frac{\overset{1}{\cancel{8}}}{\underset{3}{\cancel{9}}} \times \frac{\overset{5}{\cancel{15}}}{\underset{2}{\cancel{16}}} = \frac{5}{6}$ $\frac{\overset{5}{\cancel{25}}}{\underset{4}{\cancel{32}}} \times \frac{\overset{3}{\cancel{24}}}{\underset{7}{\cancel{35}}} = \frac{15}{28}$

7. $\frac{\overset{1}{\cancel{2}}}{\underset{3}{\cancel{9}}} \times \frac{\overset{1}{\cancel{2}}}{\underset{1}{\cancel{7}}} \times \frac{\overset{2}{\cancel{14}}}{\underset{3}{\cancel{15}}} = \frac{2}{9}$ $\frac{\overset{3}{\cancel{6}}}{\underset{1}{\cancel{7}}} \times \frac{\overset{1}{\cancel{7}}}{\underset{\underset{1}{\cancel{4}}}{\cancel{8}}} \times \frac{\overset{1}{\cancel{4}}}{\cancel{5}} = \frac{3}{5}$ $\frac{\overset{1}{\cancel{11}}}{\underset{\underset{1}{\cancel{3}}}{\cancel{15}}} \times \frac{\overset{\overset{1}{\cancel{2}}}{\cancel{10}}}{\underset{1}{\cancel{11}}} \times \frac{\overset{1}{\cancel{3}}}{\underset{2}{\cancel{4}}} = \frac{1}{2}$

8. $\frac{\overset{1}{\cancel{9}}}{\underset{5}{\cancel{10}}} \times \frac{1}{\underset{1}{\cancel{4}}} \times \frac{\overset{\overset{1}{\cancel{2}}}{\cancel{8}}}{\underset{1}{\cancel{9}}} = \frac{1}{5}$ $\frac{\overset{1}{\cancel{5}}}{\underset{3}{\cancel{6}}} \times \frac{\overset{2}{\cancel{14}}}{\underset{3}{\cancel{15}}} \times \frac{\overset{1}{\cancel{2}}}{\underset{3}{\cancel{21}}} = \frac{2}{27}$ $\frac{\overset{\overset{1}{\cancel{4}}}{\cancel{20}}}{\underset{7}{\cancel{21}}} \times \frac{\overset{3}{\cancel{9}}}{\underset{\underset{1}{\cancel{4}}}{\cancel{16}}} \times \frac{\overset{1}{\cancel{4}}}{\underset{1}{\cancel{8}}} = \frac{3}{7}$

9. $\frac{5}{\underset{1}{\cancel{8}}} \times \frac{\overset{3}{\cancel{24}}}{1} = \frac{15}{1} = 15$ $\frac{9}{\underset{2}{\cancel{10}}} \times \frac{\overset{9}{\cancel{45}}}{1} = \frac{81}{2} = 40\frac{1}{2}$ $\frac{3}{\underset{1}{\cancel{7}}} \times \frac{\overset{4}{\cancel{28}}}{1} = \frac{12}{1} = 12$

   $\frac{4}{\underset{1}{\cancel{11}}} \times \frac{\overset{5}{\cancel{55}}}{1} = \frac{20}{1} = 20$

10. $\dfrac{\overset{4}{\cancel{12}}}{1} \times \dfrac{7}{\underset{3}{\cancel{9}}} = \dfrac{28}{3} = 9\dfrac{1}{3}$ $\dfrac{\overset{7}{\cancel{35}}}{1} \times \dfrac{8}{\underset{3}{\cancel{15}}} = \dfrac{56}{3} = 18\dfrac{2}{3}$

$\dfrac{\overset{6}{\cancel{42}}}{1} \times \dfrac{12}{\underset{5}{\cancel{35}}} = \dfrac{72}{5} = 14\dfrac{2}{5}$ $\dfrac{\overset{3}{\cancel{24}}}{1} \times \dfrac{5}{\underset{2}{\cancel{16}}} = \dfrac{15}{2} = 7\dfrac{1}{2}$

11. $\dfrac{\overset{5}{\cancel{15}}}{\underset{2}{\cancel{4}}} \times \dfrac{\overset{1}{\cancel{2}}}{\underset{1}{\cancel{3}}} = \dfrac{5}{2} = 2\dfrac{1}{2}$ $\dfrac{\overset{12}{\cancel{24}}}{7} \times \dfrac{3}{\underset{5}{\cancel{10}}} = \dfrac{36}{35} = 1\dfrac{1}{35}$

$\dfrac{5}{\underset{2}{\cancel{8}}} \times \dfrac{\overset{5}{\cancel{20}}}{9} = \dfrac{25}{18} = 1\dfrac{7}{18}$ $\dfrac{\overset{1}{\cancel{8}}}{\underset{3}{\cancel{15}}} \times \dfrac{\overset{5}{\cancel{25}}}{\underset{2}{\cancel{16}}} = \dfrac{5}{6}$

12. $\dfrac{\overset{2}{\cancel{18}}}{\underset{1}{\cancel{7}}} \times \dfrac{\overset{4}{\cancel{28}}}{\underset{1}{\cancel{9}}} = \dfrac{8}{1} = 8$ $\dfrac{\overset{10}{\cancel{20}}}{11} \times \dfrac{7}{\underset{3}{\cancel{6}}} = \dfrac{70}{33} = 2\dfrac{4}{33}$

$\dfrac{\overset{2}{\cancel{14}}}{\underset{3}{\cancel{9}}} \times \dfrac{\overset{4}{\cancel{12}}}{\underset{1}{\cancel{7}}} = \dfrac{8}{3} = 2\dfrac{2}{3}$ $\dfrac{7}{\underset{1}{\cancel{8}}} \times \dfrac{\overset{4}{\cancel{32}}}{\underset{5}{\cancel{15}}} = \dfrac{28}{5} = 5\dfrac{3}{5}$

13. $\dfrac{\overset{3}{\cancel{21}}}{\cancel{16}} \times \dfrac{\overset{1}{\cancel{20}}}{\cancel{7}} \times \dfrac{\overset{3}{\cancel{12}}}{\cancel{5}} = \dfrac{9}{1} = 9$ $\dfrac{\overset{5}{\cancel{15}}}{8} \times \dfrac{\overset{1}{\cancel{2}}}{\cancel{4}} \times \dfrac{\overset{5}{\cancel{20}}}{\cancel{9}} = \dfrac{25}{8} = 3\dfrac{1}{8}$ $\dfrac{\overset{9}{\cancel{27}}}{\cancel{20}} \times \dfrac{\overset{1}{\cancel{16}}}{\cancel{3}} \times \dfrac{\overset{1}{\cancel{5}}}{\cancel{4}} = \dfrac{9}{1} = 9$

14. $\dfrac{2}{\underset{1}{\cancel{5}}} \times \dfrac{\overset{2500}{\cancel{12,500}}}{1} = \$5,000$ 15. $5 \times 4\dfrac{1}{3} =$

$\dfrac{5}{1} \times \dfrac{13}{3} = \dfrac{65}{3} = 21\dfrac{2}{3}$ yds.

16. $7\dfrac{1}{2} \times 7.00 =$ 17. $3\dfrac{3}{4} \times 68 =$

$\dfrac{15}{\underset{1}{\cancel{2}}} \times \dfrac{\overset{3.50}{\cancel{7.00}}}{1} = \$52.50$ $\dfrac{15}{\underset{1}{\cancel{4}}} \times \dfrac{\overset{17}{\cancel{68}}}{1} = \$2.55$

18. $\frac{2}{3} \times 540 =$

$\frac{2}{\cancel{3}} \times \frac{\cancel{540}^{180}}{1} = 360$ albums

19. $8\frac{2}{3} \times \$3.60 =$

$\frac{26}{\cancel{3}} \times \frac{\cancel{3.60}^{1.20}}{1} = \$31.20$

20. $\frac{3}{8} \times 184 =$

$\frac{3}{\cancel{8}} \times \frac{\cancel{184}^{23}}{1} = \$69$

DIVIDING FRACTIONS

1. $\frac{5}{\cancel{6}_2} \times \frac{\cancel{3}^1}{2} = \frac{5}{4} = 1\frac{1}{4}$ $\frac{\cancel{3}^1}{\cancel{8}_2} \times \frac{\cancel{4}^1}{\cancel{3}_1} = \frac{1}{2}$ $\frac{\cancel{9}^3}{\cancel{10}_2} \times \frac{\cancel{5}^1}{\cancel{3}_1} = \frac{3}{2} = 1\frac{1}{2}$ $\frac{7}{\cancel{9}_3} \times \frac{\cancel{6}^2}{5} = \frac{14}{15}$

2. $\frac{1}{\cancel{3}_1} \times \frac{\cancel{6}^2}{1} = \frac{2}{1} = 2$ $\frac{5}{9} \times \frac{4}{3} = \frac{20}{27}$ $\frac{11}{\cancel{12}_4} \times \frac{\cancel{3}^1}{2} = \frac{11}{8} = 1\frac{3}{8}$ $\frac{\cancel{15}^5}{\cancel{16}_8} \times \frac{\cancel{14}^7}{\cancel{9}_3} = \frac{35}{24} = 1\frac{11}{24}$

3. $\frac{\cancel{8}^2}{1} \times \frac{5}{\cancel{4}_1} = \frac{10}{1} = 10$ $\frac{\cancel{12}^6}{1} \times \frac{3}{\cancel{2}_1} = \frac{18}{1} = 18$ $\frac{\cancel{9}^3}{1} \times \frac{7}{\cancel{6}_2} = \frac{21}{2} = 10\frac{1}{2}$ $\frac{7}{1} \times \frac{4}{3} = \frac{28}{3} = 9\frac{1}{3}$

4. $\frac{\cancel{10}^2}{1} \times \frac{6}{\cancel{5}_1} = \frac{12}{1} = 12$ $\frac{\cancel{6}^3}{1} \times \frac{9}{\cancel{4}_2} = \frac{27}{2} = 13\frac{1}{2}$

   $\frac{4}{1} \times \frac{8}{3} = \frac{32}{3} = 10\frac{2}{3}$ $\frac{\cancel{15}^3}{1} \times \frac{11}{\cancel{10}_2} = \frac{33}{2} = 16\frac{1}{2}$

5. $\frac{1}{5} \div \frac{5}{1} =$ $\frac{2}{3} \div \frac{12}{1} =$ $\frac{3}{4} \div \frac{24}{1} =$ $\frac{5}{8} \div \frac{2}{1} =$

   $\frac{1}{5} \times \frac{1}{5} = \frac{1}{25}$ $\frac{\cancel{2}^1}{3} \times \frac{1}{\cancel{12}_6} = \frac{1}{18}$ $\frac{\cancel{3}^1}{4} \times \frac{1}{\cancel{24}_8} = \frac{1}{32}$ $\frac{5}{8} \times \frac{1}{2} = \frac{5}{16}$

6. $\frac{4}{5} \div \frac{9}{1} =$ $\frac{7}{8} \div \frac{7}{1} =$ $\frac{6}{11} \div \frac{3}{1} =$ $\frac{12}{13} \div \frac{8}{1} =$

   $\frac{4}{5} \times \frac{1}{9} = \frac{4}{45}$ $\frac{\cancel{7}^1}{8} \times \frac{1}{\cancel{7}_1} = \frac{1}{8}$ $\frac{\cancel{6}^2}{11} \times \frac{1}{\cancel{3}_1} = \frac{2}{11}$ $\frac{\cancel{12}^3}{13} \times \frac{1}{\cancel{8}_2} = \frac{3}{26}$

7. $\dfrac{9}{10} \div \dfrac{3}{2} =$ $\qquad$ $\dfrac{5}{6} \div \dfrac{14}{3} =$ $\qquad$ $\dfrac{14}{1} \div \dfrac{7}{3} =$ $\qquad$ $\dfrac{20}{1} \div \dfrac{16}{5} =$

$\dfrac{\cancel{9}^{3}}{\cancel{10}_{5}} \times \dfrac{\cancel{2}^{1}}{\cancel{3}_{1}} = \dfrac{3}{5}$ $\qquad$ $\dfrac{5}{\cancel{6}_{2}} \times \dfrac{\cancel{3}^{1}}{14} = \dfrac{5}{28}$ $\qquad$ $\dfrac{\cancel{14}^{2}}{1} \times \dfrac{3}{\cancel{7}_{1}} = \dfrac{6}{1} = 6$ $\qquad$ $\dfrac{\cancel{20}^{5}}{1} \times \dfrac{5}{\cancel{16}_{4}} = \dfrac{25}{4} = 6\dfrac{1}{4}$

8. $\dfrac{11}{2} \div \dfrac{11}{12} =$ $\qquad$ $\dfrac{21}{5} \div \dfrac{21}{1} =$ $\qquad$ $\dfrac{10}{3} \div \dfrac{25}{27} =$ $\qquad$ $\dfrac{14}{5} \div \dfrac{1}{7} =$

$\dfrac{\cancel{11}^{1}}{\cancel{2}_{1}} \times \dfrac{\cancel{12}^{6}}{\cancel{11}_{1}} = \dfrac{6}{1} = 6$ $\qquad$ $\dfrac{\cancel{21}^{1}}{5} \times \dfrac{1}{\cancel{21}_{1}} = \dfrac{1}{5}$ $\qquad$ $\dfrac{\cancel{10}^{2}}{\cancel{3}_{1}} \times \dfrac{\cancel{27}^{9}}{\cancel{25}_{5}} = \dfrac{18}{5} = 3\dfrac{3}{5}$ $\qquad$ $\dfrac{14}{5} \times \dfrac{7}{1} = \dfrac{98}{5} = 19\dfrac{3}{5}$

9. $\dfrac{20}{9} \div \dfrac{8}{3} =$ $\qquad$ $\dfrac{27}{8} \div \dfrac{21}{4} =$ $\qquad$ $\dfrac{7}{3} \div \dfrac{14}{9} =$ $\qquad$ $\dfrac{35}{6} \div \dfrac{25}{8} =$

$\dfrac{\cancel{20}^{5}}{\cancel{9}_{3}} \times \dfrac{\cancel{3}^{1}}{\cancel{8}_{2}} = \dfrac{5}{6}$ $\qquad$ $\dfrac{\cancel{27}^{9}}{\cancel{8}_{2}} \times \dfrac{\cancel{4}^{1}}{\cancel{21}_{7}} = \dfrac{9}{14}$ $\qquad$ $\dfrac{\cancel{7}^{1}}{\cancel{3}_{1}} \times \dfrac{\cancel{9}^{3}}{\cancel{14}_{2}} = \dfrac{3}{2} = 1\dfrac{1}{2}$ $\qquad$ $\dfrac{\cancel{35}^{7}}{\cancel{6}_{3}} \times \dfrac{\cancel{8}^{4}}{\cancel{25}_{5}} = \dfrac{28}{15} = 1\dfrac{13}{15}$

10. $4\dfrac{1}{2} \div 3 =$

$\dfrac{9}{2} \div \dfrac{3}{1} =$

$\dfrac{\cancel{9}^{3}}{2} \times \dfrac{1}{\cancel{3}_{1}} = \dfrac{3}{2} = 1\dfrac{1}{2}$ ft.

11. $20 \div \dfrac{1}{4} =$

$\dfrac{20}{1} \times \dfrac{4}{1} = \dfrac{80}{1} = 80$ cans

12. $24\dfrac{1}{2} \div 3\dfrac{1}{2} =$

$\dfrac{49}{2} \div \dfrac{7}{2} =$

$\dfrac{\cancel{49}^{7}}{\cancel{2}_{1}} \times \dfrac{\cancel{2}^{1}}{\cancel{7}_{1}} = \dfrac{7}{1} = 7$ strips

13. $18\dfrac{3}{4} \div 5 =$

$\dfrac{75}{4} \div \dfrac{5}{1} =$

$\dfrac{\cancel{75}^{15}}{4} \times \dfrac{1}{\cancel{5}_{1}} = \dfrac{15}{4} = 3\dfrac{3}{4}$ lb.

14. $13\dfrac{1}{2} \div \dfrac{3}{8} =$

$\dfrac{\cancel{27}^{9}}{\cancel{2}_{1}} \times \dfrac{\cancel{8}^{4}}{\cancel{3}_{1}} = \dfrac{36}{1} = 36$ slices

15. $16 \div 2\dfrac{1}{3} =$

$\dfrac{16}{1} \div \dfrac{7}{3} =$

$\dfrac{16}{1} \times \dfrac{3}{7} = \dfrac{48}{7} = 6\dfrac{6}{7}$ $\qquad$ The tailor can make 6 pairs of trousers.

ANSWERS AND SOLUTIONS—FRACTIONS SKILLS TEST

1. $\frac{2}{3}$

2. $\frac{7}{9}$

3. $\frac{15}{40}$

4. $\frac{28}{6} = 4\frac{4}{6} = 4\frac{2}{3}$

5. $3\frac{5}{8} = \frac{29}{8}$

6. $18 \div 36 = \frac{\overset{1}{\cancel{18}}}{1} \times \frac{1}{\underset{2}{\cancel{36}}} = \frac{1}{2}$ yard

7. $9\frac{6}{7}$

8. $11\frac{7}{5} = 12\frac{2}{5}$

9. $\begin{array}{r} 1\frac{5}{12} \\ + \ 4\frac{9}{12} \\ \hline 5\frac{14}{12} = 6\frac{2}{12} = 6\frac{1}{6} \end{array}$

10. $\begin{array}{r} 8\frac{12}{18} \\ 3\frac{14}{18} \\ + \ 2\frac{9}{18} \\ \hline 13\frac{35}{18} = 14\frac{17}{18} \end{array}$

11. $\begin{array}{r} 3\frac{1}{2} = 3\frac{2}{4} \\ + \ 5\frac{3}{4} = 5\frac{3}{4} \\ \hline 8\frac{5}{4} = 9\frac{1}{4} \text{ hrs.} \end{array}$

12. $\begin{array}{r} 64\frac{1}{2} = 64\frac{4}{8} \\ + \ 5\frac{7}{8} = \ 5\frac{7}{8} \\ \hline 69\frac{11}{8} = 70\frac{3}{8} \text{ in.} \end{array}$

13. $4\frac{4}{12} = 4\frac{1}{3}$

14. $\begin{array}{r} 7\frac{10}{16} \\ - \ 2\frac{5}{16} \\ \hline 5\frac{5}{16} \end{array}$

15. $\begin{array}{r} 11\frac{7}{7} \\ - \ 9\frac{3}{7} \\ \hline 2\frac{4}{7} \end{array}$

16. $\begin{array}{r} 3\frac{11}{9} \\ - \ 2\frac{5}{9} \\ \hline 1\frac{6}{9} = 1\frac{2}{3} \end{array}$

17. $\begin{array}{r} 8\frac{10}{15} = 7\frac{25}{15} \\ - \ 2\frac{12}{15} = 2\frac{12}{15} \\ \hline 5\frac{13}{15} \end{array}$

18. $\begin{array}{r} 5\frac{1}{3} = 5\frac{2}{6} = 4\frac{8}{6} \\ - \ 2\frac{1}{2} = 2\frac{3}{6} = 2\frac{3}{6} \\ \hline 2\frac{5}{6} \text{ yd.} \end{array}$

19. $\begin{array}{r} 132 \ = 131\frac{4}{4} \\ - \ \ 8\frac{3}{4} = \ \ 8\frac{3}{4} \\ \hline 123\frac{1}{4} \text{ lb.} \end{array}$

20. $\frac{3}{5} \times \frac{4}{7} = \frac{12}{35}$

21. $\frac{1}{2} \times \frac{5}{\underset{2}{\cancel{6}}} \times \frac{\overset{1}{\cancel{3}}}{4} = \frac{5}{16}$

22. $\dfrac{\cancel{9}^{3}}{\cancel{10}_{1}} \times \dfrac{\cancel{20}^{2}}{\cancel{21}_{7}} = \dfrac{6}{7}$

23. $\dfrac{\cancel{16}^{8}}{1} \times \dfrac{5}{\cancel{6}_{3}} = \dfrac{40}{3} = 13\dfrac{1}{3}$

24. $\dfrac{3}{\cancel{4}_{1}} \times \dfrac{\cancel{16}^{4}}{5} = \dfrac{12}{5} = 2\dfrac{2}{5}$

25. $\dfrac{\cancel{14}^{2}}{\cancel{9}_{3}} \times \dfrac{\cancel{24}^{8}}{\cancel{7}_{1}} = \dfrac{16}{3} = 5\dfrac{1}{3}$

26. $3 \times 62\dfrac{1}{2} =$

$\dfrac{3}{1} \times \dfrac{125}{2} = \dfrac{375}{2} = 187\dfrac{1}{2}$ lb.

27. $4\dfrac{2}{3} \times 2.40 =$

$\dfrac{14}{\cancel{3}_{1}} \times \dfrac{\overset{.80}{\cancel{2.40}}}{1} = \$11.20$

28. $\dfrac{\cancel{3}^{1}}{8} \times \dfrac{7}{\cancel{6}_{2}} = \dfrac{7}{16}$

29. $\dfrac{\cancel{9}^{3}}{1} \times \dfrac{11}{\cancel{6}_{2}} = \dfrac{33}{2} = 16\dfrac{1}{2}$

30. $\dfrac{3}{4} \div \dfrac{2}{1} =$

$\dfrac{3}{4} \times \dfrac{1}{2} = \dfrac{3}{8}$

31. $\dfrac{3}{10} \div \dfrac{16}{5} =$

$\dfrac{3}{\cancel{10}_{2}} \times \dfrac{\cancel{5}^{1}}{16} = \dfrac{3}{32}$

32. $\dfrac{22}{15} \div \dfrac{26}{9} =$

$\dfrac{\cancel{22}^{11}}{\cancel{15}_{5}} \times \dfrac{\cancel{9}^{3}}{\cancel{26}_{13}} = \dfrac{33}{65}$

33. $5\dfrac{1}{4} \div 3 = \dfrac{21}{4} \div \dfrac{3}{1} =$

$\dfrac{\cancel{21}^{7}}{4} \times \dfrac{1}{\cancel{3}_{1}} = \dfrac{7}{4} = 1\dfrac{3}{4}$ yd.

34. $24 \div \dfrac{3}{4} =$

$\dfrac{\cancel{24}^{8}}{1} \times \dfrac{4}{\cancel{3}_{1}} = \dfrac{32}{1} = 32$ cans

DECIMALS

UNDERSTANDING DECIMALS

Decimals are special kinds of fractions. We use decimals every day when we handle money. A penny, written as $.01, is a decimal. It is also a fraction and represents *one hundredth* of a dollar. Thirty cents, written as $.30, is a decimal and a fraction which represents *thirty hundredths* or, if you reduce it, *three tenths* of a dollar.

There are two main differences between decimals and fractions. First, we do not write the denominators (bottom numbers) of decimals. Second, only certain numbers can be denominators for decimals. Any whole number except zero is an acceptable denominator for a fraction. The only numbers that work as denominators for decimals are 10, 100, 1000, 10,000 and so forth, but, again, we never write these denominators. The name of a decimal is determined by the number of places occupied to the right of the decimal point. Any digit at the left of the decimal point is in a whole number position. Any number to the right of the decimal point is in a decimal position.

The chart below gives the names of the first six decimal places as well as examples and the examples written as proper fractions.

Number of Places		Decimal Name	Example		Proper Fraction
one place	=	tenths	.7	=	$\frac{7}{10}$
two places	=	hundredths	.23	=	$\frac{23}{100}$
three places	=	thousandths	.016	=	$\frac{16}{1000}$
four places	=	ten-thousandths	.0037	=	$\frac{37}{10,000}$
five places	=	hundred-thousandths	.00008	=	$\frac{8}{100,000}$
six places	=	millionths	.000125	=	$\frac{125}{1,000,000}$

The decimal point is a separation between whole numbers and decimal fractions. The point is not a place. *Mixed decimals* are numbers with both whole numbers and decimals. A decimal point separates the two parts. For example 25.6 is a mixed decimal. We read it as twenty-five and six tenths. 25 is the whole number and .6 is the decimal.

READING DECIMALS

To read a decimal or a mixed decimal, first find the decimal point. Any digits to the *left* of the decimal point form a whole number. Any digits to the *right* of the decimal point form a decimal fraction. Read the whole number. Say "and" for the decimal point. Read the decimal fraction according to the number of places at the right of the point. Study the following examples carefully.

EXAMPLE: Read .038

Step 1.   Find the decimal point. Every digit is to the right of the decimal point. There is no whole number.

Step 2.   Count the number of places. The decimal has three places. Three places are thousandths.

Step 3.   Read .038 as "thirty-eight thousandths."

EXAMPLE: Read 20.0007

Step 1.   Find the decimal point. There are two digits to the left of the point. The digits at the left are the whole number twenty.

Step 2.   Count the digits to the right of the point. There are four digits to the right. Four digits are ten-thousandths.

Step 3.   Read 20.0007 as "twenty and seven ten-thousandths."

Write each of the following decimals or mixed decimals in words:

1.   .3 =   .9 =

2.   .14 =   .08 =

3.   6.2 =   4.03 =

4.   .005 =   .092 =

5.   36.01 =   9.54 =

6.   .0058 =   2.0003 =

7.   .349 =   30.006 =

8.   720.4 =   .00487 =

9.   .0249 =   .00052 =

10.   .000006 =   .000048 =

Answers begin on page 154.

WRITING DECIMALS

To write decimals from words, first decide how many places you need. Use zeros for any places that are not occupied. Use a decimal point to replace the word *and* in a mixed decimal. Study the following examples carefully.

EXAMPLE: Write fourteen thousandths as a decimal.

Step 1.   Thousandths require three places.

Step 2.   Fourteen uses two places. Hold the first place with a zero.   *Answer:*   .014

EXAMPLE: Write twenty and five ten-thousandths as a mixed decimal.

Step 1.   The whole number twenty requires two places to the left of the point. Ten-thousandths require four places to the right of the point.

Step 2. Five uses only one of the decimal places. Hold the first three places with zeros.

Answer: 20.0005

Write the following as decimals or mixed decimals.

1. three tenths =   three hundredths =

2. six thousandths =   twenty-four thousandths =

3. eight ten-thousandths =   five millionths =

4. one hundred twelve thousandths =

5. sixty and seventy-five thousandths =

6. nine hundred forty and two thousandths =

7. seventeen and thirty-eight hundred-thousandths =

8. two thousand five hundred thirty and four tenths =

9. one and two hundred sixty-four ten-thousandths =

10. nine and eight hundred twenty-seven millionths =

Answers begin on page 154.

CHANGING DECIMALS TO FRACTIONS

As you learned, decimals are special kinds of fractions. It is easy to change a decimal (or a mixed decimal) to a common fraction (or a mixed number). Write the digits in the decimal as the top number of a fraction. Write the bottom number of the fraction according to the number of places in the decimal. Then reduce the fraction.

EXAMPLE: Change .04 to a common fraction and reduce.

Step 1.   Write 4 as the top number. It is not necessary to write the zero because it has no value.

$\dfrac{4}{}$

Step 2.   Two decimal places are hundredths. Write 100 as the bottom number.

$\dfrac{4}{100}$

Step 3.   Reduce $\dfrac{4}{100}$ by 4.

$\dfrac{4}{100} = \dfrac{1}{25}$

EXAMPLE: Change 6.8 to a mixed number and reduce.

Step 1.   Write 6 as a whole number and 8 as the top number of the fraction.

$6\dfrac{8}{}$

Step 2.   One decimal place is tenths. Write 10 as the bottom number.

$6\dfrac{8}{10}$

Step 3.   Reduce $\dfrac{8}{10}$ by 2.

$6\dfrac{8}{10} = 6\dfrac{4}{5}$

Write each of the following as a common fraction or a mixed number and reduce.

1.   .5 =   .36 =   .15 =

2.   .025 =   .002 =   .375 =

3.   4.2 =   10.05 =   3.065 =

4.   .0045 =   .00125 =   .000002 =

5. 6.014 =   200.84 =   100.8 =

Answers begin on page 155.

CHANGING FRACTIONS TO DECIMALS

The line which separates the top number from the bottom number in a fraction means to divide. The fraction $\frac{1}{2}$ means "one divided by 2." To change a common fraction to a decimal, divide the bottom number into the top number. Place a decimal point and zeros to the right of the top number. Sometimes one zero will be enough. Usually two are necessary.

EXAMPLE: Change $\frac{1}{2}$ to a decimal.

Step 1.   Divide 2 into 1.

Step 2.   Place a decimal point and a zero to the right of 1.

Step 3.   Divide and bring the decimal point up into the answer. Notice that in this example one zero was enough.

$$\begin{array}{r} .5 \\ 2\overline{)1.0} \\ \underline{1\,0} \end{array}$$

EXAMPLE: Change $\frac{2}{25}$ to a decimal.

Step 1.   Divide 25 into 2.

Step 2.   Place a decimal point and two zeros to the right of 2. One zero is not enough. 25 will not divide into 20.

Step 3.   Divide and bring the decimal point up into the answer. Notice that in this example we put a zero in the tenths place because 25 cannot divide into 20.

$$\begin{array}{r} .08 \\ 25\overline{)2.00} \\ \underline{2\,00} \end{array}$$

EXAMPLE: Change $\frac{2}{9}$ to a decimal.

Step 1.   Divide 9 into 2.

Step 2.   Place a decimal point and two zeros to the right of 2.

Step 3.   Divide and bring the decimal point up into the answer. Notice that in this example the division does not come

$$\begin{array}{r} .22\frac{2}{9} \\ 9\overline{)2.00} \\ \underline{1\,8} \\ 20 \\ \underline{18} \\ 2 \end{array}$$

out even. If we added more zeros, the answer would still not come out even. After two decimal places, write the remainder as a fraction over the number you divided by. Reduce this fraction if possible.

Change each of the following to decimals.

1. $\frac{3}{4} =$ $\frac{4}{5} =$ $\frac{3}{8} =$ $\frac{2}{3} =$

2. $\frac{7}{9} =$ $\frac{5}{6} =$ $\frac{5}{8} =$ $\frac{1}{3} =$

3. $\frac{7}{10} =$ $\frac{3}{7} =$ $\frac{1}{12} =$ $\frac{1}{20} =$

Answers begin on page 155.

COMPARING DECIMALS

PROBLEM: Which of the following is longer, a piece of metal that is .06 inch long or a piece of metal that is .4 inch long?

SOLUTION: Give each decimal the same number of decimal places. Then decide which decimal is larger.

Step 1. At the right of .4 place a zero. This does not change its value because 4 is still in the tenths place.

Step 2. Compare .06 and .40. Forty hundredths is larger than six hundredths. The piece of metal which measures .4 inch is longer.

EXAMPLE: Which is larger, .3 or .097?

Step 1.   Give each decimal the same number of places. At the right of .3 place two zeros.

Step 2.   Compare .300 and .097. Three hundred thousandths is larger than ninety-seven thousandths.

Underline the larger decimal in each of the following pairs.

1.   .08 or .008   .101 or .11   .06 or .601

2.   .0013 or .03   .92 or .902   .625 or .65

3.   .071 or .17   .1023 or .012   .05 or .0075

4.   .304 or .32   .0704 or .47   .0019 or .001

Answers begin on page 155.

ADDING DECIMALS

PROBLEM: The distance from Mr. Munro's home to the gas station is .9 mile. The distance from the gas station to Mr. Munro's factory is .7 mile. What is the distance from Mr. Munro's home to the factory by way of the gas station?

SOLUTION: Add the decimals.

Step 1.   Line up the decimals with *point under point*.

Step 2.   Add and bring down the decimal point. Notice that nine tenths and seven tenths add to give a two-digit sum. Only one digit can go in the tenths column. Carry the other digit to the next column, the units.

$$\begin{array}{r} .9 \\ + .7 \\ \hline 1.6 \text{ mi.} \end{array}$$

PROBLEM: A carton weighs two pounds. The contents of the carton weigh 6.5 pounds. What is the combined weight of the carton and the contents?

SOLUTION: Add the numbers.

Step 1.   Line up the numbers with *point under point*. Remember that any whole number is understood to have a decimal point at its right.

$$\begin{array}{r} 2. \\ +\ 6.5 \\ \hline 8.5 \text{ pounds} \end{array}$$

Step 2.   Add and bring down the decimal point.

Add the following.

1.   .3 + .4 + .7 =   .08 + .9 + .263 =

2.   .084 + 12 + 2.65 =   3.4 + .034 + .34 =

3.   9.006 + .49 + 3 =   1.26 + 21 + .044 =

4.   23 + 2.67 + .358 =   .0056 + 7.203 + 4.1 =

5.   3.2 + 16 + .48 =   .2 + 2 + .002 =

Answers begin on page 155.

Applying Addition of Decimals Skills

In the following problems watch for key words such as *total*, *sum*, and *altogether*. Put the correct label such as $ or meters next to each answer.

---

6. At the grocery Ethel bought 1.75 pounds of roast beef, 3 pounds of cheese, and 2.4 pounds of ground beef. Find the total weight of her purchases.

7. In 1800 there were 5.3 million people living in the United States. In 1900 there were 70.6 million more people than in 1800. Find the U.S. population in 1900.

8. Monday morning Tom drove 101.3 miles. Monday afternoon he drove 89.6 miles. Monday night he drove 104.2 miles. How many miles did Tom drive altogether on Monday?

9. The distance from Los Angeles to San Francisco is 402.7 miles. The distance from San Francisco to Seattle is 1,460.8 miles. Find the total distance from Los Angeles to Seattle by way of San Francisco.

10. Mike mailed three packages. One of them weighed .65 kilograms, another weighed 4.2 kilograms, and the third one weighed 3.85 kilograms. What was the combined weight of the three packages?

Answers begin on page 156.

SUBTRACTING DECIMALS

PROBLEM: The price of a gallon of gasoline went from 89.6¢ to 94¢.
            By how much did the price increase?

SOLUTION: Subtract the old price from the new price.

Step 1.   Put the larger number on top and line up point under
          point. Remember that a whole number is understood
          to have a point at its right.

Step 2.   Put a zero at the right of 94. This does not change the
          value of 94, but it helps remind you to borrow.

Step 3.   Borrow, subtract, and bring down the decimal point.

$$
\begin{array}{r}
94.0¢ \\
-\ 89.6 \\
\hline
4.4¢
\end{array}
$$

Subtract the following.

1. $4.7 - 2.79 =$ $8 - 6.23 =$ $.4 - .175 =$

2. $.9 - .2 =$ $14 - 2.078 =$ $.06 - .059 =$

3. $10 - .38 =$ $.7 - .25 =$ $3 - 1.296 =$

4. $3.4 - 2 =$ $12.56 - 4 =$ $80 - .23 =$

Answers begin on page 156.

Applying Subtraction of Decimals Skills

In the following problems watch for phrases that tell you to subtract such as: *How much more? How much less? How much was left?* Give each answer the correct label.

---

5. Robert is 1.65 meters tall. His son John is 1.49 meters tall. How much taller is Robert than John?

6. In one year 41.7 million passengers use Chicago's O'Hare airport. In one year 27.3 million passengers use Atlanta's airport. Find the difference between the number of passengers using Chicago's O'Hare airport and the number using Atlanta's airport.

7. The area of the Soviet Union is 8.65 million square miles. The area of the United States is 3.62 million square miles. How much greater is the area of the Soviet Union than the area of the United States?

8. Steve has a can that contained 8 liters of gasoline. He poured 1.35 liters of the gasoline into his lawn mower. How many liters were left in the can?

9. In 1960, 1.9 million students graduated from high school in the United States. In 1977, 3.2 million students graduated from high school. How many more students graduated in 1977 than in 1960?

Answers begin on page 156.

10. The distance from Jane's house to her job is exactly 10 miles. She drops her children off at school which is 3.6 miles from their house. After she drops the children off, how much farther does Jane have to drive to get to work?

MULTIPLYING DECIMALS BY WHOLE NUMBERS

PROBLEM: One inch contains 2.54 centimeters. How many centimeters are there in six inches?

SOLUTION: Multiply the number of centimeters in one inch by six.

Step 1. Line up the numbers for convenient multiplication. It is not necessary to put point under point.

Step 2. Multiply the numbers as you would multiply whole numbers.

Step 3. Count the number of decimal places in both numbers that you multiplied. Put that total number of places in your answer.

$$
\begin{array}{r}
2.54 \quad \text{(two decimal places)} \\
\times \; 6 \quad \text{(no decimal places)} \\
\hline
15.24 \quad \text{(two decimal places)} \\
\end{array}
$$

15.24 centimeters

Multiply the following.

1. $8 \times 2.28 =$ $71.4 \times 6 =$ $7 \times .445 =$

2. $6.34 \times 9 =$ $3 \times 8.63 =$ $.208 \times 4 =$

3. $12 \times .893 =$ $34.6 \times 15 =$ $20 \times .647 =$

4. $3.07 \times 16 =$ $23 \times 93.9 =$ $.389 \times 18 =$

Answers begin on page 157.

MULTIPLYING DECIMALS BY DECIMALS

PROBLEM: Patrick earns $4.30 an hour. How much does he earn in 7.5 hours?

SOLUTION: Multiply the amount that Patrick earns in one hour by the number of hours.

Step 1.   Line up the numbers for convenient multiplication.

Step 2.   Multiply the numbers as you would multiply whole numbers.

Step 3.   Count the number of decimal places in both numbers that you multiplied. Put that total number of places in your answer.

$$
\begin{array}{r}
\$4.30 \text{ (two places)} \\
\times \quad 7.5 \text{ (one place)} \\
\hline
2\ 150 \\
30\ 10 \\
\hline
\$32.250 \text{ (three places)} \\
\$32.25
\end{array}
$$

Notice that in this problem the answer has three places. However, money has only two places. We drop the last zero to make the answer easier to read.

Sometimes it is necessary to add zeros to an answer.

EXAMPLE: Multiply .03 by .5

Step 1.   Line up the numbers for convenient multiplication.

Step 2. Multiply the numbers as you would multiply whole numbers.

Step 3. Count the number of decimal places in both numbers that you multiplied. Put that total number of places in your answer.

$$\begin{array}{r} .03 \text{ (two places)} \\ \times \quad .5 \text{ (one place)} \\ \hline .015 \text{ (three places)} \end{array}$$

In this example we need three decimal places. We add the zero in order to get three places.

Multiply the following.

5. .7 × 81.6 =   1.18 × .4 =   .92 × .56 =

6. .06 × 4.8 =   54.3 × .09 =   .007 × 2.4 =

7. .515 × 2.3 =   1.4 × 29.4 =   .628 × .13 =

8. .012 × .16 =   2.8 × .027 =   .0016 × .09 =

Answers begin on page 157.

MULTIPLYING DECIMALS BY 10, 100, AND 1000

To multiply a decimal by 10, move the decimal point *one place to the right*.

EXAMPLE: Multiply .37 by 10 $37 \times 10 = 3.7 = 3.7$

To multiply a decimal by 100, move the decimal point *two places to the right*.

EXAMPLE: Multiply 100 by .3

$100 \times .3 = 30 = 30$. Notice that we had to add one zero in order to move the point two places.

To multiply a decimal by 1000, move the decimal point *three places to the right*.

EXAMPLE: Multiply 2.8 by 1000

$2.8 \times 1000 = 2.800 = 2800$. Notice that we had to add two zeros in order to move the point three places.

Write the answer to each of the following.

9. $10 \times .7 =$ $10 \times 2.86 =$ $1.4 \times 10 =$ $.499 \times 10 =$

10. $100 \times 3.2 =$ $100 \times .26 =$ $.387 \times 100 =$ $46.2 \times 100 =$

11. $1000 \times .4 =$ $1000 \times .97 =$ $7.4 \times 1000 =$ $.397 \times 1000 =$

Answers begin on page 158.

Applying Multiplication of Decimals Skills

In the following problems watch for situations that tell you to multiply such as: find the cost of several things when you have the cost of one thing, or find the weight of several things when you know the weight of one thing. Put the correct label beside each answer.

12. On the highway John drives at an average speed of 45.6 miles per hour. How many miles can he drive in 3.5 hours?

13. Cynthia earns $5.20 an hour. How much does she earn for 36.5 hours of work?

14. One can of tomatoes weighs .688 pounds. How much do 24 cans of tomatoes weigh?

15. One yard of material costs $2.70. How much do 4.5 yards of the material cost?

16. An average of 18.4 people walk into Tom's Record Shop every hour. Tom's shop is open 8.5 hours a day. How many people come into Tom's shop on a normal day?

17. One pound equals 0.45 kilograms. Richard weighs 180 pounds. What is Richard's weight in kilograms?

Answers begin on page 158.

DIVIDING DECIMALS BY WHOLE NUMBERS

PROBLEM: David has a board 4.25 yards long. He wants to cut the board into five equal pieces. How long will each piece be?

SOLUTION: Divide the length of the board by 5.

Step 1.   Set the problem up as you would for whole number division.

Step 2.   Divide and bring the decimal point up into the answer directly above its position in the problem.

$$\begin{array}{r} .85 \text{ yd.} \\ 5\overline{)4.25} \\ 4\,0 \\ \hline 25 \\ 25 \\ \hline \end{array}$$

Sometimes you will have to put zeros in your answer.

EXAMPLE:
$$\begin{array}{r} .03 \\ 8\overline{)\,.24} \end{array}$$

The zero holds the tenths place in the answer and shows that the decimal point comes before the tenths.

Divide the following.

1. $9\overline{)32.4}$ $6\overline{)1.62}$ $5\overline{)\,.365}$ $4\overline{)39.2}$

2. $7\overline{)2.772}$ $3\overline{)7.71}$ $8\overline{)363.2}$ $2\overline{)6.16}$

3. $12\overline{)\,.804}$ $27\overline{)31.32}$ $36\overline{)1.908}$ $15\overline{)655.5}$

4. $91\overline{)312.13}$ $52\overline{)2.912}$ $16\overline{)4.912}$ $43\overline{)3.483}$

Answers begin on page 158.

DIVIDING DECIMALS BY DECIMALS

PROBLEM: One mile equals 1.6 kilometers. How many miles are there in 6.72 kilometers?

SOLUTION: Divide 6.72 kilometers by the number of kilometers in one mile.

Step 1.   Set the problem up as you would to divide whole numbers.

$$1.6\overline{)6.72}$$

Step 2.   Change the *divisor* (the number outside the bracket) into a whole number. Move the decimal point to the right as far as it will go in the divisor. In this problem the point moves one place.

$$1.6\overline{)6.72}$$

Step 3.   Change the *dividend* (the number inside the bracket) by moving the decimal point the same number of places to the right that you moved the point in the divisor. In this problem the point moves one place.

$$1.6\overline{)6.7\,2}$$

Step 4.   Bring the point up in the answer directly above its new position in the dividend and divide.

$$\begin{array}{r} 4.2 \text{ miles} \\ 1.6\overline{)6.7\,2} \\ 6\,4 \\ \hline 3\,2 \\ 3\,2 \\ \hline \end{array}$$

This operation often causes students trouble. Be sure that you understand this example well before you try the problems below.

---

5. $.8\overline{)2.88}$ $.9\overline{)42.3}$ $.25\overline{)1.275}$ $.16\overline{).0752}$

6. $.006\overline{).01404}$ $.09\overline{)17.37}$ $.015\overline{).2835}$ $.07\overline{)24.15}$

In the following problems you will need to add zeros to the dividend in order to have enough places to move the decimal point.

7. $.09\overline{)4.5}$ $.014\overline{).84}$ $.03\overline{)7.2}$ $.007\overline{)3.64}$

8. $.06\overline{)48.6}$ $.008\overline{)2.96}$ $.022\overline{)2.86}$ $.013\overline{)5.59}$

Answers begin on page 159.

DIVIDING WHOLE NUMBERS BY DECIMALS

PROBLEM: Mr. Rigby has a hardware store. He wants to package nine pounds of tacks into boxes that each contain .25 pounds of tacks. How many boxes can he fill?

SOLUTION: Divide the total weight of tacks that Mr. Rigby has by the weight each box should contain.

Step 1. Set the problem up as you would to divide whole numbers.

$.25\overline{)9}$

Step 2. Change the *divisor* (the number outside the bracket) into a whole number. Move the decimal point to the right as far as it will go. In this problem the point moves two places.

$.25\overline{)9}$

Step 3. Change the *dividend* (the number inside the bracket) by moving the decimal point the same number of places to the right that you moved the point in the divisor. In this problem the point after the 9 moves two places. Write two zeros to give two places.

$.25\overline{)9.00}$

Step 4. Bring the point up in the answer directly above its new position in the dividend and divide.

$$.25\overline{)9.00} \quad \begin{array}{r} 36. \text{ boxes} \\ \hline 7\,5 \\ \hline 1\,50 \\ 1\,50 \\ \hline \end{array}$$

Divide the following.

9. $.4\overline{)8}$ $.03\overline{)12}$ $.005\overline{)23}$ $.08\overline{)16}$

10. $.009\overline{)54}$ $.28\overline{)644}$ $.06\overline{)75}$ $.12\overline{)492}$

11. $3.2\overline{)1120}$ $4.8\overline{)2880}$ $.016\overline{)368}$ $3.6\overline{)144}$

12. $.042\overline{)336}$ $.21\overline{)105}$ $.058\overline{)522}$ $.064\overline{)768}$

Answers begin on page 160.

DIVIDING DECIMALS BY 10, 100, AND 1000

To divide a decimal by 10, move the decimal point *one place to the left*.

EXAMPLE: $4.7 \div 10 = 4.7 = .47$

To divide a decimal by 100, move the decimal point *two places to the left*.

EXAMPLE: $3.9 \div 100 = 03.9 = .039$ Notice that we had to add a zero in order to move the point two places.

To divide a decimal by 1000, move the decimal point *three places to the left*.

EXAMPLE: $.27 \div 1000 = 000.27 = .00027$ Notice that we had to add three zeros in order to move the point three places.

Write the answer to each of the following.

13. $8.2 \div 10 =$ $.7 \div 10 =$ $1.36 \div 10 =$ $42.8 \div 10 =$

14. $36.5 \div 100 =$ $497 \div 100 =$ $1.2 \div 100 =$ $23.8 \div 100 =$

15. $1.9 \div 1000 =$ $387 \div 1000 =$ $1964 \div 1000 =$ $14.6 \div 1000 =$

Answers begin on page 160.

Applying Division of Decimals Skills

In the following problems watch for words that tell you to divide such as *share*, *cut*, or *split*. Put the thing being divided inside the $)$ sign. Give every answer the correct label.

---

16. Andrew has a board 1.68 meters long. He wants to cut it into four equal pieces. How long will each piece be?

17. There are 2.54 centimeters in an inch. How many inches are there in 60.96 centimeters?

18.   The price of 3.8 pounds of chicken is $3.42. What is the price of one pound of chicken?

19.   Mr. Hoffman drove 182 miles in 3.5 hours. What was his average speed in miles per hour?

20.   Mary earns $136.80 in one week. She earns $3.80 an hour. How many hours does she work in one week?

21.   The price of 6.5 yards of lumber is $7.15. Find the price of one yard of lumber?

22.   Jeff sells shoes on commission. In five days Jeff earned $306.15 in commissions. What was his average daily commission?

Answers begin on page 160.

DECIMALS SKILLS TEST

Before going on to percents, try this review of your decimals skills. Check your answers with those beginning on page 161. Then use the Decimals Skills Test Evaluation on page 153 to decide what you need to study more.

1.   Write the decimal .027 in words.

2.   Write the mixed decimal 10.07 in words.

3. Write eight thousandths as a decimal.

4. Write forty and thirty-eight ten-thousandths as a mixed decimal.

5. Change .045 to a common fraction and reduce.

6. Change 3.06 to a mixed number and reduce.

7. Change $\frac{2}{5}$ to a decimal.

8. Change $\frac{4}{7}$ to a decimal.

9. Underline the larger decimal: .06 or .037

10. Underline the larger decimal: .0027 or .005

11. $3.8 + 17 + .039 =$ 12. $.037 + 4.2 + 31 =$

13. Amy carried 4.8 pounds of groceries, 3.75 pounds of books, and 5 pounds of cleaning items from her car to her kitchen. Find the total weight of the things that she carried.

14. $12 - 2.39 =$ 15. $.8 - .673 =$ 16. $6 - .582 =$

17. Dorothy is 1.48 meters tall. Her daughter Renee is 1.56 meters
     tall. How much taller is Renee than her mother?

18. $14 \times 2.56 =$ 19. $.28 \times 4.9 =$ 20. $.083 \times 2.7 =$

21. $10 \times 4.6 =$ 22. $3.257 \times 100 =$ 23. $1000 \times .38 =$

24. One can of soup weighs .485 pounds. Find the weight of 16
     cans of soup.

25. $8\overline{)45.6}$ 26. $6\overline{).258}$ 27. $.7\overline{)3.43}$

28. $.09\overline{)7.2}$ 29. $1.2\overline{)60}$ 30. $.003\overline{)21}$

31. $9.6 \div 10 =$ 32. $387.3 \div 100 =$ 33. $4.73 \div 1000 =$

34. A train traveled 312 miles in 6.5 hours. What was the average speed of the train in miles per hour?

DECIMALS SKILLS TEST EVALUATION

Problem Number	Practice Pages	Problem Number	Practice Pages
1–2	129–130	18	140–141
3–4	130–131	19–20	141–142
5–6	131–132	21–23	142–143
7–8	133–134	24	143–144
9–10	134–135	25–26	144–145
11–12	135–136	27–28	146–147
13	137	29–30	147–148
14–16	138	31–33	148–149
17	139–140	34	149–150

Passing score: 27 out of 34 problems.
Your score: ___ out of 34 problems.

If you had less than a passing score, review the practice pages for the problems you got wrong. Then repeat this test before going on to the percent unit.

If you had a passing score, correct any problem you got wrong, and go to the percent unit.

ANSWERS AND SOLUTIONS—DECIMALS SKILLS EXERCISES

READING DECIMALS

1. three tenths   nine tenths

2. fourteen hundredths   eight hundredths

3. six and two tenths   four and three hundredths

4. five thousandths   ninety-two thousandths

5. thirty-six and one hundredth   nine and fifty-four hundredths

6. fifty-eight ten-thousandths   two and three ten-thousandths

7. three hundred forty-nine thousandths   thirty and six thousandths

8. seven hundred twenty and four tenths   four hundred eighty-seven hundred-thousandths

9. two hundred forty-nine ten-thousandths   fifty-two hundred-thousandths

10. six millionths   forty-eight millionths

WRITING DECIMALS

1. .3   .03

2. .006   .024

3. .0008   .000005

4. .112

5. 60.075

6. 940.002

7. 17.00038

8. 2,530.4

9. 1.0264

10. 9.000827

CHANGING DECIMALS TO FRACTIONS

1. $\dfrac{5}{10} = \dfrac{1}{2}$ $\dfrac{36}{100} = \dfrac{9}{25}$ $\dfrac{15}{100} = \dfrac{3}{20}$

2. $\dfrac{25}{1000} = \dfrac{1}{40}$ $\dfrac{2}{1000} = \dfrac{1}{500}$ $\dfrac{375}{1000} = \dfrac{3}{8}$

3. $4\dfrac{2}{10} = 4\dfrac{1}{5}$ $10\dfrac{5}{100} = 10\dfrac{1}{20}$ $3\dfrac{65}{1000} = 3\dfrac{13}{200}$

4. $\dfrac{45}{10,000} = \dfrac{9}{2000}$ $\dfrac{125}{100,000} = \dfrac{1}{800}$ $\dfrac{2}{1,000,000} = \dfrac{1}{500,000}$

5. $6\dfrac{14}{1000} = 6\dfrac{7}{500}$ $200\dfrac{84}{100} = 200\dfrac{21}{25}$ $100\dfrac{8}{10} = 100\dfrac{4}{5}$

CHANGING FRACTIONS TO DECIMALS

1. $\dfrac{3}{4} = \overset{.75}{4\overline{)3.00}}$ $\dfrac{4}{5} = \overset{.8}{5\overline{)4.0}}$ $\dfrac{3}{8} = \overset{.37\frac{1}{2}}{8\overline{)3.00}}$ or $.375$ $\dfrac{2}{3} = \overset{.66\frac{2}{3}}{3\overline{)2.00}}$

2. $\dfrac{7}{9} = \overset{.77\frac{7}{9}}{9\overline{)7.00}}$ $\dfrac{5}{6} = \overset{.83\frac{1}{3}}{6\overline{)5.00}}$ $\dfrac{5}{8} = \overset{.62\frac{1}{2}}{8\overline{)5.00}}$ or $.625$ $\dfrac{1}{3} = \overset{.33\frac{1}{3}}{3\overline{)1.00}}$

3. $\dfrac{7}{10} = \overset{.7}{10\overline{)7.0}}$ $\dfrac{3}{7} = \overset{.42\frac{6}{7}}{7\overline{)3.00}}$ $\dfrac{1}{12} = \overset{.08\frac{1}{3}}{12\overline{)1.00}}$ $\dfrac{1}{20} = \overset{.05}{20\overline{)1.00}}$

COMPARING DECIMALS

1. .08   .11   .601

2. .03   .92   .65

3. .17   .1023   .05

4. .32   .47   .0019

ADDING DECIMALS

1.
```
     .3          .08
     .4          .9
  +  .7       +  .263
    1.4         1.243
```
2.
```
    .084        3.4
  12.           .034
+  2.65      +  .34
  14.734       3.774
```

3.
```
   9.006       1.26
    .49       21.
+  3.       +  .044
  12.496      22.304
```
4.
```
  23.          .0056
   2.67        7.203
+  .358     +  4.1
  26.028      11.3086
```

5. $\begin{array}{r} 3.2 \\ 16. \\ +\ .48 \\ \hline 19.68 \end{array}$ $\begin{array}{r} .2 \\ 2. \\ +\ .002 \\ \hline 2.202 \end{array}$ 6. $\begin{array}{r} 1.75 \\ 3. \\ +\ 2.4 \\ \hline 7.15 \end{array}$ pounds

7. $\begin{array}{r} 5.3 \\ +\ 70.6 \\ \hline 75.9 \end{array}$ million   8. $\begin{array}{r} 101.3 \\ 89.6 \\ +\ 104.2 \\ \hline 295.1 \end{array}$ miles

9. $\begin{array}{r} 402.7 \\ +\ 1,460.8 \\ \hline 1,863.5 \end{array}$ miles   10. $\begin{array}{r} .65 \\ 4.2 \\ +\ 3.85 \\ \hline 8.70 \end{array}$ kilograms

SUBTRACTING DECIMALS

1. $\begin{array}{r} 4.70 \\ -\ 2.79 \\ \hline 1.91 \end{array}$ $\begin{array}{r} 8.00 \\ -\ 6.23 \\ \hline 1.77 \end{array}$ $\begin{array}{r} .400 \\ -\ .175 \\ \hline .225 \end{array}$

2. $\begin{array}{r} .9 \\ -\ .2 \\ \hline .7 \end{array}$ $\begin{array}{r} 14.000 \\ -\ 2.078 \\ \hline 11.922 \end{array}$ $\begin{array}{r} .060 \\ -\ .059 \\ \hline .001 \end{array}$

3. $\begin{array}{r} 10.00 \\ -\ .38 \\ \hline 9.62 \end{array}$ $\begin{array}{r} .70 \\ -\ .25 \\ \hline .45 \end{array}$ $\begin{array}{r} 3.000 \\ -\ 1.296 \\ \hline 1.704 \end{array}$

4. $\begin{array}{r} 3.4 \\ -\ 2.0 \\ \hline 1.4 \end{array}$ $\begin{array}{r} 12.56 \\ -\ 4.00 \\ \hline 8.56 \end{array}$ $\begin{array}{r} 80.00 \\ -\ .23 \\ \hline 79.77 \end{array}$

5. $\begin{array}{r} 1.65 \\ -\ 1.49 \\ \hline 0.16 \end{array}$ meters   6. $\begin{array}{r} 41.7 \\ -\ 27.3 \\ \hline 14.4 \end{array}$ million

7. $\begin{array}{r} 8.65 \\ -\ 3.62 \\ \hline 5.03 \end{array}$ million square miles   8. $\begin{array}{r} 8.00 \\ -\ 1.35 \\ \hline 6.65 \end{array}$ liters

9. $\begin{array}{r} 3.2 \\ -\ 1.9 \\ \hline 1.3 \end{array}$ million students   10. $\begin{array}{r} 10.0 \\ -\ 3.6 \\ \hline 6.4 \end{array}$ miles

MULTIPLYING DECIMALS

1.
```
   2.28        71.4         .445
 ×    8       ×   6        ×   7
  18.24       428.4        3.115
```

2.
```
   6.34        8.63         .208
 ×    9       ×   3        ×   4
  57.06       25.89         .832
```

3.
```
    .893       34.6         .647
 ×   12       ×  15        ×  20
  1 786       173 0       12.940
  8 93         346
 10.716       519.0
```

4.
```
   3.07        93.9         .389
 ×  16        ×  23        ×  18
  18 42       281 7        3 112
  30 7        1 878        3 89
  49.12      2,159.7       7.002
```

5.
```
   81.6        1.18          .92
 ×  .7        ×  .4        ×  .56
  57.12        .472         552
                            460
                           .5152
```

6.
```
    4.8        54.3          2.4
 ×  .06       ×  .09       ×  .007
   .288       4.887         .0168
```

7.
```
    .515       29.4         .628
 ×  2.3       ×  1.4       ×  .13
   1545       11 76        1884
  1 030       29 4          628
  1.1845      41.16        .08164
```

8.
```
    .012        2.8         .0016
 ×  .16       × .027       ×   .09
     72         196        .000144
     12          56
   .00192      .0756
```

9. $10 \times .7 = 7$ $10 \times 2.86 = 28.6$ $1.4 \times 10 = 14$ $.499 \times 10 = 4.99$

10. $100 \times 3.2 = 320$ $100 \times .26 = 26$ $.387 \times 100 = 38.7$ $46.2 \times 100 = 4,620$

11. $1000 \times .4 = 400$ $1000 \times .97 = 970$ $7.4 \times 1000 = 7,400$ $.397 \times 1000 = 397$

12.
```
     45.6
  ×   3.5
    22 80
   136 8
   159.6Ø miles
```

13.
```
     36.5
  ×   5.20
    7 300
  182 5
  $189.80Ø
```

14.
```
     .688
  ×    24
    2 752
   13 76
   16.512 pounds
```

15.
```
    $2.70
  ×   4.5
    1 350
   10 80
   $12.15Ø
```

16.
```
     18.4
  ×   8.5
     9 20
   147 2
   156.4Ø people
```

17.
```
      180
  ×    .45
     9 00
    72 0
    81.0Ø kilograms
```

DIVIDING DECIMALS

1.
```
        3.6            .27           .073            9.8
    9)32.4        6)1.62        5).365          4)39.2
      27            1 2           35              36
       5 4            42           15               3 2
       5 4            42           15               3 2
```

2.
```
       .396          2.57          45.4            3.08
    7)2.772       3)7.71        8)363.2         2)6.16
      2 1            6            32              6
       67            1 7          43             0 16
       63            1 5          40               16
       42            21            3 2
       42            21            3 2
```

3.
```
       .067              1.16              .053              43.7
   12).804          27)31.32          36)1.908          15)655.5
      72               27                1 80              60
      ──               ──               ────              ──
      84                4 3              108               55
      84                2 7             108                45
      ──               ───              ───              ──
                       1 62                               10 5
                       1 62                               10 5
                       ────                               ────
```

4.
```
      3.43               .056              .307              .081
   91)312.13         52)2.912          16)4.912          43)3.483
      273               2 60              4 8              3 44
      ───               ────              ──               ───
       39 1             312              112                43
       36 4             312              112                43
       ────             ───              ───               ──
        2 73
        2 73
        ────
```

5.
```
        3.6                 4 7              5.1               .47
    .8)2.8 8          .9)42.3        .25)1.27 5        .16).07 52
       2 4               36              1 25               6 4
       ───               ──             ────               ───
        4 8               6 3             2 5               1 12
        4 8               6 3             2 5               1 12
        ───               ───            ───               ────
```

6.
```
         2.34              1 93              18.9              3 45
  .006).014 04      .09)17.37       .015).283 5         .07)24.15
        12                 9               15                 21
       ────                ──             ───                ──
         2 0               8 3            133                3 1
         1 8               8 1            120                2 8
        ────               ───           ───                ───
          24                27            13 5                35
          24                27            13 5                35
         ───               ───           ────                ──
```

7.
```
         50                 60              2 40               520
  .09)4.50         .014).840         .03)7.20          .007)3.640
       4 5                 84               6                 3 5
       ───                 ──              ──                 ───
                                          1 2                 14
                                          12                  14
                                          ──                  ──
```

8.
```
        8 10               370              130                430
  .06)48.60        .008)2.960       .022)2.860        .013)5.590
      48                   2 4              2 2                5 2
      ──                   ───              ───                ───
       6                    56               66                39
       6                    56               66                39
       ─                    ──               ──                ──
```

9.
```
        2 0              4 00             4,600             2 00
   .4)8.0,        .03)12.00,        .005)23.000       .08)16.00,
      8               12                 20                16
                                         3 0
                                         3 0
```

10.
```
      6,000            2,300             1,250            4,100
  .009)54.000      .28)644.00,       .06)75.00,      .12)492.00,
       54               56                 6               48
                        84                15               12
                        84                12               12
                                          3 0
                                          3 0
```

11.
```
       35 0            60 0             23,000             4 0
  3.2)1120.0,     4.8)2880.0,      .016)368.000      3.6)144.0,
       96              288                32               144
      160                                48
      160                                48
```

12.
```
       8,000            5 00             9,000            12,000
  .042)336.000     .21)105.00,      .058)522.000     .064)768.000,
       336             105                522               64
                                                          128
                                                          128
```

13. $8.2 \div 10 = .82$ $.7 \div 10 = .07$ $1.36 \div 10 = .136$ $42.8 \div 10 = 4.28$

14. $36.5 \div 100 = .365$ $497 \div 100 = 4.97$ $1.2 \div 100 = .012$ $23.8 \div 100 = .238$

15. $1.9 \div 1000 = .0019$ $387 \div 1000 = .387$ $1964 \div 1000 = 1.964$

$14.6 \div 1000 = .0146$

16.
```
       .42 meter
    4)1.68
      1 6
        8
        8
```

17.
```
           24 inches
    2.54)60.96,
         50 8
         10 16
         10 16
```

18.
$$\begin{array}{r} \$\ \ \ .90 \\ 3.8\overline{)\ \$3.4,20} \\ 3\ 4\ 2 \end{array}$$

19.
$$\begin{array}{r} 5\ 2\ \text{mph} \\ 3.5\overline{)182.0,} \\ 175 \\ \hline 7\ 0 \\ 7\ 0 \end{array}$$

20.
$$\begin{array}{r} 36\ \text{hours} \\ 3.80\overline{)136.80,} \\ 114\ 0 \\ \hline 22\ 80 \\ 22\ 80 \end{array}$$

21.
$$\begin{array}{r} \$\ \ 1.10 \\ 6.5\overline{)\$7.1,50} \\ 6\ 5 \\ \hline 6\ 5 \\ 6\ 5 \end{array}$$

22.
$$\begin{array}{r} \$\ 61.23 \\ 5\overline{)\$306.15} \\ 30 \\ \hline 06 \\ 5 \\ \hline 1\ 1 \\ 1\ 0 \\ \hline 15 \\ 15 \end{array}$$

ANSWERS AND SOLUTIONS—DECIMALS SKILLS TEST

1. twenty-seven thousandths

2. ten and seven hundredths

3. .008

4. 40.0038

5. $\dfrac{45}{1000} = \dfrac{9}{200}$

6. $3\dfrac{6}{100} = 3\dfrac{3}{50}$

7.
$$\begin{array}{r} .4 \\ 5\overline{)2.0} \end{array}$$

8.
$$\begin{array}{r} .57\frac{1}{7} \\ 7\overline{)4.00} \end{array}$$

9. .06 or .037

10. .0027 or .005

11.
```
      3.8
     17.
  +   .039
  ─────────
     20.839
```

12.
```
        .037
       4.2
  +  31
  ─────────
     35.237
```

13.
```
      4.8
      3.75
  +  5
  ─────────
     13.55  pounds
```

14.
```
     12.00
  -   2.39
  ─────────
      9.61
```

15.
```
     .800
  -  .673
  ────────
     .127
```

16.
```
     6.000
  -   .582
  ─────────
     5.418
```

17.
```
     1.56
  -  1.48
  ────────
      .08  meters
```

18.
```
       2.56
  ×      14
  ─────────
      10 24
      25 6
  ─────────
      35.84
```

19.
```
       4.9
  ×    .28
  ─────────
       392
        98
  ─────────
     1.372
```

20.
```
       .083
  ×     2.7
  ─────────
       581
       166
  ─────────
      .2241
```

21. $10 \times 4.6 = 46$

22. $3.257 \times 100 = 325.7$

23. $1000 \times .38 = 380$

24.
```
       .485
  ×      16
  ─────────
      2 910
      4 85
  ─────────
     7.76Ø  pounds
```

25.
```
        5.7
    ┌────────
  8 )45.6
     40
     ────
      5 6
      5 6
```

26.
```
        .043
    ┌────────
  6 ).258
      24
      ────
       18
       18
```

27.
```
        4.9
    ┌────────
  .7 )3.4 3
      2 8
      ────
        6 3
        6 3
```

28.
```
         80
     ┌────────
  .09 )7.20
        7 2
```

29.
$$
\begin{array}{r}
5\,0 \\
1.2\,)\overline{60.0} \\
\underline{60}
\end{array}
$$

30.
$$
\begin{array}{r}
7{,}000 \\
.003\,)\overline{21.000} \\
\underline{21}
\end{array}
$$

31. $9.6 \div 10 = .96$

32. $387.3 \div 100 = 3.873$

33. $4.73 \div 1000 = .00473$

34.
$$
\begin{array}{r}
4\,8 \text{ mph} \\
6.5\,)\overline{312.0} \\
\underline{260} \\
52\,0 \\
\underline{52\,0}
\end{array}
$$

PERCENT

UNDERSTANDING PERCENT

Percent is a common term in the business world. Percent is used to measure interest rates, commissions, mark-ups, discounts, and tax rates. In the unit on decimals you learned that decimals are special kinds of fractions. Percents are even more special kinds of fractions. The only denominator that percent uses is 100, but the denominator is not written. The symbol % means "per 100." 25% means 25 things out of 100 things. As a fraction 25% is $\frac{25}{100}$ or $\frac{1}{4}$. As a decimal 25% is .25 or twenty-five hundredths.

CHANGING DECIMALS TO PERCENTS

Decimals and percents are very closely related. To change a decimal into a percent, *move the decimal point two places to the right* and *write a % sign*.

EXAMPLE: Change .15 to a percent. $.15 = .15\% = 15\%$

Since the decimal point moved to the right end of the number, we do not need to write it.

EXAMPLE: Change .4 to a percent. $.4 = .40\% = 40\%$

In order to move the decimal point two places, we had to write a zero.

EXAMPLE: Change .016 to a percent. $.016 = .016\% = 1.6\%$

In this example the decimal point comes in the middle of the percent.

EXAMPLE: Change $.16\frac{2}{3}$ to a percent. $.16\frac{2}{3} = .16\frac{2}{3}\% = 16\frac{2}{3}\%$

Notice that it is not necessary to place a decimal point between a digit and a fraction.

Change each of the following to a percent.

1. .07 =   .75 =   .035 = $.33\frac{1}{3}$ =

2. .9 =   1.5 =   .004 =   .65 =

3. .1 = $.66\frac{2}{3}$ = $.08\frac{1}{3}$ =   .05 =

Answers begin on page 192.

CHANGING PERCENTS TO DECIMALS

To change a percent to a decimal, *move the decimal point two places to the left* and *drop the % sign.*

EXAMPLE: Change 35% to a decimal. $35\% = \underset{\smile}{35.} = .35$

The decimal point that we moved in 35% is understood to be at the right.

EXAMPLE: Change 80% to a decimal. $80\% = \underset{\smile}{80.} = .8$

We can drop the zero in .80 because the zero does not affect the value of the decimal.

EXAMPLE: Change 5.7% to a decimal. $5.7\% = \underset{\smile}{05.7} = .057$

In order to move the decimal point two places, we had to write a zero.

EXAMPLE: Change $83\frac{1}{3}\%$ to a decimal. $83\frac{1}{3}\% = \underset{\smile}{83.\frac{1}{3}} = .83\frac{1}{3}$

The decimal point that we moved in $83\frac{1}{3}\%$ was understood to be between the digit 3 and the fraction.

Change each of the following to a decimal.

1. 9% =   35% =   4.8% = $22\frac{2}{9}\%$ =

2. 60% =   125% =   .3% =   95% =

3. 20% = $33\frac{1}{3}\%$ = $6\frac{1}{4}\%$ =   3% =

Answers begin on page 192.

CHANGING FRACTIONS TO PERCENTS

To change a fraction to a percent, multiply the fraction by 100%.

EXAMPLE: Change $\frac{1}{2}$ to a percent.

$$\frac{1}{2} \times 100\% = \frac{1}{\overset{}{\underset{1}{2}}} \times \frac{\overset{50}{\cancel{100}}\%}{1} = 50\%$$

EXAMPLE: Change $\frac{5}{9}$ to a percent.

$$\frac{5}{9} \times 100\% = \frac{5}{9} \times \frac{100\%}{1} = \frac{500}{9} = 55\frac{5}{9}\%$$

Another method for changing a fraction to a percent is to first change the fraction into a decimal. Then change the decimal to a percent.

EXAMPLE: Change $\frac{1}{2}$ to a percent.

Step 1.   Change $\frac{1}{2}$ to a decimal.

$$2\overline{)1.0}^{\,.5}$$

Step 2.   Change .50 to a percent.

$$.5 = .50 = 50\%$$

These methods are equally acceptable. Use the method that you prefer in the next problems.

Change each of the following to a percent.

1. $\frac{1}{4} =$ $\frac{3}{5} =$ $\frac{1}{6} =$ $\frac{9}{10} =$

2. $\frac{2}{3} =$ $\frac{3}{4} =$ $\frac{3}{8} =$ $\frac{4}{7} =$

3. $\dfrac{5}{6} =$ $\dfrac{3}{10} =$ $\dfrac{2}{5} =$ $\dfrac{1}{12} =$

4. $\dfrac{1}{20} =$ $\dfrac{5}{12} =$ $\dfrac{5}{8} =$ $\dfrac{4}{5} =$

Answers begin on page 193.

CHANGING PERCENTS TO FRACTIONS

To change a percent to a fraction, place the percent over 100 and reduce.

EXAMPLE: Change 45% to a fraction. $45\% = \dfrac{45}{100} = \dfrac{9}{20}$

EXAMPLE: Change 8% to a fraction. $8\% = \dfrac{8}{100} = \dfrac{2}{25}$

Change each of the following to a fraction and reduce.

1. $25\% =$ $6\% =$ $20\% =$ $85\% =$

2. $16\% =$ $90\% =$ $50\% =$ $48\% =$

3. $10\% =$ $125\% =$ $30\% =$ $75\% =$

Answers begin on page 194.

To change a percent that contains decimal places to a fraction, first change the percent to a decimal. Then change the decimal to a fraction.

EXAMPLE: Change 2.5% to a fraction.

Step 1.   Change 2.5% to a decimal. $2.5\% = .025$

Step 2.   Change .025 to a fraction and reduce.

$$.025 = \frac{25}{1000} = \frac{1}{40}$$

Change each of the following to a fraction and reduce.

4. $7.5\% =$ $12.5\% =$ $4.4\% =$ $1.25\% =$

5. $0.8\% =$ $0.15\% =$ $9.5\% =$ $87.5\% =$

Answers begin on page 194.

Percents with fractions in them, such as $16\frac{2}{3}\%$, are the most difficult to change. Remember that the line which separates the top number from the bottom number of a fraction means to divide. When you write the percent over 100, it is difficult to reduce the new fraction. Instead of reducing, divide the top by the bottom. Study the following example carefully.

EXAMPLE: Change $16\frac{2}{3}\%$ to a fraction.

Step 1.   Write the percent over 100. $16\frac{2}{3}\% = \dfrac{16\frac{2}{3}}{100}$

Step 2. Divide the top of the new fraction by the bottom.

$$16\tfrac{2}{3} \div 100 = \frac{50}{3} \div \frac{100}{1} = \frac{\overset{1}{\cancel{50}}}{3} \times \frac{1}{\underset{2}{\cancel{100}}} = \frac{1}{6}$$

Change each of the following to a fraction.

6. $8\tfrac{1}{3}\% =$ $33\tfrac{1}{3}\% =$ $83\tfrac{1}{3}\% =$

7. $6\tfrac{1}{4}\% =$ $22\tfrac{2}{9}\% =$ $66\tfrac{2}{3}\% =$

8. $42\tfrac{6}{7}\% =$ $6\tfrac{2}{3}\% =$ $12\tfrac{1}{2}\% =$

Answers begin on page 194.

COMMON PERCENTS AND FRACTIONS

The table that follows includes the most common fractions and asks for the percents that they are equal to. You have already changed most of these fractions to percents. Fill in the table. Then take the time to memorize this list. You will save time later on if you know this table. Many of the fractions in this table are much easier to use than the percents.

Fraction		Percent		Fraction		Percent
$\frac{1}{2}$	=			$\frac{1}{8}$	=	
$\frac{1}{4}$	=			$\frac{3}{8}$	=	
$\frac{3}{4}$	=			$\frac{5}{8}$	=	
$\frac{1}{5}$	=			$\frac{7}{8}$	=	
$\frac{2}{5}$	=			$\frac{1}{10}$	=	
$\frac{3}{5}$	=			$\frac{3}{10}$	=	
$\frac{4}{5}$	=			$\frac{7}{10}$	=	
$\frac{1}{3}$	=			$\frac{9}{10}$	=	
$\frac{2}{3}$	=			$\frac{1}{6}$	=	
				$\frac{5}{6}$	=	

FINDING A PERCENT OF A NUMBER

Answers begin on page 195.

PROBLEM: Sam earns $12,000 a year. He spends 15% of his income for rent. How much does Sam spend on rent in a year?

SOLUTION: Find 15% of Sam's income. To find a percent of a number, change the percent to a decimal or to a fraction and multiply.

Method 1.

Step 1.   Change 15% to a decimal. $15\% = .15$

Step 2.   Multiply $12,000 by .15

$$\begin{array}{r} \$12{,}000 \\ \times \quad .15 \\ \hline 600\ 00 \\ 1\ 200\ 0 \\ \hline \$1{,}800.00 \end{array}$$

Method 2.

    Step 1. Change 15% to a fraction. $15\% = \frac{15}{100} = \frac{3}{20}$

    Step 2. Multiply $12,000 by $\frac{3}{20}$

$$\frac{3}{\cancel{20}_{\,1}} \times \frac{\overset{600}{\cancel{\$12,000}}}{1} = \$1,800$$

Use the method that you find easier to solve the following problems.

1. 20% of 800 =   75% of 640 =   30% of 350 =

2. 80% of 65 =   25% of 32 =   10% of 120 =

3. 6% of 3,400 =   100% of 236 =   84% of 1,500 =

4. 8% of 450 =   4.5% of 600 =   .2% of 80 =

Answers begin on page 195.

Before going on, try the problems above again and use the other method.

Complex percents with fractions in them, such as $83\frac{1}{3}\%$, are sometimes difficult to use. The easiest method is to replace the percent with the fraction it is equal to. The table on page 170 gives some of the most common examples.

EXAMPLE: Find $83\frac{1}{3}\%$ of 120.

Step 1. Change the percent to a fraction. $83\frac{1}{3}\% = \frac{5}{6}$

Step 2. Multiply 120 by the fraction. $\frac{5}{\cancel{6}_1} \times \frac{\cancel{120}^{20}}{1} = 100$

If you do not know what fraction a complex percent is equal to, write the percent as an improper fraction. Then multiply by the other number over 100.

EXAMPLE: Find $6\frac{1}{4}\%$ of 48.

Step 1. Change the percent to an improper fraction. $6\frac{1}{4} = \frac{25}{4}$

Step 2. Put 48 over 100 and multiply by the improper fraction.

$$\frac{\cancel{25}^1}{\cancel{4}_1} \times \frac{\cancel{48}^{12}}{\cancel{100}_4} = \frac{12}{4} = 3$$

Find the following.

5. $16\frac{2}{3}\%$ of 96 = $33\frac{1}{3}\%$ of 75 = $37\frac{1}{2}\%$ of 120 =

6. $6\frac{2}{3}\%$ of 60 = $8\frac{1}{3}\%$ of 132 = $3\frac{3}{4}\%$ of 800 =

7. $83\frac{1}{3}\%$ of 156 = $12\frac{1}{2}\%$ of 200 = $4\frac{1}{2}\%$ of 1000 =

Answers begin on page 196.

Finding a Percent of a Number: Applying Your Skills

When you find a percent of a number, you find a part of that number. The label of your answer should be the same as the label of the number in the problem.

8.   Hilda earns a gross salary of $240 each week. Her employer deducts 15% of her salary for taxes and social security. How much does her employer deduct each week from Hilda's check?

9.   The number of registered voters in Centerville is 36,000. At the last election 45% of the people who were registered actually voted. How many people voted in Centerville in the last election?

10. The sales tax in Mike's state is 6%. Mike bought a sweater for $20. How much was the sales tax for the sweater?

11. Mr. and Mrs. Spohn are buying a house which costs $34,000. They made a down payment of 12% on the house. Find the amount of the down payment.

12. Jim earns $10,000 a year. Next year he will get a 6.5% raise. How much more will Jim earn next year?

13. Tom took a math test with 60 problems on it. His score was 85% correct. How many of the problems did Tom get right?

Answers begin on page 196.

In many practical situations involving percent, you must first find a percent of a number and then add or subtract this new amount.

EXAMPLE: Charles bought an electric drill for $24. What was the price of the drill including 7% for sales tax?

Step 1.   Change 7% to a decimal. $7\% = .07$

Step 2.   Multiply $24 by .07

$$\begin{array}{r} \$24 \\ \times\ .07 \\ \hline \$1.68 \end{array}$$

Step 3.   Add the new amount to $24.

$$\begin{array}{r} \$24.00 \\ +\ 1.68 \\ \hline \$25.68 \end{array}$$

EXAMPLE: A coat was originally marked $60. It was on sale for "15% off." Find the sale price of the coat.

Step 1.   Change 15% to a decimal.   15% = .15

Step 2.   Multiply $60 by .15

$$\begin{array}{r} \$60 \\ \times\,.15 \\ \hline 300 \\ 60 \\ \hline \$9.00 \end{array}$$

Step 3.   Subtract the new amount from $60.

$$\begin{array}{r} \$60 \\ -\,9 \\ \hline \$51 \end{array}$$

Read each of the following problems carefully to decide whether you need to add or subtract the new amount.

---

14.   There are usually 30 students in Warren's math class. One January day 20% of the students were absent. How many students were present that day?

15.   Richard earns a gross salary of $280 a week. His employer deducts 18% of his salary for taxes and social security. What is Richard's weekly pay after deductions?

16.   In 1970 the population of Central County was 120,000. In 1980 the population of Central County was 30% more that it had been in 1970. What was the population of Central County in 1980?

17. Kathy bought new living room furniture for $540. The sales tax in Kathy's state is 8%. Find the price of the furniture including sales tax.

18. Mr. Clay owns an appliance store. He pays $80 to a wholesale dealer for a portable television. Mr. Clay charges his customers 20% more than the wholesale price. What is the price that Mr. Clay charges his customers for the portable television?

19. Mr. Clay usually charges his customers $360 for a three-piece stereo system. During a Labor Day sale, Mr. Clay sold the stereo system for 10% off the usual price. What was the sale price of the stereo system?

Answers begin on page 197.

Finding a Percent of a Number: Rounding Off

Percent problems often involve money, and often the answer to a percent problem has too many decimal places. Our money system has two decimal places, dimes and pennies, which correspond to the tenths and hundredths of the decimal system.

When a money answer has more than two decimal places, you must *round off* your answer to the nearest cent.

If the digit in the third decimal place is *4 or less, leave the answer* with the first two decimal places as they are.

If the digit in the third decimal place is *5 or more, raise the answer* to the next cent.

EXAMPLE: Find 6% of $3.86

Step 1.   Change 6% to a decimal. $6\% = .06$

Step 2. Multiply $3.86 by .06

$$\begin{array}{r} \$3.86 \\ \times\ \ .06 \\ \hline \$.2316 \end{array}$$

Step 3. Since there is a 1 in the third decimal place, leave the answer as $.23.

EXAMPLE: Find 5% of $8.95

 Step 1. Change 5% to a decimal. 5% = .05

 Step 2. Multiply $8.95 by .05

$$\begin{array}{r} \$8.95 \\ \times\ \ .05 \\ \hline \$.4475 \end{array}$$

Step 3. Since there is a 7 in the third decimal place, raise the answer to $.45.

Round off each answer to the nearest cent.

20. 8% of $2.59 =   12% of $14.70 =   3% of $6.42 =

21. 9% of $.84 =   15% of $64.75 =   4.5% of $305.16 =

22. 1.5% of $9.70 =   7% of $19.80 =   11% of $8.95 =

Answers begin on page 197.

Finding a Percent of a Number: Interest

Interest is one of the most common applications of finding a percent of a number. You pay interest whenever you take out a loan. You earn interest whenever you have money in a savings account.

The formula for finding interest is **I = PRT** where:

I is the *interest* in dollars;
P is the *principal*, the amount of money borrowed or saved;
R is the *rate* in percent; and
T is the *time* in years.

We read the formula as interest is equal to the principal times the rate times the time.

EXAMPLE: Find the interest on $800 at 6% annual interest for one year.

SOLUTION: Change 6% to a fraction and substitute each number into the formula.

$$\overset{8}{\cancel{\$800}} \times \frac{6}{\underset{1}{\cancel{100}}} \times 1 = \$48$$

EXAMPLE: Find the interest on $600 at 4.3% annual interest for one year.

SOLUTION: Change 4.3% to a decimal and substitute each number into the formula.

$$
\begin{array}{r}
\$600 \\
\times\ .043 \\
\hline
1\,800 \\
24\,00 \\
\hline
\$25.80\cancel{0}
\end{array}
$$

---

23.   Find the interest on $400 at 9% annual interest for one year.

24. Find the interest on $1,200 at $4\frac{1}{2}\%$ annual interest for one year.

25. Find the interest on $650 at 6% annual interest for one year.

26. Find the interest on $700 at 5.5% annual interest for one year.

27. Find the interest on $1,500 at 12% annual interest for one year.

Answers begin on page 197.

When the time period for interest is not one year, write the time as a fraction of a year.

EXAMPLE: Find the interest on $900 at 6% annual interest for eight months.

Step 1. Change 6% to a fraction. $6\% = \frac{6}{100}$

Step 2. Write eight months as a fraction of a year.

$$\frac{8 \text{ months}}{12 \text{ months per year}} = \frac{2}{3} \text{ year}$$

Step 3. Substitute each number into the formula.

$$\frac{\overset{9}{\cancel{\$900}}}{1} \times \frac{\overset{}{\cancel{6}}}{\underset{1}{\cancel{100}}} \times \frac{2}{\underset{1}{\cancel{3}}} = \$36$$

EXAMPLE: Find the interest on $800 at 5% annual interest for one year and three months.

Step 1.   Change 5% to a fraction. $5\% = \frac{5}{100}$

Step 2.   Write one year and three months as an improper fraction.

$$1 \text{ year } 3 \text{ months} = 1\frac{3}{12} \text{ years} = 1\frac{1}{4} = \frac{5}{4} \text{ years}$$

Step 3.   Substitute each number into the formula.

$$\frac{\overset{2}{\cancel{\$800}}}{1} \times \frac{5}{\underset{1}{\cancel{100}}} \times \frac{5}{\underset{1}{\cancel{4}}} = \$50$$

---

28.   Find the interest on $750 at 10% annual interest for four months.

29.   Find the interest on $1000 at 4% annual interest for six months.

30.   Find the interest on $1600 at $3\frac{1}{2}\%$ annual interest for nine months.

31.   Find the interest on $510 at 3% annual interest for one year and four months.

32. Find the interest on $2,000 at $5\frac{1}{2}\%$ annual interest for two years and three months.

33. Find the interest on $500 at 12% annual interest for one year and eight months.

Answers begin on page 198.

FINDING WHAT PERCENT ONE NUMBER IS OF ANOTHER

PROBLEM: Martha works 40 hours a week. She spends 15 hours each week filing. What percent of Martha's work week does she spend filing?

SOLUTION: Find what percent 15 is of 40. To find what percent one number is of another, make a fraction by putting the *part over the whole*. (The part is usually the smaller number, and the whole is usually the larger number.) Then reduce the fraction and change it to a percent.

Step 1. Put the part over the whole and reduce. $\frac{15}{40} = \frac{3}{8}$

Step 2. Change the fraction to a percent.

$$\frac{3}{\overset{}{\underset{2}{8}}} \times \frac{\overset{25}{\cancel{100}}\%}{1} = \frac{75}{2} = 37\frac{1}{2}\%$$

Find the following.

1. 7 is what % of 21?   45 is what % of 90?   48 is what % of 60?

2. 24 is what % of 32?   35 is what % of 56?   160 is what % of 640?

3. 45 is what % of 54?   33 is what % of 55?   108 is what % of 120?

4. 18 is what % of 48?   150 is what % of 225?   30 is what % of 72?

Answers begin on page 198.

Finding What Percent One Number Is of Another:
Applying Your Skills

In the following problems be sure to put the part over the whole.

5. Susan had 18 problems right out of a total of 20 problems on a test. What percent of the problems did she get right?

6. Arthur earns $600 a month. He spends $150 a month for rent. What percent of his income does Arthur spend for rent?

7. There are three feet in a yard. A foot is what percent of a yard?

8. In a factory with 400 employees there are 150 women. What percent of the employees are women?

9. Mr. and Mrs. Shaeffer bought a house which cost $32,000. So far, they have paid $24,000 toward the total cost of the house. What percent of the total price have they paid?

10. There should be 24 students in Mr. Johnson's history class. One day in January only 18 students attended the class. What percent of the class was there?

Answers begin on page 198.

Sometimes, when you are looking for what percent one number is of another, you must compare a changing amount to some original amount.

EXAMPLE: The price of a dozen eggs went from 80¢ to 90¢ a dozen. By what percent did the price of a dozen eggs increase?

SOLUTION: Find out how much the price of a dozen eggs increased. Then find what percent this amount is of the original price.

Step 1.   To find out how much the price increased, subtract the old price from the new price.

$$
\begin{array}{r}
90¢ \\
-80 \\
\hline
10¢
\end{array}
$$

Step 2.   Put the change in price (the increase) over the original amount (80¢) and change the fraction to a percent.

$$\frac{10¢}{80¢} = \frac{1}{8} \qquad \frac{1}{\cancel{8}_{2}} \times \frac{\cancel{100}^{25}}{1} = \frac{25}{2} = 12\frac{1}{2}\%$$

EXAMPLE: A shirt originally selling for \$8 was on sale for \$6. Find the percent of discount.

SOLUTION: Find the discount. Then find what percent this number is of the original price.

Step 1.   Subtract the new price from the original price.

$$
\begin{array}{r}
\$8 \\
-6 \\
\hline
\$2
\end{array}
$$

Step 2.   Put the change in price (the discount) over the original amount (\$8) and change the fraction to a percent.

$$\frac{\$2}{\$8} = \frac{1}{4} \qquad \frac{1}{\cancel{4}_{1}} \times \frac{\cancel{100}^{25}}{1} = 25\%$$

---

11.   In 1980 the population of Smithtown was 30,000. In 1988 the population was 36,000. By what percent did the population increase from 1980 to 1988?

12. Paul bought a new car last year for $3200. This year the car is worth $2800. By what percent did the value of the car decrease?

13. Mr. Clay pays a wholesale dealer $20 for a portable radio. Mr. Clay charges the customers in his store $28 for the radio. By what percent does Mr. Clay increase the price of the radio for his customers?

14. In June Mark weighed 180 pounds. He went on a diet and by November he weighed 150 pounds. What percent of Mark's weight did he lose?

15. Mary wants to buy a coat that originally cost $60. It is now on sale for $54. What percent of the original price can Mary save if she buys the coat on sale?

16. A local tenants' association had 150 members last year. After a few months of campaigning, the association now has 250 members. By what percent did the membership increase?

Answers begin on page 199.

FINDING A NUMBER WHEN A PERCENT OF IT IS GIVEN

PROBLEM: The Lake Street Block Association has raised $300 for planting trees. The amount they have raised represents 75% of the amount that they need. Find the total amount that the block association needs for their project.

SOLUTION: You must find the number that, when you take 75% of it, gives an answer of 300. To find the missing number, change the percent to a fraction or a decimal. Then divide the amount you have by this fraction or decimal.

Method 1.

   Step 1. Change 75% to a fraction. $75\% = \frac{75}{100} = \frac{3}{4}$

   Step 2. Divide $300 by this fraction.

$$\$300 \div \frac{3}{4} = \frac{\overset{100}{\cancel{\$300}}}{1} \times \frac{4}{\underset{1}{\cancel{3}}} = \$400$$

Method 2.

   Step 1. Change 75% to a decimal. $75\% = .75$

   Step 2. Divide $300 by this decimal.

$$
\begin{array}{r}
\$4\ 00. \\
.75\overline{)\$300.00} \\
\underline{300} \\
0\ 00
\end{array}
$$

Use the method that you find easier to solve the following problems.

1. 50% of what number is 24?   40% of what number is 36?

2. 25% of what number is 62? $33\frac{1}{3}$% of what number is 84?

3. 60% of what number is 99? $16\frac{2}{3}$% of what number is 25?

4. $37\frac{1}{2}$% of what number is 240?   90% of what number is 270?

5. 4.5% of what number is 36?   6.7% of what number is 134?

Answers begin on page 200.

Finding a Number When a Percent of It Is Given:
Applying Your Skills

To find the missing number in these problems, divide by the percent. Change the percent into either a decimal or a fraction.

6. Tom has paid $2,850 on his automobile loan. This represents 75% of the total loan. Find the total amount of Tom's loan.

7. At a recent meeting of the Heywood School Parents' Association 245 parents were present. Those parents represent 35% of the parents with children in the school. If every parent had attended the meeting, how many would have been there?

8. On a math test Becky received a score of 85% correct. She got 34 of the problems correct. How many problems were on the test?

9. Mr. Clay pays a wholesaler $24 for a portable fan. The $24 represents 60% of the price that Mr. Clay charges his customers. How much does a customer pay for the portable fan?

10. In a recent election for mayor, Mr. Prouty received 4,420 votes. These votes represented 52% of the total number of votes that were cast for mayor. How many people voted for mayor in that election?

11. The Frey family spends an average of $43 a month for utilities. This represents 5% of their monthly expenses. What are the Frey family's monthly expenses?

Answers begin on page 200.

PERCENT SKILLS TEST

Before going on to the final test, try this review of your percent skills. Check your answers with those beginning on page 201. Then use the Percent Skills Test Evaluation to decide what you need to study more.

1. Change .06 to a percent.

2. Change .057 to a percent.

3. Change 80% to a decimal.

4. Change .9% to a decimal.

5. Change $\frac{4}{5}$ to a percent.

6. Change $\frac{2}{7}$ to a percent.

7. Change 35% to a fraction and reduce.

8. Change 84% to a fraction and reduce.

9. Change $58\frac{1}{3}\%$ to a fraction and reduce.

10. Find 40% of 310.

11. Find 6.2% of 250.

12.   Find $66\frac{2}{3}\%$ of 96.   13.   Find $12\frac{1}{2}\%$ of 120.

14.   Steve bought a car which cost $4,200. He made a down payment of 15% of the price. Find the amount of Steve's down payment.

15.   Carolyn bought a pair of shoes for $24.50. The sales tax in her state is 6%. Find the cost of the shoes including sales tax.

16.   Find 8% of $84.79 to the nearest cent.

17.   Find the interest on $900 at 4.5% annual interest for one year.

18.   Find the interest on $1200 at 6% annual interest for one year and four months.

19.   12 is what % of 20?   20.   42 is what % of 48?

21. 15 is what % of 60?   22. 48 is what % of 72?

23. In Ms. Miller's English class there are 25 students. 15 of the students are female. What percent of the class is female?

24. Paco bought a camera on sale for $75. The regular price of the camera was $125. What percent of the regular price did Paco save by buying the camera on sale?

25. 20% of what number is 17?   26. 70% of what number is 161?

27. $12\frac{1}{2}$% of what number is 24?   28. 15% of what number is 48?

29. Marcia bought a washing machine on sale for $240. The sale price represents 80% of the regular price. Find the regular price of the washing machine.

30. Douglas missed six problems on a math test. The six problems represent 5% of the total number of problems on the test. How many problems were on the test?

PERCENT SKILLS TEST EVALUATION

Problem Number	Practice Pages	Problem Number	Practice Pages
1–2	164–165	16	176–177
3–4	165	17	178–179
5–6	166–167	18	179–181
7–8	167	19–22	181–182
9	168–169	23	182–183
10–11	170–171	24	184–185
12–13	172–173	25–28	186–187
14	173–174	29–30	188
15	174–176		

Passing score: <u>24</u> out of 30 problems.
Your score: __ out of 30 problems.

If you had less than a passing score, review the practice pages for the problems you got wrong. Then repeat this test before going on to the final test.

If you had a passing score, correct any problem you got wrong, and go to the final test.

ANSWERS AND SOLUTIONS—PERCENT SKILLS EXERCISES

CHANGING DECIMALS TO PERCENTS

1. $.07 = 7\%$ $.75 = 75\%$ $.035 = 3.5\%$ $.33\frac{1}{3} = 33\frac{1}{3}\%$

2. $.9 = 90\%$ $1.5 = 150\%$ $.004 = .4\%$ $.65 = 65\%$

3. $.1 = 10\%$ $.66\frac{2}{3} = 66\frac{2}{3}\%$ $.08\frac{1}{3} = 8\frac{1}{3}\%$ $.05 = 5\%$

CHANGING PERCENTS TO DECIMALS

1. $9\% = .09$ $35\% = .35$ $4.8\% = .048$ $22\frac{2}{9}\% = .22\frac{2}{9}$

2. $60\% = .6$ $125\% = 1.25$ $.3\% = .003$ $95\% = .95$

3. $20\% = .2$ $33\frac{1}{3}\% = .33\frac{1}{3}$ $6\frac{1}{4}\% = .06\frac{1}{4}$ $3\% = .03$

CHANGING FRACTIONS TO PERCENTS

1. $\dfrac{1}{\overset{}{\underset{1}{4}}} \times \dfrac{\overset{25}{100}}{1} = 25\%$ $\qquad$ $\dfrac{3}{\overset{}{\underset{1}{5}}} \times \dfrac{\overset{20}{100}}{1} = 60\%$

$\dfrac{1}{\overset{}{\underset{3}{6}}} \times \dfrac{\overset{50}{100}}{1} = \dfrac{50}{3} = 16\frac{2}{3}\%$ $\qquad$ $\dfrac{9}{\overset{}{\underset{1}{10}}} \times \dfrac{\overset{10}{100}}{1} = 90\%$

2. $\dfrac{2}{3} \times \dfrac{100}{1} = \dfrac{200}{3} = 66\frac{2}{3}\%$ $\qquad$ $\dfrac{3}{\overset{}{\underset{1}{4}}} \times \dfrac{\overset{25}{100}}{1} = 75\%$

$\dfrac{3}{\overset{}{\underset{2}{8}}} \times \dfrac{\overset{25}{100}}{1} = \dfrac{75}{2} = 37\frac{1}{2}\%$ $\qquad$ $\dfrac{4}{7} \times \dfrac{100}{1} = \dfrac{400}{7} = 57\frac{1}{7}\%$

3. $\dfrac{5}{\overset{}{\underset{3}{6}}} \times \dfrac{\overset{50}{100}}{1} = \dfrac{250}{3} = 83\frac{1}{3}\%$ $\qquad$ $\dfrac{3}{\overset{}{\underset{1}{10}}} \times \dfrac{\overset{10}{100}}{1} = 30\%$

$\dfrac{2}{\overset{}{\underset{1}{5}}} \times \dfrac{\overset{20}{100}}{1} = 40\%$ $\qquad$ $\dfrac{1}{\overset{}{\underset{3}{12}}} \times \dfrac{\overset{25}{100}}{1} = \dfrac{25}{3} = 8\frac{1}{3}\%$

4. $\dfrac{1}{\overset{}{\underset{1}{20}}} \times \dfrac{\overset{5}{100}}{1} = 5\%$ $\qquad$ $\dfrac{5}{\overset{}{\underset{3}{12}}} \times \dfrac{\overset{25}{100}}{1} = 41\frac{2}{3}\%$

$\dfrac{5}{\overset{}{\underset{2}{8}}} \times \dfrac{\overset{25}{100}}{1} = \dfrac{125}{2} = 62\frac{1}{2}\%$ $\qquad$ $\dfrac{4}{\overset{}{\underset{1}{5}}} \times \dfrac{\overset{20}{100}}{1} = 80\%$

CHANGING PERCENTS TO FRACTIONS

1. $\dfrac{25}{100} = \dfrac{1}{4}$ $\dfrac{6}{100} = \dfrac{3}{50}$ $\dfrac{20}{100} = \dfrac{1}{5}$ $\dfrac{85}{100} = \dfrac{17}{20}$

2. $\dfrac{16}{100} = \dfrac{4}{25}$ $\dfrac{90}{100} = \dfrac{9}{10}$ $\dfrac{50}{100} = \dfrac{1}{2}$ $\dfrac{48}{100} = \dfrac{12}{25}$

3. $\dfrac{10}{100} = \dfrac{1}{10}$ $\dfrac{125}{100} = \dfrac{5}{4} = 1\dfrac{1}{4}$ $\dfrac{30}{100} = \dfrac{3}{10}$ $\dfrac{75}{100} = \dfrac{3}{4}$

4. $.075 = \dfrac{75}{1000} = \dfrac{3}{40}$ $.125 = \dfrac{125}{1000} = \dfrac{1}{8}$

$.044 = \dfrac{44}{1000} = \dfrac{11}{250}$ $.0125 = \dfrac{125}{10,000} = \dfrac{1}{80}$

5. $.008 = \dfrac{8}{1000} = \dfrac{1}{125}$ $.0015 = \dfrac{15}{10,000} = \dfrac{3}{2000}$

$.095 = \dfrac{95}{1000} = \dfrac{19}{200}$ $.875 = \dfrac{875}{1000} = \dfrac{7}{8}$

6. $\dfrac{25}{3} \div \dfrac{100}{1} = \dfrac{\overset{1}{\cancel{25}}}{3} \times \dfrac{1}{\underset{4}{\cancel{100}}} = \dfrac{1}{12}$ $\dfrac{100}{3} \div \dfrac{100}{1} = \dfrac{\overset{1}{\cancel{100}}}{3} \times \dfrac{1}{\underset{1}{\cancel{100}}} = \dfrac{1}{3}$

$\dfrac{250}{3} \div \dfrac{100}{1} = \dfrac{\overset{5}{\cancel{250}}}{3} \times \dfrac{1}{\underset{2}{\cancel{100}}} = \dfrac{5}{6}$

7. $\dfrac{25}{4} \div \dfrac{100}{1} = \dfrac{\overset{1}{\cancel{25}}}{4} \times \dfrac{1}{\underset{4}{\cancel{100}}} = \dfrac{1}{16}$ $\dfrac{200}{9} \div \dfrac{100}{1} = \dfrac{\overset{2}{\cancel{200}}}{9} \times \dfrac{1}{\underset{1}{\cancel{100}}} = \dfrac{2}{9}$

$\dfrac{200}{3} \div \dfrac{100}{1} = \dfrac{\overset{2}{\cancel{200}}}{3} \times \dfrac{1}{\underset{1}{\cancel{100}}} = \dfrac{2}{3}$

8. $\dfrac{300}{7} \div \dfrac{100}{1} = \dfrac{\overset{3}{\cancel{300}}}{7} \times \dfrac{1}{\underset{1}{\cancel{100}}} = \dfrac{3}{7}$ $\dfrac{20}{3} \div \dfrac{100}{1} = \dfrac{\overset{1}{\cancel{20}}}{3} \times \dfrac{1}{\underset{5}{\cancel{100}}} = \dfrac{1}{15}$

$$\frac{25}{2} \div \frac{100}{1} = \frac{\overset{1}{\cancel{25}}}{2} \times \frac{1}{\underset{4}{\cancel{100}}} = \frac{1}{8}$$

Fraction		Percent		Fraction		Percent
$\frac{1}{2}$	=	50%		$\frac{1}{8}$	=	$12\frac{1}{2}\%$
$\frac{1}{4}$	=	25%		$\frac{3}{8}$	=	$37\frac{1}{2}\%$
$\frac{3}{4}$	=	75%		$\frac{5}{8}$	=	$62\frac{1}{2}\%$
$\frac{1}{5}$	=	20%		$\frac{7}{8}$	=	$87\frac{1}{2}\%$
$\frac{2}{5}$	=	40%		$\frac{1}{10}$	=	10%
$\frac{3}{5}$	=	60%		$\frac{3}{10}$	=	30%
$\frac{4}{5}$	=	80%		$\frac{7}{10}$	=	70%
$\frac{1}{3}$	=	$33\frac{1}{3}\%$		$\frac{9}{10}$	=	90%
$\frac{2}{3}$	=	$66\frac{2}{3}\%$		$\frac{1}{6}$	=	$16\frac{2}{3}\%$
				$\frac{5}{6}$	=	$83\frac{1}{3}\%$

FINDING A PERCENT OF A NUMBER

1.
```
    800          640          350
  × .20        × .75        × .30
  160.00        32 00       105.00
               448 0
               480.00
```

2.
```
     65           32          120
   × .85        × .25        × .10
   52.00         1 60        12.00
                 6 4
                 8.00
```

3.
$$\begin{array}{r} 3400 \\ \times\ .06 \\ \hline 204.0\!\!\!/0\!\!\!/ \end{array}$$
$$\begin{array}{r} 236 \\ \times 1.00 \\ \hline 236.0\!\!\!/0\!\!\!/ \end{array}$$
$$\begin{array}{r} 1500 \\ \times\ .84 \\ \hline 60\ 00 \\ 1200\ 0 \\ \hline 1260.0\!\!\!/0\!\!\!/ \end{array}$$

4.
$$\begin{array}{r} 450 \\ \times\ .08 \\ \hline 36.0\!\!\!/0\!\!\!/ \end{array}$$
$$\begin{array}{r} 600 \\ \times .045 \\ \hline 3\ 000 \\ 24\ 00 \\ \hline 27.0\!\!\!/0\!\!\!/0\!\!\!/ \end{array}$$
$$\begin{array}{r} 80 \\ \times .002 \\ \hline .16\!\!\!/0\!\!\!/ \end{array}$$

5. $\dfrac{1}{\cancel{6}} \times \dfrac{\overset{16}{\cancel{96}}}{1} = 16$

$\dfrac{1}{\cancel{3}} \times \dfrac{\overset{25}{\cancel{75}}}{1} = 25$

$\dfrac{3}{8} \times \dfrac{\overset{15}{\cancel{120}}}{1} = 45$

6. $\dfrac{\overset{1}{\cancel{20}}}{\cancel{3}} \times \dfrac{\overset{20}{\cancel{60}}}{\underset{5}{\cancel{100}}} = \dfrac{20}{5} = 4$

$\dfrac{\overset{1}{\cancel{25}}}{\cancel{3}} \times \dfrac{\overset{44}{\cancel{132}}}{\underset{4}{\cancel{100}}} = \dfrac{44}{4} = 11$

$\dfrac{\overset{3}{\cancel{15}}}{\cancel{4}} \times \dfrac{\overset{200}{\cancel{800}}}{\underset{20}{\cancel{100}}} = \dfrac{600}{20} = 30$

7. $\dfrac{5}{\cancel{6}} \times \dfrac{\overset{26}{\cancel{156}}}{1} = 130$

$\dfrac{1}{\cancel{8}} \times \dfrac{\overset{25}{\cancel{200}}}{1} = 25$

$\dfrac{9}{2} \times \dfrac{1000}{100} = \dfrac{9000}{200} = 45$

8.
$$\begin{array}{r} 240 \\ \times\ .15 \\ \hline 12\ 00 \\ 24\ 0 \\ \hline \$36.00 \end{array}$$

9.
$$\begin{array}{r} 36{,}000 \\ \times\ .45 \\ \hline 1\ 800\ 00 \\ 14\ 400\ 0 \\ \hline 16{,}200.0\!\!\!/0\!\!\!/ \text{ people} \end{array}$$

10.
$$\begin{array}{r} \$20 \\ \times\ .06 \\ \hline \$1.20 \end{array}$$

11.
$$\begin{array}{r} \$34{,}000 \\ \times\ .12 \\ \hline 680\ 00 \\ 3\ 400\ 0 \\ \hline \$4{,}080.00 \end{array}$$

12.
$$\begin{array}{r} \$10{,}000 \\ \times\ .065 \\ \hline 50\ 000 \\ 600\ 00 \\ \hline \$650.00\!\!\!/0\!\!\!/ \end{array}$$

13.
$$\begin{array}{r} 60 \\ \times\ .85 \\ \hline 3\ 00 \\ 48\ 0 \\ \hline 51.0\!\!\!/0\!\!\!/ \text{ problems} \end{array}$$

14.
```
     30          30
   × .20        −  6
   ------       ----
   6.00          24
```

15.
```
    280         $280.00
   × .18       −  50.40
   -----       --------
   22 40       $229.60
   28 0
   ------
   $50.40
```

16.
```
   120,000        120,000
   ×    .30      + 36,000
   ---------     --------
   36,000.00     156,000 people
```

17.
```
    $540        $540.00
   × .08       +  43.20
   -----       -------
   $43.20      $583.20
```

18.
```
    $80          $80
   × .20        + 16
   ------       ----
   $16.00        $96
```

19.
```
    $360         $360
   × .10        −  36
   ------       ----
   $36.00       $324
```

20.
```
   $2.59              14.70              $6.42
   × .08             ×  .12             × .03
   --------          ------             --------
   .2072 = $.21       2940              .1926 = $.19
                     1 470
                     ------
                     1.7640 = $1.76
```

21.
```
    $.84             $64.75            $305.16
   ×  .09            ×  .15            ×  .045
   ------------      -------           ----------
   $.0756 = $.08     3 2375            1 52580
                     6 475             12 2064
                     -------           -----------
                     9.7125 = $9.71    13.73220 = $13.73
```

22.
```
   $9.70             $19.80             $8.95
   × 0.15            × .07             × .11
   ------------      -------------      -----------
   4850              1.3860 = $1.39     895
    970                                 895
   ------------                         -----------
   .14550 = $.15                        .9845 = $.98
```

23.
$$\frac{\overset{4}{\cancel{400}}}{1} \times \frac{9}{\underset{1}{\cancel{100}}} \times 1 = \$36$$

24.
$$\frac{\overset{600}{\cancel{1200}}}{100} \times \frac{9}{\underset{1}{\cancel{2}}} \times 1 = \frac{5400}{100} = \$54$$

25.
$$\frac{\overset{13}{\cancel{650}}}{1} \times \frac{6}{\underset{2}{\cancel{100}}} \times 1 = \frac{78}{2} = \$39$$

26.
```
    $700
   × .055
   -------
   3 500
   35 00
   -------
   $38.500
```

27. $\dfrac{\overset{15}{\cancel{1500}}}{1} \times \dfrac{12}{\underset{2}{\cancel{100}}} \times 1 = \$180$

28. $\dfrac{4}{12} = \dfrac{1}{3}$

$\dfrac{\overset{15}{\cancel{750}}}{1} \times \dfrac{10}{\underset{2}{\cancel{100}}} \times \dfrac{1}{3} = \dfrac{150}{6} = \$25$

29. $\dfrac{6}{12} = \dfrac{1}{2}$

$\dfrac{\overset{10}{\cancel{1000}}}{1} \times \dfrac{4}{\underset{1}{\cancel{100}}} \times \dfrac{1}{2} = \$20$

30. $\dfrac{9}{12} = \dfrac{3}{4}$

$\dfrac{\overset{\overset{\overset{2}{\cancel{8}}}{\cancel{6}}}{\cancel{1600}}}{\underset{1}{\cancel{100}}} \times \dfrac{7}{\underset{1}{\cancel{2}}} \times \dfrac{3}{\underset{1}{\cancel{4}}} = \$42$

31. $1\dfrac{4}{12} = 1\dfrac{1}{3} = \dfrac{4}{3}$

$\dfrac{\overset{51}{\cancel{510}}}{1} \times \dfrac{\overset{1}{\cancel{3}}}{\underset{\underset{5}{\cancel{10}}}{\cancel{100}}} \times \dfrac{\overset{2}{\cancel{4}}}{\underset{1}{\cancel{3}}} = \dfrac{102}{5} = \$20.40$

32. $2\dfrac{3}{12} = 2\dfrac{1}{4} = \dfrac{9}{4}$

$\dfrac{\overset{\overset{5}{\cancel{20}}}{\cancel{2000}}}{\underset{1}{\cancel{100}}} \times \dfrac{11}{2} \times \dfrac{9}{\underset{1}{\cancel{4}}} = \dfrac{495}{2} = \$247.50$

33. $1\dfrac{8}{12} = 1\dfrac{2}{3} = \dfrac{5}{3}$

$\dfrac{\overset{5}{\cancel{500}}}{1} \times \dfrac{\overset{4}{\cancel{12}}}{\underset{1}{\cancel{100}}} \times \dfrac{5}{\underset{1}{\cancel{3}}} = \$100$

FINDING WHAT PERCENT ONE NUMBER IS OF ANOTHER

1. $\dfrac{7}{21} = \dfrac{1}{3}$

$\dfrac{1}{3} \times \dfrac{100}{1} = \dfrac{100}{3} = 33\dfrac{1}{3}\%$

$\dfrac{45}{90} = \dfrac{1}{2}$

$\dfrac{1}{\underset{1}{\cancel{2}}} \times \dfrac{\overset{50}{\cancel{100}}}{1} = 50\%$

$\dfrac{48}{60} = \dfrac{4}{5}$

$\dfrac{4}{\underset{1}{\cancel{5}}} \times \dfrac{\overset{20}{\cancel{100}}}{1} = 80\%$

2. $\dfrac{24}{32} = \dfrac{3}{4}$

$\dfrac{3}{\underset{1}{\cancel{4}}} \times \dfrac{\overset{25}{\cancel{100}}}{1} = 75\%$

$\dfrac{35}{56} = \dfrac{5}{8}$

$\dfrac{5}{\underset{2}{\cancel{8}}} \times \dfrac{\overset{25}{\cancel{100}}}{1} = \dfrac{125}{2} = 62\dfrac{1}{2}\%$

$\dfrac{160}{640} = \dfrac{1}{4}$

$\dfrac{1}{\underset{1}{\cancel{4}}} \times \dfrac{\overset{25}{\cancel{100}}}{1} = 25\%$

3. $\dfrac{45}{54} = \dfrac{5}{6}$

$\dfrac{5}{6} \times \dfrac{100}{1} = \dfrac{250}{3} = 83\dfrac{1}{3}\%$

$\dfrac{33}{55} = \dfrac{3}{5}$

$\dfrac{3}{\cancel{5}} \times \dfrac{\cancel{100}^{20}}{1} = 60\%$

$\dfrac{108}{120} = \dfrac{9}{10}$

$\dfrac{9}{\cancel{10}} \times \dfrac{\cancel{100}^{10}}{1} = 90\%$

4. $\dfrac{18}{48} = \dfrac{3}{8}$

$\dfrac{3}{\cancel{8}_2} \times \dfrac{\cancel{100}^{25}}{1} = \dfrac{75}{2} = 37\dfrac{1}{2}\%$

$\dfrac{150}{225} = \dfrac{2}{3}$

$\dfrac{2}{3} \times \dfrac{100}{1} = \dfrac{200}{3} = 66\dfrac{2}{3}\%$

$\dfrac{30}{72} = \dfrac{5}{12}$

$\dfrac{5}{\cancel{12}_3} \times \dfrac{\cancel{100}^{25}}{1} = \dfrac{125}{3} = 41\dfrac{2}{3}\%$

5. $\dfrac{18}{20} = \dfrac{9}{10}$

$\dfrac{9}{10} \times \dfrac{100}{1} = 90\%$

6. $\dfrac{150}{600} = \dfrac{1}{4}$

$\dfrac{1}{4} \times \dfrac{100}{1} = 25\%$

7. $\dfrac{1}{3} \times \dfrac{100}{1} = \dfrac{100}{3} = 33\dfrac{1}{3}\%$

8. $\dfrac{150}{400} = \dfrac{3}{8}$

$\dfrac{3}{\cancel{8}_2} \times \dfrac{\cancel{100}^{25}}{1} = \dfrac{75}{2} = 37\dfrac{1}{2}\%$

9. $\dfrac{24,000}{32,000} = \dfrac{3}{4}$

$\dfrac{3}{\cancel{4}_1} \times \dfrac{\cancel{100}^{25}}{1} = 75\%$

10. $\dfrac{18}{24} = \dfrac{3}{4}$

$\dfrac{3}{\cancel{4}_1} \times \dfrac{\cancel{100}^{25}}{1} = 75\%$

11. $\begin{array}{r} 36,000 \\ -\ 30,000 \\ \hline 6,000 \end{array}$ $\dfrac{6,000}{30,000} = \dfrac{1}{5}$

$\dfrac{1}{5} \times \dfrac{100}{1} = 20\%$

12. $\begin{array}{r} 3,200 \\ -\ 2,800 \\ \hline 400 \end{array}$ $\dfrac{400}{3200} = \dfrac{1}{8}$

$\dfrac{1}{\cancel{8}_2} \times \dfrac{\cancel{100}^{25}}{1} = \dfrac{25}{2} = 12\dfrac{1}{2}\%$

13. $\begin{array}{r} 28 \\ -\ 20 \\ \hline 8 \end{array}$ $\dfrac{8}{20} = \dfrac{2}{5}$

$\dfrac{2}{\cancel{5}_1} \times \dfrac{\cancel{100}^{20}}{1} = 40\%$

14. $\begin{array}{r} 180 \\ -\ 150 \\ \hline 30 \end{array}$ $\dfrac{30}{180} = \dfrac{1}{6}$

$\dfrac{1}{\cancel{6}_3} \times \dfrac{\cancel{100}^{50}}{1} = \dfrac{50}{3} = 16\dfrac{2}{3}\%$

15. $\begin{array}{r} 60 \\ -\ 54 \\ \hline 6 \end{array}$ $\dfrac{6}{60} = \dfrac{1}{10}$ 16. $\begin{array}{r} 250 \\ -\ 150 \\ \hline 100 \end{array}$ $\dfrac{100}{150} = \dfrac{2}{3}$

$\dfrac{1}{10} \times \dfrac{100}{1} = 10\%$ $\dfrac{2}{3} \times \dfrac{100}{1} = \dfrac{200}{3} = 66\dfrac{2}{3}\%$

FINDING A NUMBER WHEN A PERCENT OF IT IS GIVEN

1. $50\% = \dfrac{1}{2}$

$24 \div \dfrac{1}{2} = \dfrac{24}{1} \times \dfrac{2}{1} = 48$

$40\% = \dfrac{2}{5}$

$36 \div \dfrac{2}{5} = \dfrac{36}{1} \times \dfrac{5}{2} = 90$

2. $25\% = \dfrac{1}{4}$

$62 \div \dfrac{1}{4} = \dfrac{62}{1} \times \dfrac{4}{1} = 248$

$33\dfrac{1}{3}\% = \dfrac{1}{3}$

$84 \div \dfrac{1}{3} = \dfrac{84}{1} \times \dfrac{3}{1} = 252$

3. $60\% = \dfrac{3}{5}$

$99 \div \dfrac{3}{5} = \dfrac{\overset{33}{\cancel{99}}}{1} \times \dfrac{5}{\underset{1}{\cancel{3}}} = 165$

$16\dfrac{2}{3}\% = \dfrac{1}{6}$

$25 \div \dfrac{1}{6} = \dfrac{25}{1} \times \dfrac{6}{1} = 150$

4. $37\dfrac{1}{2}\% = \dfrac{3}{8}$

$240 \div \dfrac{3}{8} = \dfrac{\overset{80}{\cancel{240}}}{1} \times \dfrac{8}{\underset{1}{\cancel{3}}} = 640$

$90\% = \dfrac{9}{10}$

$270 \div \dfrac{9}{10} = \dfrac{\overset{30}{\cancel{270}}}{1} \times \dfrac{10}{\underset{1}{\cancel{9}}} = 300$

5. $4.5\% = .045$

$\begin{array}{r} 800 \\ .045\,\overline{)36.000} \\ 36\ 0 \end{array}$

$6.7\% = .067$

$\begin{array}{r} 2\ 000 \\ .067\,\overline{)134.000} \\ 134 \end{array}$

6. $75\% = \dfrac{3}{4}$

$2850 \div \dfrac{3}{4} = \dfrac{\overset{950}{\cancel{2850}}}{1} \times \dfrac{4}{\underset{1}{\cancel{3}}} = \$3800$

7. $35\% = .35$

$\begin{array}{r} 700\ \text{parents} \\ .35\,\overline{)245.00} \\ 245 \end{array}$

8. $85\% = .85$

$$.85 \overline{)34.00} \quad \text{40 problems}$$
$$\underline{34\ 0}$$

9. $60\% = \frac{3}{5}$

$$24 \div \frac{3}{5} = \frac{24}{1} \times \frac{5}{3} = \$40$$

10. $52\% = .52$

$$.52 \overline{)4420.00} \quad \text{8500 people}$$
$$\underline{416}$$
$$260$$
$$\underline{260}$$

11. $5\% = \frac{1}{20}$

$$43 \div \frac{1}{20} = \frac{43}{1} \times \frac{20}{1} = \$860$$

ANSWERS AND SOLUTIONS—PERCENT SKILLS TEST

1. $.06 = 6\%$

2. $.057 = 5.7\%$

3. $80\% = .8$

4. $.9\% = .009$

5. $\frac{4}{\cancel{5}} \times \frac{\cancel{100}^{20}}{1} = 80\%$
    ^{1}

6. $\frac{2}{7} \times \frac{100}{1} = \frac{200}{7} = 28\frac{4}{7}\%$

7. $\frac{35}{100} = \frac{7}{20}$

8. $\frac{84}{100} = \frac{21}{25}$

9. $58\frac{1}{3} \div 100 = \frac{173}{3} \div \frac{100}{1} = \frac{\cancel{175}^{7}}{3} \times \frac{1}{\cancel{100}_{4}} = \frac{7}{12}$

10.
$$\begin{array}{r} 310 \\ \times\ .40 \\ \hline 124.00 \end{array}$$

11.
$$\begin{array}{r} 250 \\ \times .062 \\ \hline 500 \\ 15\ 00 \\ \hline 15.50\cancel{0} \end{array}$$

12. $\frac{2}{\cancel{3}} \times \frac{\cancel{96}^{32}}{1} = 64$
     ^{1}

13. $\frac{1}{\cancel{8}} \times \frac{\cancel{120}^{15}}{1} = 15$
     ^{1}

14.
$$
\begin{array}{r}
4{,}200 \\
\times\ .15 \\
\hline
210\ 00 \\
420\ 0 \\
\hline
\$630.00
\end{array}
$$

15.
$$
\begin{array}{r}
24.50 \\
\times\ .06 \\
\hline
\$1.4700
\end{array}
\qquad
\begin{array}{r}
24.50 \\
+\ 1.47 \\
\hline
\$25.97
\end{array}
$$

16.
$$
\begin{array}{r}
84.79 \\
\times\ .08 \\
\hline
6.7832 = \$6.78
\end{array}
$$

17.
$$
\begin{array}{r}
900 \\
\times\ .045 \\
\hline
4\ 500 \\
36\ 00 \\
\hline
\$40.50\cancel{0}
\end{array}
$$

18. $1\frac{4}{12} = 1\frac{1}{3} = \frac{4}{3}$

$$\frac{\overset{12}{\cancel{1200}}}{1} \times \frac{\overset{2}{\cancel{6}}}{\underset{1}{\cancel{100}}} \times \frac{4}{\underset{1}{\cancel{3}}} = \$96$$

19. $\frac{12}{20} = \frac{3}{5}$

$$\frac{3}{\underset{1}{\cancel{5}}} \times \frac{\overset{20}{\cancel{100}}}{1} = 60\%$$

20. $\frac{42}{48} = \frac{7}{8}$

$$\frac{7}{\underset{2}{\cancel{8}}} \times \frac{\overset{25}{\cancel{100}}}{1} = \frac{175}{2} = 87\frac{1}{2}\%$$

21. $\frac{15}{60} = \frac{1}{4}$

$$\frac{1}{\underset{1}{\cancel{4}}} \times \frac{\overset{25}{\cancel{100}}}{1} = 25\%$$

22. $\frac{48}{72} = \frac{2}{3}$

$$\frac{2}{3} \times \frac{100}{1} = \frac{200}{3} = 66\frac{2}{3}\%$$

23. $\frac{15}{25} = \frac{3}{5}$

$$\frac{3}{\underset{1}{\cancel{5}}} \times \frac{\overset{20}{\cancel{100}}}{1} = 60\%$$

24.
$$
\begin{array}{r}
125 \\
-\ 75 \\
\hline
50
\end{array}
\qquad
\frac{50}{125} = \frac{2}{5}
$$

$$\frac{2}{\underset{1}{\cancel{5}}} \times \frac{\overset{20}{\cancel{100}}}{1} = 40\%$$

25. $20\% = \frac{1}{5}$

$$17 \div \frac{1}{5} = \frac{17}{1} \times \frac{5}{1} = 85$$

26. $70\% = \frac{7}{10}$

$$161 \div \frac{7}{10} = \frac{\overset{23}{\cancel{161}}}{1} \times \frac{10}{\underset{1}{\cancel{7}}} = 230$$

27. $12\frac{1}{2}\% = \frac{1}{8}$

$24 \div \frac{1}{8} = \frac{24}{1} \times \frac{8}{1} = 192$

28. $15\% = .15$

$$.15 \overline{)48.00}$$

3 20

45

3 0

3 0

29. $80\% = \frac{4}{5}$

$240 \div \frac{4}{5} = \frac{240}{1} \times \frac{5}{4} = \$300$

60

1

30. $5\% = .05$

120 problems

$.05 \overline{)6.00}$

POST-TEST: Finding Out What You Know about Whole Numbers, Fractions, Decimals and Percent

Solve each problem. There is additional work space on page 215. Then write your answer on the blank beside the number that corresponds to the problem. Answers to these problems begin on page 216.

1. _____   1. In 487 the 8 is in what place?

2. _____   2. What is the value of the 6 in 264,089?

3. _____   3. Write seven million, five thousand twenty as a whole number.

4. _____   4.   247,306   5. $16 + 2,075 + 134,836 =$
                           $+ 322,571$
5. _____

6. _____   6. Thursday night 985 people attended the Central School basketball tournament. Friday night 1,280 people attended the tournament. Saturday night 1,478 people attended. What was the total attendance for the three-day tournament?

7. _____   7. Last month Mr. and Mrs. Munro spent $10.85 for gas, $17.32 for electricity, and $41.64 for the telephone. What was the total amount they paid for these utilities?

8. _____   8. At Central School there are 847 freshmen, 812 sophomores, 763 juniors, and 729 seniors. What is the total number of students at Central School?

9. _____

9. 74,283
   − 23,251

10. 3,000,060 − 974,238 =

10. _____

11. _____

11. Debbie bought a winter coat on sale for $79.95. The regular price was $110. How much did Debbie save by buying the coat on sale?

12. _____

12. Mrs. Bennett shopped for groceries on Saturday. The bill came to a total of $41.79. She paid with $50. How much change did she receive?

13. _____

13. Jack is driving from his house to his parents' house which is 243 miles away. When he has driven 168 miles, how much farther does he have to drive?

14. _____

14. 423
   × 32

15. 1209
   × 67

15. _____

16. _____

16. 794 × 58 =

17. 623 × 1000 =

17. _____

18. _____

18. Colin drove at an average speed of 57 miles per hour for six hours. How far did he drive?

19. _____   19. Matt earns $5.80 an hour. How much does he make when he works 42 hours?

20. _____   20. $7\overline{)413}$ 21. $64\overline{)4,702}$

21. _____

22. _____   22. $15,466 \div 38 =$ 23. $30,464 \div 476 =$

23. _____

24. _____   24. Last year Fumio paid a total of $2724 for rent. How much rent did he pay each month?

25. _____   25. There are 16 ounces in a pound. How many pounds are there in 672 ounces?

26. _____   26. Reduce $\frac{36}{48}$ 27. Raise $\frac{4}{9}$ to 36ths.

27. _____

28. _____   28. Change $\frac{44}{8}$ to a mixed number and reduce.

29. _____   29. Change $7\frac{5}{6}$ to an improper fraction.

30. _____   30. A yard contains 36 inches. 20 inches is what fractional part of a yard?

31. _____   31. $\begin{array}{r} 8\frac{5}{9} \\ + 6\frac{1}{9} \\ \hline \end{array}$ 32. $\begin{array}{r} 4\frac{5}{12} \\ 8\frac{2}{3} \\ + 7\frac{3}{8} \\ \hline \end{array}$

32. _____

33. _____   33. Ellis is $73\frac{1}{2}$ inches tall. His son Howard is $2\frac{7}{8}$ inches taller than Ellis. How tall is Howard?

34. _____   34. Gordon is painting his apartment. On Friday he worked $2\frac{1}{2}$ hours. On Saturday he worked $6\frac{3}{4}$ hours. On Sunday he worked $5\frac{3}{4}$ hours. What was the total number of hours Gordon spent painting his apartment?

35. _____   35. Diana bought a turkey that weighed $12\frac{5}{16}$ pounds, a roast beef that weighed $3\frac{1}{4}$ pounds, and $2\frac{7}{8}$ pounds of chicken. What was the total weight of her purchases?

36. _____

37. _____

36.
$$8\frac{5}{7}$$
$$-\ 2\frac{6}{7}$$

37.
$$14\frac{5}{9}$$
$$-\ 9\frac{5}{6}$$

38. _____

38. From a piece of cloth 48 inches long, Senta cut a piece that was $17\frac{3}{8}$ inches long. How long was the piece that was left?

39. _____

39. Shirley usually works $7\frac{1}{2}$ hours a day. Friday she left $2\frac{3}{4}$ hours early in order to go to the dentist. How many hours did Shirley work on Friday?

40. _____

40. Herbert's suitcase weighed $28\frac{1}{4}$ pounds when it was full. The empty suitcase weighs only $4\frac{9}{16}$ pounds. What was the weight of the items inside Herbert's suitcase?

41. _____

42. _____

43. _____

41. $\frac{5}{8} \times \frac{1}{2} \times \frac{12}{25} =$ 42. $20 \times \frac{4}{5} =$ 43. $3\frac{5}{9} \times 3\frac{3}{4} =$

44. _____

44. Jane wanted to sell 200 tickets to her school's bazaar. In one week she sold $\frac{5}{8}$ of the tickets. How many tickets did Jane sell that week?

45. _____   45. Carl is a tailor. He needs $3\frac{2}{3}$ yards of material to make a suit. How many yards does he need to make five suits?

46. _____   46. $\frac{3}{4} \div \frac{7}{8} =$ 47. $18 \div \frac{3}{5} =$

47. _____

48. _____   48. $\frac{5}{6} \div 30 =$ 49. $6\frac{2}{3} \div 1\frac{5}{9} =$

49. _____

50. _____   50. Bill has a piece of lumber that is $7\frac{1}{2}$ feet long. He wants to split it into three equal pieces for shelves. How long will each piece be?

51. _____   51. How many strips of paper, each $4\frac{1}{2}$ inches long, can be cut from a roll of paper that is $112\frac{1}{2}$ inches long?

52. _____   52. Write .0006 in words.

53. _____   53. Write seventy-nine millionths as a decimal.

54. _____   54. Write forty and seventeen thousandths as a mixed decimal.

55. _____   55. Change .035 to a fraction and reduce.

56. _____   56.   Change $\frac{3}{200}$ to a decimal.

57. _____   57.   Which decimal is larger: .083 or .0308?

58. _____   58. $4.923 + 85 + 16.37 =$

59. _____   59.   Rachel's normal temperature is 98.6°. When she was sick, her temperature went up 4.5°. What was Rachel's temperature when she was sick?

60. _____   60.   On a regular weekday morning, Maxine drives 4.3 miles to her children's school, 6 miles to work, and 5.8 miles back home. What is the total distance that Maxine drives in one regular day?

61. _____   61. $14 - .248 =$

62. _____   62.   Last year Central City spent $3.9 million for education and $4.2 million for police and fire protection. How much more did Central City spend for police and fire protection than for education?

63. _____ 63. On Monday morning the reading on the mileage gauge of Dave's car was 20,243.6 miles. On Friday night the reading was 21,431.2 miles. How far did Dave drive between Monday morning and Friday night?

64. _____ 64. .387 × 15 =   65. 6.3 × .29 =

65. _____

66. _____ 66. 1000 × 2.36 =

67. _____ 67. Robert pays 98.4¢ for a gallon of gasoline. How much does he pay for 12.5 gallons?

68. _____ 68. One jar of ketchup weighs .631 pound. How much do 24 jars of ketchup weigh?

69. _____ 69. $12\overline{).3672}$ 70. $.06\overline{).01674}$ 71. $.024\overline{)11.592}$

70. _____

71. _____

72. _____ 72. $.004\overline{)8}$ 73. .385 ÷ 100 =

73. _____

74. _____ 74. Nancy bought 4.3 pounds of roast beef for $6.88. What was the price of one pound of roast beef?

75. _____ 75. Bill earned $36 in 7.5 hours of work. How much did he earn in one hour?

76. _____ 76. Change .015 to a percent.

77. _____ 77. Change 8% to a decimal.

78. _____ 78. Change $\frac{6}{25}$ to a percent.

79. _____ 79. Change 4% to a fraction and reduce.

80. _____ 80. Change $13\frac{1}{3}$% to a fraction and reduce.

81. _____ 81. Find 70% of 350.

82. _____ 82. Find 2.6% of 800.

83. _____   83. Find $12\frac{1}{2}\%$ of 728.

84. _____   84. 14,260 people are registered to vote in Central City. At the last election 65% of them actually voted. How many people voted in Central City's last election?

85. _____   85. John and Corinne bought a house that cost $38,500. They made a down payment of 15%. Find the amount of their down payment.

86. _____   86. This year Susan paid $2440 for rent. Next year she will pay 8.5% more for rent. What will her yearly rent be next year?

87. _____   87. Ira bought a camera on sale for 20% off. The original price was $229.89. Find the sale price of the camera to the nearest penny.

88. _____   88. Find the interest on $1,200 at $6\frac{1}{2}\%$ annual interest for one year and eight months.

89. _____   89. 45 is what % of 60?

90. _____   90. 56 is what % of 84?

91. _____   91. 32 is what % of 400?

92. _____   92. Joyce took a test with 120 questions. She got 84 of the questions right. What percent of the questions did she get right?

93. _____   93. There are 36 inches in a yard. 30 inches are what percent of a yard?

94. _____   94. In January Sheila weighed 175 pounds. By June she weighed 140 pounds. What percent of her weight did Sheila lose from January to June?

95. _____   95. The Thompsons bought a house in 1960 for $24,500. They sold it in 1980 for $35,525. By what percent did the value of the Thompsons' house increase in twenty years?

96. _____   96. 75% of what number is 90?

97. _____   97. $62\frac{1}{2}$% of what number is 45?

98. _____   98. At Central Hospital there are 390 women employees. Women represent 65% of the total number of employees. How many people work at Central Hospital?

99. _____   99. Mark bought an electric drill on sale for $22.40. This was 80% of the original price. Find the original price of the drill.

100. _____   100. The town of Central City is running a fund raising campaign to get money to build a new community center. So far they have collected $65,000 which is 52% of the total that they need. How much does Central City need for the new center?

_____

Do your work here

ANSWERS AND SOLUTIONS—POST-TEST

1. tens

2. 60,000

3. 7,005,020

4. 569,877

5. 136,927

```
        16
     2,075
 + 134,836
   136,927
```

6. 3,743

```
      985
    1,280
  + 1,478
    3,743
```

7. $69.81

```
  $10.85
   17.32
 + 41.64
  $69.81
```

8. 3,151 students

```
    847
    812
    763
  + 729
  3,151
```

9. 51,032

10. 2,025,822

```
  3,000,060
  − 974,238
  2,025,822
```

11. $30.05

```
  $110.00
  − 79.95
  $30.05
```

12. $8.21

```
  $50.00
  − 41.79
   $8.21
```

13. 75 miles

```
    243
  − 168
     75
```

14. 13,536

```
      423
    × 32
      846
   12 69
   13,536
```

15. 81,003

```
    1,209
   × 67
    8 463
   72 54
   81,003
```

16. 46,052

```
      794
    × 58
    6 352
   39 70
   46,052
```

17. 623,000

$$
\begin{array}{r}
623 \\
\times\ 1000 \\
\hline
623{,}000
\end{array}
$$

18. 342 miles

$$
\begin{array}{r}
57 \\
\times\ 6 \\
\hline
342
\end{array}
$$

19. $243.60

$$
\begin{array}{r}
\$5.80 \\
\times\ 42 \\
\hline
11\ 60 \\
232\ 0 \\
\hline
\$243.60
\end{array}
$$

20. 59

$$
\begin{array}{r}
59 \\
7\,\overline{)413} \\
35 \\
\hline
63 \\
63 \\
\hline
\end{array}
$$

21. 73r30

$$
\begin{array}{r}
73r30 \\
64\,\overline{)4{,}702} \\
4\ 48 \\
\hline
222 \\
192 \\
\hline
30
\end{array}
$$

22. 407

$$
\begin{array}{r}
407 \\
38\,\overline{)15{,}466} \\
15\ 2 \\
\hline
266 \\
266 \\
\hline
\end{array}
$$

23. 64

$$
\begin{array}{r}
64 \\
476\,\overline{)30{,}464} \\
28\ 56 \\
\hline
1\ 904 \\
1\ 904 \\
\hline
\end{array}
$$

24. $227

$$
\begin{array}{r}
\$\ 227 \\
12\,\overline{)\$2724} \\
24 \\
\hline
32 \\
24 \\
\hline
84 \\
84 \\
\hline
\end{array}
$$

25. 42 lbs.

$$
\begin{array}{r}
42 \\
16\,\overline{)672} \\
64 \\
\hline
32 \\
32 \\
\hline
\end{array}
$$

26. $\frac{3}{4}$

$$
\frac{36}{48} = \frac{3}{4}
$$

27. $\frac{16}{36}$

$$
\frac{4}{9} = \frac{16}{36}
$$

28. $5\frac{1}{2}$

$$
5\frac{4}{8} = 5\frac{1}{2}
$$

$$
\begin{array}{r}
8\,\overline{)44} \\
40 \\
\hline
4
\end{array}
$$

29. $\dfrac{47}{6}$

$$7\tfrac{5}{6} = \dfrac{47}{6}$$

30. $\dfrac{5}{9}$

$$\dfrac{20}{36} = \dfrac{5}{9}$$

---

31. $14\tfrac{2}{3}$

$$14\tfrac{6}{9} = 14\tfrac{2}{3}$$

32. $20\tfrac{11}{24}$

$$
\begin{aligned}
4\tfrac{5}{12} &= 4\tfrac{10}{24}\\
8\tfrac{2}{3} &= 8\tfrac{16}{24}\\
+\;7\tfrac{3}{8} &= 7\tfrac{9}{24}\\
\hline
19\tfrac{35}{24} &= 20\tfrac{11}{24}
\end{aligned}
$$

---

33. $76\tfrac{3}{8}$ in.

$$
\begin{aligned}
73\tfrac{1}{2} &= 73\tfrac{4}{8}\\
+\;2\tfrac{7}{8} &= 2\tfrac{7}{8}\\
\hline
75\tfrac{11}{8} &= 76\tfrac{3}{8}
\end{aligned}
$$

34. 15 hrs.

$$
\begin{aligned}
2\tfrac{1}{2} &= 2\tfrac{2}{4}\\
6\tfrac{3}{4} &= 6\tfrac{3}{4}\\
+\;5\tfrac{3}{4} &= 5\tfrac{3}{4}\\
\hline
13\tfrac{8}{4} &= 15
\end{aligned}
$$

---

35. $18\tfrac{7}{16}$ lbs.

$$
\begin{aligned}
12\tfrac{5}{16} &= 12\tfrac{5}{16}\\
3\tfrac{1}{4} &= 3\tfrac{4}{16}\\
+\;2\tfrac{7}{8} &= 2\tfrac{14}{16}\\
\hline
17\tfrac{23}{16} &= 18\tfrac{7}{16}
\end{aligned}
$$

36. $5\tfrac{6}{7}$

$$
\begin{aligned}
8\tfrac{5}{7} &= 7\tfrac{12}{7}\\
-\;2\tfrac{6}{7} &= 2\tfrac{6}{7}\\
\hline
5\tfrac{6}{7}
\end{aligned}
$$

---

37. $4\tfrac{13}{18}$

$$
\begin{aligned}
14\tfrac{5}{9} &= 14\tfrac{10}{18} = 13\tfrac{28}{18}\\
-\;9\tfrac{5}{6} &= 9\tfrac{15}{18} = 9\tfrac{15}{18}\\
\hline
&\qquad\qquad\quad 4\tfrac{13}{18}
\end{aligned}
$$

38. $30\tfrac{5}{8}$ in.

$$
\begin{aligned}
48 &= 47\tfrac{8}{8}\\
-\;17\tfrac{3}{8} &= 17\tfrac{3}{8}\\
\hline
30\tfrac{5}{8}
\end{aligned}
$$

---

39. $4\tfrac{3}{4}$ hrs.

$$
\begin{aligned}
7\tfrac{1}{2} &= 7\tfrac{2}{4} = 6\tfrac{6}{4}\\
-\;2\tfrac{3}{4} &= 2\tfrac{3}{4} = 2\tfrac{3}{4}\\
\hline
&\qquad\qquad\quad 4\tfrac{3}{4}
\end{aligned}
$$

40. $23\tfrac{11}{16}$ lbs.

$$
\begin{aligned}
28\tfrac{1}{4} &= 28\tfrac{4}{16} = 27\tfrac{20}{16}\\
-\;4\tfrac{9}{16} &= 4\tfrac{9}{16} = 4\tfrac{9}{16}\\
\hline
&\qquad\qquad\quad 23\tfrac{11}{16}
\end{aligned}
$$

41. $\frac{3}{20}$

$$\frac{\overset{1}{\cancel{6}}}{\underset{2}{\cancel{8}}} \times \frac{1}{2} \times \frac{\overset{3}{\cancel{12}}}{\underset{5}{\cancel{25}}} = \frac{3}{20}$$

42. 16

$$\frac{\overset{4}{\cancel{20}}}{1} \times \frac{4}{\underset{1}{\cancel{5}}} = 16$$

43. $13\frac{1}{3}$

$$3\frac{5}{9} \times 3\frac{3}{4} =$$

$$\frac{\overset{8}{\cancel{32}}}{\underset{3}{\cancel{9}}} \times \frac{\overset{5}{\cancel{15}}}{\underset{1}{\cancel{4}}} = \frac{40}{3} = 13\frac{1}{3}$$

44. 125 tickets

$$\frac{5}{\underset{2}{\cancel{8}}} \times \frac{\overset{50}{\cancel{200}}}{1} = 125$$

45. $18\frac{1}{3}$ yds.

$$5 \times 3\frac{2}{3} =$$

$$\frac{5}{1} \times \frac{11}{3} = \frac{55}{3} = 18\frac{1}{3}$$

46. $\frac{6}{7}$

$$\frac{3}{\underset{1}{\cancel{4}}} \times \frac{\overset{2}{\cancel{8}}}{7} = \frac{6}{7}$$

47. 30

$$\frac{\overset{6}{\cancel{18}}}{1} \times \frac{5}{\underset{1}{\cancel{3}}} = 30$$

48. $\frac{1}{36}$

$$\frac{\overset{1}{\cancel{5}}}{6} \times \frac{1}{\underset{6}{\cancel{30}}} = \frac{1}{36}$$

49. $4\frac{2}{7}$

$$\frac{20}{3} \div \frac{14}{9} =$$

$$\frac{\overset{10}{\cancel{20}}}{\underset{1}{\cancel{3}}} \times \frac{\overset{3}{\cancel{9}}}{\underset{7}{\cancel{14}}} = \frac{30}{7} = 4\frac{2}{7}$$

50. $2\frac{1}{2}$ ft.

$$7\frac{1}{2} \div 3 =$$

$$\frac{\overset{5}{\cancel{15}}}{2} \times \frac{1}{\underset{1}{\cancel{3}}} = \frac{5}{2} = 2\frac{1}{2}$$

51. 25 strips

$$112\frac{1}{2} \div 4\frac{1}{2} =$$

$$\frac{225}{2} \div \frac{9}{2} =$$

$$\frac{\overset{25}{\cancel{225}}}{\underset{1}{\cancel{2}}} \times \frac{\overset{1}{\cancel{2}}}{\underset{1}{\cancel{9}}} = 25$$

52. six ten-thousandths

53. .000079

54. 40.017

55. $\dfrac{7}{200}$

   $.035 = \dfrac{35}{1000} = \dfrac{7}{200}$

56. .015

   $$\begin{array}{r} .015 \\ 200\overline{)3.000} \\ \underline{2\ 00} \\ 1\ 000 \\ \underline{1\ 000} \end{array}$$

57. .083

   .0830 or .0308

58. 106.293

   $$\begin{array}{r} 4.923 \\ 85.0 \\ +\ 16.37 \\ \hline 106.293 \end{array}$$

59. 103.1°

   $$\begin{array}{r} 98.6 \\ +\ 4.5 \\ \hline 103.1 \end{array}$$

60. 16.1 mi.

   $$\begin{array}{r} 4.3 \\ 6.0 \\ +\ 5.8 \\ \hline 16.1 \end{array}$$

61. 13.752

   $$\begin{array}{r} 14.000 \\ -\ .248 \\ \hline 13.752 \end{array}$$

62. $.3 million

   $$\begin{array}{r} \$4.2\ \text{million} \\ -\ 3.9\ \text{million} \\ \hline \$\ \ .3\ \text{million} \end{array}$$

63. 1,187.6 mi.

   $$\begin{array}{r} 21,431.2 \\ -\ 20,243.6 \\ \hline 1,187.6 \end{array}$$

64. 5.805

   $$\begin{array}{r} .387 \\ \times\ 15 \\ \hline 1935 \\ 387 \\ \hline 5.805 \end{array}$$

65. 1.827

   $$\begin{array}{r} 6.3 \\ \times\ .29 \\ \hline 567 \\ 126 \\ \hline 1.827 \end{array}$$

66. 2,360

   $$\begin{array}{r} 1000 \\ \times\ 2.36 \\ \hline 60\ 00 \\ 300\ 0 \\ 2\ 000 \\ \hline 2,360.00 \end{array}$$

67. $12.30

```
      $.984
    ×  12.5
      4920
      1968
       984
    $12.3000
```

68. 15.144 lbs.

```
      .631
    ×  24
     2 524
     12 62
    15.144
```

69. .0306

```
        .0306
    12)‾.3672
        36
        072
         72
```

70. .279

```
          .279
    .06)‾.01 674
          1 2
           47
           42
           54
           54
```

71. 483

```
           483
    .024)‾11.592
          9 6
          1 99
          1 92
            72
            72
```

72. 2000

```
          2000
    .004)‾8.000
```

73. .00385

```
    .385 ÷ 100 = .00385
```

74. $1.60

```
           1.60
    4.3)‾$6.8.80
         4 3
         2 5 8
         2 5 8
```

75. $4.80

```
            4.80
    7.5)‾$36.0.00
         30 0
         6 00
         6 00
```

76. 1.5%

```
    .015 = .01 5 = 1.5%
```

77. .08

$$8\% = .08$$

78. 24%

$$\frac{6}{\underset{1}{\cancel{25}}} \times \frac{\overset{4}{\cancel{100}}}{1} = 24\%$$

79. $\frac{1}{25}$

$$\frac{4}{100} = \frac{1}{25}$$

80. $\frac{2}{15}$

$$13\frac{1}{3} \div 100 =$$

$$\frac{\overset{2}{\cancel{40}}}{3} \times \frac{1}{\underset{5}{\cancel{100}}} = \frac{2}{15}$$

81. 245

$$70\% = .7$$

$$\begin{array}{r} 350 \\ \times\ .7 \\ \hline 245.0 \end{array}$$

82. 20.8

$$2.6\% = .026$$

$$\begin{array}{r} 800 \\ \times\ .026 \\ \hline 4\ 800 \\ 16\ 00\ \ \ \\ \hline 20.800 \end{array}$$

83. 91

$$12\frac{1}{2}\% = \frac{1}{8}$$

$$\frac{1}{\cancel{8}} \times \frac{\overset{91}{\cancel{728}}}{1} = 91$$

84. 9,269 people

$$65\% = .65$$

$$\begin{array}{r} 14,260 \\ \times\ .65 \\ \hline 713\ 00 \\ 8556\ 0\ \ \ \\ \hline 9269.\cancel{0}\cancel{0} \end{array}$$

85. $5,775

$$15\% = .15$$

$$\begin{array}{r} \$38,500 \\ \times\ .15 \\ \hline 1\ 925\ 00 \\ 3\ 850\ 0\ \ \ \\ \hline \$5,775.00 \end{array}$$

86. $2,647.40

$$8.5\% = .085$$

$$\begin{array}{r} \$2,440 \\ \times\ .085 \\ \hline 12\ 200 \\ 195\ 20\ \ \ \\ \hline \$207.40\cancel{0} \end{array} \qquad \begin{array}{r} 2440.00 \\ +\ 207.40 \\ \hline \$2,647.40 \end{array}$$

87. $183.91

$$20\% = .2$$

$$\begin{array}{r} 229.89 \\ \times\ .2 \\ \hline 45.978 \end{array} \qquad \begin{array}{r} 229.89 \\ -\ 45.98 \\ \hline \$183.91 \end{array}$$

$45.978 rounds off to $45.98

88. $130

$$1\text{ yr. }8\text{ mos.} = 1\frac{8}{12} = 1\frac{2}{3} = \frac{5}{3}$$

$$\frac{13}{\cancel{2}_{1}} \times \frac{\cancel{1200}^{\,2}}{\cancel{100}_{1}} \times \frac{5}{\cancel{3}_{1}} = \$130$$

89. 75%

$$\frac{45}{60} = \frac{3}{4}$$

$$\frac{3}{\cancel{4}_{1}} \times \frac{\cancel{100}^{25}}{1} = 75\%$$

90. $66\frac{2}{3}\%$

$$\frac{56}{84} = \frac{2}{3}$$

$$\frac{2}{3} \times \frac{100}{1} = \frac{200}{3} = 66\frac{2}{3}\%$$

91. 8%

$$\frac{32}{400} = \frac{2}{25}$$

$$\frac{2}{\cancel{25}_{1}} \times \frac{\cancel{100}^{4}}{1} = 8\%$$

92. 70%

$$\frac{84}{120} = \frac{7}{10}$$

$$\frac{7}{\cancel{10}_{1}} \times \frac{\cancel{100}^{10}}{1} = 70\%$$

93. $83\frac{1}{3}\%$

$$\frac{30}{36} = \frac{5}{6}$$

$$\frac{5}{\cancel{6}_{3}} \times \frac{\cancel{100}^{50}}{1} = \frac{250}{3} = 83\frac{1}{3}\%$$

94. 20%

$$\begin{array}{r} 175 \\ -\ 140 \\ \hline 35 \end{array} \qquad \frac{35}{175} = \frac{1}{5}$$

$$\frac{1}{\cancel{5}_{1}} \times \frac{\cancel{100}^{20}}{1} = 20\%$$

95. 45%

$$\begin{array}{r} 35,525 \\ -\ 24,500 \\ \hline \$11,025 \end{array} \qquad \frac{11,025}{24,500} = \frac{9}{20}$$

$$\frac{9}{\cancel{20}_{1}} \times \frac{\cancel{100}^{5}}{1} = 45\%$$

96. 120

$$75\% = \frac{3}{4}$$

$$90\% \div \frac{3}{4} = \frac{\cancel{90}^{30}}{1} \times \frac{4}{\cancel{3}_{1}} = 120$$

97. 72

$$62\tfrac{1}{2}\% = \frac{5}{8}$$

$$45 \div \frac{5}{8} = \frac{\overset{9}{\cancel{45}}}{1} \times \frac{8}{\underset{1}{\cancel{5}}} = 72$$

98. 600 people

$$65\% = .65$$

$$\begin{array}{r} 6\,00 \\ .65\overline{)390.00} \\ \underline{390} \end{array}$$

99. \$28

$$80\% = .8$$

$$\begin{array}{r} \$28.00 \\ .8\overline{)\$22.4\,00} \\ \underline{16} \\ 64 \\ \underline{64} \end{array}$$

100. \$125,000

$$52\% = .52$$

$$\begin{array}{r} \$125{,}000. \\ .52\overline{)65{,}000{,}00} \\ \underline{52}\phantom{{,}000{,}00} \\ 130\phantom{{,}00{,}00} \\ \underline{104}\phantom{{,}00{,}00} \\ 260\phantom{{,}0{,}00} \\ \underline{260}\phantom{{,}0{,}00} \end{array}$$

POST-TEST EVALUATION

A passing score is 80 out of 100 problems correct.

Following is a list of the problems on the test and the topics to which each problem belongs. If you had less than a passing score, study the sections in the book that correspond to the problems you got wrong. Then try the test again. If you had a passing score, correct any problems that you missed.

Problems	*Topics*
	WHOLE NUMBERS
1, 2, 3	Understanding Whole Numbers
4, 5	Adding Whole Numbers
6, 7, 8	Applying Addition Skills
9, 10	Subtracting Whole Numbers
11, 12, 13	Applying Subtraction Skills
14, 15, 16, 17	Multiplying Whole Numbers
18, 19	Applying Multiplication Skills
20, 21, 22, 23	Dividing Whole Numbers
24, 25	Applying Division Skills
	FRACTIONS
26, 27, 28, 29, 30	Understanding Fractions
31, 32	Adding Fractions
33, 34, 35	Applying Addition of Fractions Skills
36, 37	Subtracting Fractions
38, 39, 40	Applying Subtraction of Fractions Skills
41, 42, 43	Multiplying Fractions
44, 45	Applying Multiplication of Fractions Skills
46, 47, 48, 49	Dividing Fractions
50, 51	Applying Division of Fractions Skills

DECIMALS

PERCENT